Tomson James Cup.

Winners W. G. C. B. Team

Scores.

F. R. Burrow 80
P. A. Lushington 85
I. M. Challinor 85
S. R. James 86
336

Colt Book

CONDITIONS.

Entries for all Competitions must be made through the Secretary of the Club of which the Competitor is a member, and must reach the **Hon. Sec. of the Union, G. D. Carr, The Garth, Malvern,** on or before **Thursday, May 10th,** *together with Entry Fees* and a statement of the qualification, handicap, and postal address of Competitor.

Members of more than one Club must give their lowest handicap.

Competitors of any handicap may enter, but will not receive more than 9 handicap.

Any question arising as to Handicapping, Qualification, or any other point will be considered by the Executive Committee of the Council of the Union, whose decision shall be final.

QUALIFICATION. The Competitions are open to all Amateur Members of Clubs belonging to the Union, but no player shall be eligible to compete at the Meeting who has played in the Union of any other County since the 31st December, 1905.

The Competitions will be held under the Rules of Golf (Special Rules for Stroke Competitions), supplemented by the Local Rules of the Worcestershire Golf Club.

The Worcestershire Golf Club have arranged to make all Competitors Temporary Members of the Club from Monday, 14th May, to Wednesday, 16th May, inclusive, without green fee.

G. D. CARR, The Garth, Malvern,

Hon. Sec. W.U.G.C.

Scratch Medals

		Tie Scores	
I. M. Challinor	81 + 80 = 161 ----	77 + 85 = 162. ---	Gold
F. A. Woolley	77 + 84 = 161 ----	81 + 82 = 163	Silver
W. W. Lowe	84 + 80 = 164 ----	84 - - - - - -	Bronze
S. R. James	84 + 80 = 164 ----	88	

Morning handicap Prize

Capt Eccles 79 - 6 = 73

Afternoon handicap Prize

S. R. James 80 - 3 = 77

The Centenary History of the Worcestershire Union of Golf Clubs

The Centenary History of the Worcestershire Union of Golf Clubs

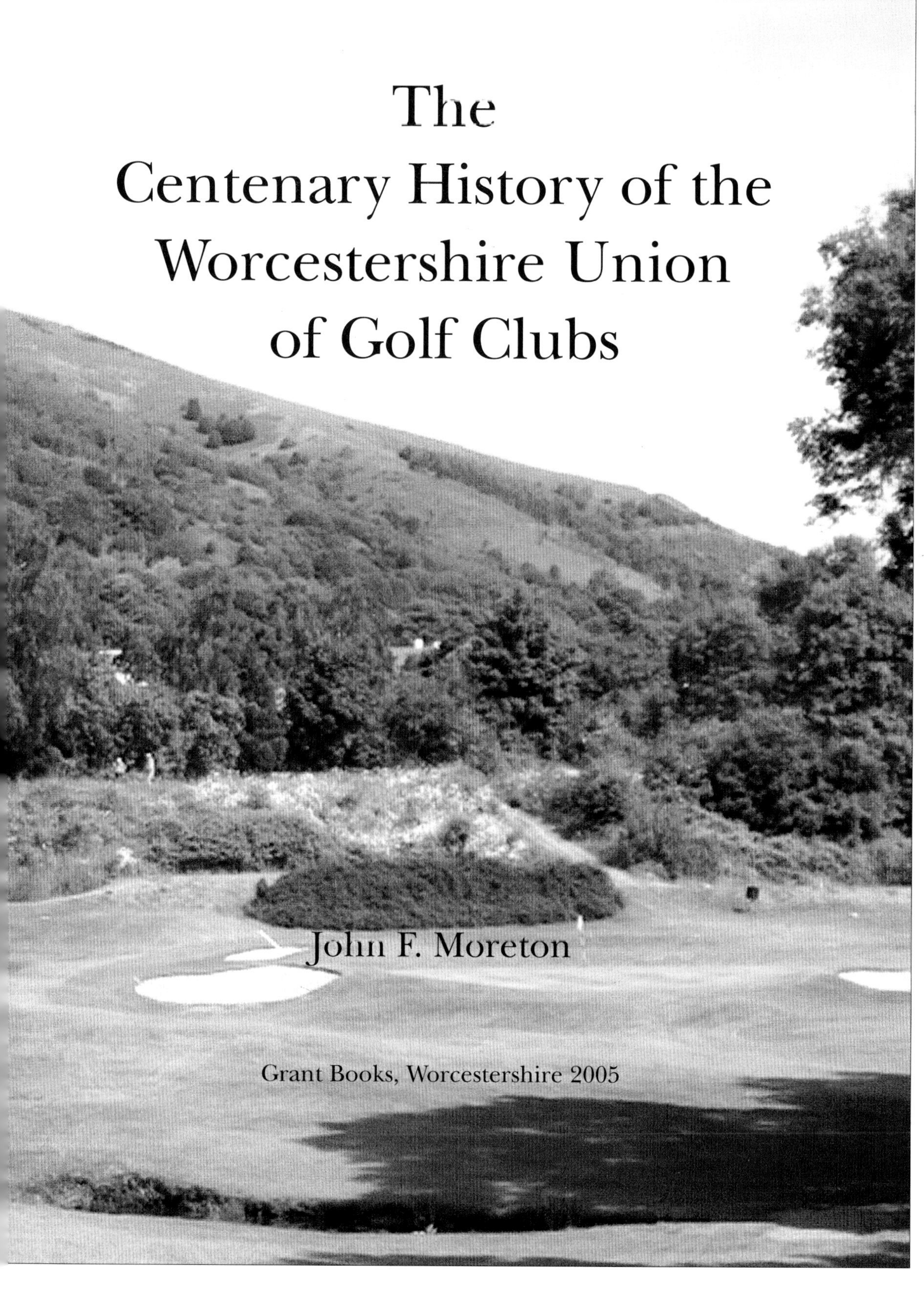

John F. Moreton

Grant Books, Worcestershire 2005

First published 2005

ISBN 0 907186 57 2

Published in a limited edition
of 1,500 copies

Typeset in 11 on 13 point New Baskerville
and printed in Great Britain by
Hughes & Company
Kempsey, Worcestershire, England

Published by
Grant Books
The Coach House, Cutnall Green,
Droitwich, Worcestershire WR9 0PQ
www.grantbooks.co.uk

Contents

Acknowledgements

I SHOULD LIKE to thank county players past and present for their memories of Worcestershire golf, and the secretaries and other members of the county's clubs who have assisted with information. The clubs which have produced centenary history books or handbooks are acknowledged in the bibliography.

Particular thanks are due to: Ray Baldwin, whose advice and meticulous attention to accuracy has been invaluable; Garnet Scott, for information on Rev. James and the early days of golf in our county; Brenda Smith, who maintained the archives so efficiently for more than half the Union's active history in addition to all her other duties; Eric Fiddian, who brought golf history alive; Denis and Maryann Hayes, for use of Dr. Tweddell's scrapbook; Peter Ricketts, for photographs and information.

The staff of Birmingham Central Library's Local Studies Department have been most helpful and understanding. The golf related items they possess have inspired numerous other areas of research.

Alan Jackson of the British Golf Collectors Society supplied the information about the defunct clubs.

The Centenary Committee consisted of Norman Bolton, Brian Peplow, Matthew Houghton, Bill Thompson, Andrew Boyd and the author.

John F. Moreton

Worcestershire Union of Golf Clubs

Founded 1905

Website: www.wugc.co.uk

President
B. Peplow
Ashton Wold
The Hundred
Nr. Leominster
Herefordshire
HR6 0HZ
Tel: 01584 711064
Fax: 01584 711189
E-mail: brian.peplow@btinternet.com

Chairman
W. Thompson
6 Teazel Avenue
Bournville
Birmingham
B30 1LZ
Tel: 0121 459 6750
Mobile: 07980 672755
E-mail: billt@blueyonder.co.uk

Captain
M. Houghton
53 Upton Road
Kidderminster
Worcestershire
DY10 2YD
Tel: 01562 747714
Mobile: 07764 710256

Secretary
A. Boyd
The Bears Den
Upper Street, Defford
Worcester WR8 9BG
Tel: 01386 750657
Mobile 07976 965036
Fax: 01386 750472
E-mail: aboydgolf@aol.com

Treasurer
C. Gupwell
Woodlands
Stock Green
Worcestershire
B96 6TB
Tel: 01386 792116

Junior Organiser
J.F. Moreton
138 Melton Road
Kings Heath
Birmingham
B14 7ES
Tel: 0121 4445347

August 2005

Dear Members

It is a great pleasure and honour for me to write this introduction to our Centenary book. Like any project of this size thanks must be expressed to the author John Moreton who has painstakingly researched records contained in minutes of meetings, newspapers, magazines and books.

We are fortunate in having John write this history since not only is he a very experienced author of golf books he is also the current junior organiser for the county and has been for the last fourteen years. I cannot thank John enough for his contribution to the affairs of the Worcestershire Union of Golf Clubs and the contents of this publication.

The pages include records of all our notable achievements for representative golf both at county, national and international levels. This book also tells the story of our founders at a time when a great expansion of golf in the UK was taking place (387 clubs in 1890, 2330 in 1900 and 4150 in 1910) and the need to organise golf beyond the boundaries of the individual clubs and counties.

The dedication and foresight of our early administrators is something we should be grateful for. The spirit and ethics of our sport were set in those early days and I earnestly hope that these traditions will continue during the next 100 years.

I am sure this book will be a source of great pleasure and may bring back fond memories to many people.

Best wishes to all our Members in this our centenary year.

Yours sincerely

Brian Peplow
President
Worcestershire Union of Golf Clubs

The Royal and Ancient Golf Club of St Andrews
Fife KY16 9JD
Telephone (01334) 460000

August 2005

Mr Brian Peplow
President
Worcestershire Union of Golf Clubs.

Dear Mr President

On behalf of the Members of The Royal and Ancient Golf Club of St Andrews I send you our warmest congratulations on the Centenary of Worcestershire Union of Golf Clubs.

We trust that your Members both present and future will enjoy their golf and the friendships made as a result.

With all good wishes for your continued success.

Yours sincerely

Richard Cole-Hamilton

RICHARD COLE-HAMILTON, CBE
Captain

Introduction

During the last quarter of the nineteenth century the "healthful and ancient pursuit of the game of golf" expanded in a fashion similar to the boom one hundred years later. By 1900 golfers in Worcestershire had the opportunity to play on ten courses within the county's boundaries.

Prior to the foundation of the county's oldest club, The Worcestershire, in 1879, Worcestershire golfers would have had to travel south to Newbury and Crookham, south-west to Westward Ho!, north to Hoylake or Manchester or make the long trek to Scotland, the rail network of that time assisting them in their journeys rather more conveniently than its modern counterpart.

Garnet Scott's history of the club records with justifiable pride that The Worcestershire was the first golf course in the English Midlands. It lay on Malvern Common and remained there until 1926 when it moved to its present location. Traces of the original course can still be seen on the common. It was another twelve years before a second course opened in the county. This was Ipsley Golf Club in Redditch which lasted until 1908, by which time the Redditch and Walkwood Club had been formed close to the site of the present Redditch club.

Clubs were founded at Moseley, Stourbridge and Kings Norton in 1892, Blackwell, Dudley, Yardley and Kidderminster (at Aggborough) a year later, and Evesham in 1894. Droitwich followed in 1897 and Worcester two years later at Tolladine. Only Moseley, Stourbridge and Blackwell occupy their original sites, while Evesham moved to its present location in 1895. Stourbridge closed in 1898 after difficulties with a new tenant farmer but the members were offered membership of Hagley Golf Club without payment of an entrance fee. Unfortunately, the Hagley club ceased to exist in 1906, hence it was not invited to join the Union, while Stourbridge was able to reopen in 1903 after coming to an agreement with a new tenant farmer. Nor did Yardley survive long enough to take advantage of affiliation, ceasing to exist about 1909.

Inter-club matches became possible and ladies of several Midland clubs were in the forefront of this movement. It should be noted that the Ladies Golf Union was formed in 1893, ten years before Mrs. Pankhurst formed the Women's Social and Political Union, after Laidlaw Purves' efforts to form an English Golf Union had failed to elicit a response from gentlemen golfers. It was not until 1924 that this body was set up, by which time Ireland, Scotland and Wales had already formed their Unions.

The time was therefore ripe for regional organisations to set up their own bodies and in 1905 The Worcestershire Golf Club took the first steps towards forming a county golf union, following the lead of Hampshire and the Isle of Wight (1893), Yorkshire (1894), Cornwall (1896), Nottinghamshire and Sussex (1899) and Lincoln in 1900.

Rev. Sydney James *J.J. Tomson*

Co-founders of the Worcestershire Union of Golf Clubs

Chapter One

Foundation

THE INITIATIVE of the senior club in Worcestershire, proposed by the Rev. S.R. James, headmaster of Malvern College, led to an invitation to thirteen clubs in the county to attend a meeting at the Star Hotel in Worcester on 17th November 1905. This proved a convenient meeting place for the delegates from eight of the invited clubs, situated as it is immediately opposite Foregate Street railway station.

The Rev. James was invited to take the chair and it was agreed that a county golf union be formed and regulations be drafted, including rules for representation. That there was enthusiasm for the proposal is clear, for Messrs. F.R. Burrow, a member of The Worcestershire and a country member of Kings Norton, and T.W. Piggott of Kings Norton presented draft general regulations which they had prepared in anticipation of the decision to proceed. These were duly adopted. One provision was that the governing body be known as the council and every member club would have a representative on this body. Clubs with fewer than one hundred members would have one representative, those with between one and two hundred members would have two representatives and clubs with more than two hundred members, three. The annual subscription of one guinea was based on the number of representatives from each club.

G.D. Carr of The Worcestershire was asked to act as secretary, *pro tem*; he remained in office until 1926, when the cup bearing his name was inaugurated as a tribute. Mr. Burrow took office as match secretary the following year.

The clubs represented at the founding meeting, in addition to The Worcestershire, were the Malvern Working Mens Club, who played on the Worcestershire club's course and assisted in its upkeep, Moseley, Stourbridge, Kings Norton, Dudley, Worcester City, Robin Hood and Evesham. Changes to Birmingham's city boundaries caused Robin Hood Golf Club to move to the Warwickshire union in 1912.

Shirley Baldwin
An early member of The Worcestershire and Kidderminster

F.R. Burrow
The first match secretary

G.D. Carr
The first secretary

F.H. Fowler

W.R. Nash

C.A. Horne

Courtesy of The Worcestershire Golf Club

A letter to the *Redditch Indicator* in January 1906 listed the representation of the member clubs, to which Kidderminster, Blackwell, Droitwich, Bromsgrove, Broadway, Alcester, Tenbury and Ipsley had been added. These clubs, except for Kidderminster, each had one representative, along with Robin Hood, Evesham and Worcester City. Kidderminster, Kings Norton, Moseley, Dudley and Stourbridge each had two, while The Worcestershire had three, presumably including one from the Malvern Working Mens Club.

In his reminiscences, published in 1920 under the title *Seventy Years*, Rev. James wrote:

What made my life specially healthy and pleasant at Malvern was the game of golf ... I always kept two hours open in the afternoon, and I should think I must have had a round of golf on an average four times a week, sometimes oftener. The nearest point of the course (now the sixteenth tee) was not two minutes walk from my house, and more than twenty of the staff were golfers, so I could always get a game. While I was at Eton I had played a good deal in the holidays at Westward Ho! and Bembridge, and for some years we had a sort of course in Windsor Park, but I had never established what might be called a consistent game; my handicap stood at about 9. When I came to Malvern I gave up football, and I never was an assiduous cricketer, so the golf was a godsend to me. Apart from other considerations, the friendly intercourse with colleagues was an excellent thing.

Largely owing to Foster (Rev. H. Foster was captain of The Worcestershire in 1883 and won the Easter Challenge Prize on three occasions) I improved fairly rapidly, and on one great day in 1900 I won two big competitions with a start of 7, doing the best scratch score in one of them, and brought down my handicap with a run by 4 strokes. Later I knocked another stroke off, and lived in hopes of improving that figure, but I left Malvern without doing so and then came the war.

He went on to describe the fun he and his colleagues had playing the Common Knockout foursomes. Strangely, he does not mention his part in the formation of our county Union.

The Rev. James and Mr. J.J. Tomson, a founder and benefactor of Kings Norton, presented the Tomson-James Cup to the Union, for competition at the annual county meeting by teams of four representing each club. Clubs were permitted to enter two teams for this event, which was first held in 1906 at The Worcestershire. The home club's "B" team were the first winners, ahead of teams from Blackwell, Worcester City, Kings Norton, Kidderminster, Robin Hood, Edgbaston, Moseley, Dudley, Stourbridge and the Malvern Working Mens Club. A brief council meeting was held on this occasion at which Messrs. James, Carr and Burrow were appointed to consider and report on handicaps. As Burrow and James were members of the winning Worcestershire "B" team it would be churlish to conclude that any skulduggery regarding handicaps was implied!

The following day, at the same venue, J.M. Challinor of The Worcestershire tied with F.A. Woolley of Kings Norton for the individual championship, with a score of 161. He subsequently beat Woolley in a thirty-six hole play-off with a score of 162. The bronze medal was won by another home player, W.W. Lowe who defeated Rev. James in another play-off.

Woolley was the only one of these gentlemen to represent Worcestershire in the first inter-county match, played against Gloucestershire at Minchinhampton on 1st June 1906. The details are as follows:

Worcestershire v Gloucestershire, 1906

	Worcestershire	*Gloucestershire*	
1	T.K. Ashton (1 up)	Hon. Denys Scott	0
1	F.A. Woolley (2 & 1)	G. Grieve	0
0	H.G. Nevile	J. Bryan (8 & 7)	1
0	T.W. Piggott	C.O.H. Sewell (19th)	1
1	S. Baldwin (2 & 1)	Rev. F.H. Fowler	0
0	W.R. Nash	A.S. Winterbottom (1 up)	1
1	F.R. Burrow (2 & 1)	E.H.T. Fowler	0
1	J.G. Baker (1 up)	E.H. Topham	0
0	J.W.G. Hill	L. Grist (4 & 3)	1
0	C.A. Horne	H.M. Newman (2 & 1)	1
1	A.C. Auster (1 up)	J.G. Wells	0
6			5

Mr. Ashton reached the semi-finals of the Amateur Championship in this year, losing to H.S. Colt, then secretary of Sunningdale and eventually to become one of the most distinguished of golf course architects. Ashton entered this tournament from Cheltenham; in 1907 it was proposed that cricket qualifications for inter-county matches be adopted, so presumably this was already tacitly in operation and Mr. Ashton's Worcestershire affiliation

Worcestershire v Nottinghamshire, 1906

was stronger than that to his Gloucestershire club – gentlemen golfers of the time were often members of more than one club. F.H. Fowler won the Parker Challenge Prize at Malvern during this year, so he, too, had divided loyalties.

At the annual meeting of the Union in 1906 a sub-committee was appointed to draw up local rules applicable to all member clubs and the Earl of Dudley was invited to become the first president of the Union. He was sufficiently addicted to the game to have his own private nine hole course at his seat, Witley Court, and to retain Andra' Kirkaldy as his personal professional. In 1902 he invited ten of the country's leading professionals to play in a tournament at Witley Court, which was won by Harry Vardon with a score of 153, despite the adverse snowy conditions.

A year later, as Lord Lieutenant of Ireland, the Earl of Dudley held a week-long tournament in Dublin, at great expense, and not greatly to the liking of local amateurs who found themselves without caddies for the week.

The county team played four more matches in 1906 after defeating Gloucestershire in the first match, beating them again at Malvern, beating Nottinghamshire at Kings Norton but losing the return match at Hollinwell and the match against Warwickshire, also at Kings Norton. The expenses for the two matches at Kings Norton came to 5s.6d. and 3s.7d. respectively and the Union concluded the season with a healthy balance in the bank of £15.4s.10d.

The Warwickshire match took place on 9th November, one month after that county's first meeting, and Frank Woolley lost a hard match against Charles Palmer, a member of Handsworth, who was also a member of Kings Norton, so the game must have been played in a spirit of friendly rivalry. One Warwickshire player was listed as A.N.Other in their victory by seven matches to four.

The sub-committee appointed to formulate the local rules for member clubs visited the clubs to fix the scratch score of each course, the basis for which was the bogey score plus five shots. This resulted in the following scores: Worcester City 71, Kidderminster 70, Moseley 72, Blackwell 72, Robin Hood 74, Bromsgrove 72, Redditch Walkwood 70, Edgbaston 66, Dudley 72, Evesham 72, Stourbridge 72, The Worcestershire 69 and Kings Norton 70.

This committee also recommended the following local rules:

1 A ball may at any time be lifted and dropped not nearer the hole under penalty of one stroke.

2 A ball lying in or touching dung may be lifted and dropped behind without penalty. (Most courses were used for grazing at this time, which helped to keep the grass at an acceptable height for golf.)

3 A ball played onto a putting green other than that of the hole being played must be lifted and dropped without penalty clear of the green but not nearer the hole and so that the line of the next shot is not made easier.

4 In the case of greens protected by posts and wire

(a) a ball lying on the putting green within two clubs length of the posts or wire in such a position that the posts or wire interfere with the stroke may be lifted and placed in a playable position no nearer the hole without penalty.

(b) if a ball played at a green strikes the post or wire between the player and the hole the player may drop a ball in or as near as possible to the original position and replay the stroke without penalty.

During this inaugural year a noted Scottish international, Edward B.H. Blackwell, was a member of Kidderminster Golf Club, which then played at Aggborough. A member of a distinguished golfing family who featured prominently in the activities of the Royal and Ancient Club of St Andrews, Blackwell was runner-up to Walter Travis in the Amateur Championship of 1904, which was played at Sandwich.

Blackwell was born in St Andrews and played for Scotland regularly from 1902 until 1912, and occasionally afterwards. He was runner-up in the Scottish Championship at the age of fifty-six. Between 1891 and 1923 he won twenty-one of the R&A's trophies. Another claim to fame was that he once drove a gutty ball a measured 366 yards, thought to be the longest recorded drive with this type of ball. After six years in California he returned to England and settled in the Midlands in 1898, taking one of Lord Dudley's farms. As a boy he was familiar with the exploits of such great names as Old and Young Tom Morris and Freddie Tait.

Frank Woolley

Edward Blackwell

Perhaps because of the indifference with which the R&A regarded the formation of county unions, this prominent member of the ruling body did not play in the Worcestershire team during the inaugural year, which was duly noted in the *Birmingham Daily Post*, which also criticised the Fosters for their non-participation. Blackwell took cognisance of this comment and changed his mind.

By the time of the council meeting on 8th February 1907, the Union had grown to fifteen member clubs, Stourbridge, Redditch Walkwood, Droitwich, Blackwell, Bromsgrove and Edgbaston having joined. At this time the Edgbaston course was situated in Warley; the club then moved to Harborne before acquiring its present site and thus becoming a member of the Warwickshire union.

The council meeting also approved the proposal to form a Midland Counties Golf Association, our delegates having attended the meeting called to discuss this initiative. The Earl of Plymouth was elected president of the Union, his secretary replying from the Earl's seat at Hewell Grange accepting the position on his Lordship's behalf.

The county championship in 1907 was held at Kings Norton and the Tomson-James Cup was won by the home club's team with a score of 322, ten clubs having entered. The gold medal was won by Frank Woolley with a score

North Worcestershire Golf Club
The opening of the extended course, 1st May 1912
Seated, left to right: Frank Wooley, James Braid, Harry Vardon, Frank Carr

of 151, and he returned the same score the following year at The Worcestershire. He became a dominant figure within the county and earned selection for England, representing his country in matches against Scotland in 1910, 1911 and 1912. He appears to have been a free-swinging, flamboyant character and was captain of Kings Norton in 1909-10. Woolley reached the quarter-finals of the Amateur Championship in 1910, losing by two holes to none other than Abe Mitchell, then still an amateur and artisan golfer.

He also enjoyed a game with the greatest golfer of the first ten years of the last century when he partnered James Braid on 1st May 1912 in an exhibition match against Harry Vardon and Frank Carr, the leading light of the Midland Counties Golf Association, to mark the opening of North Worcestershire's extended course. Braid had designed the new holes as well as the first nine but lost to Vardon in a medal played in the morning, Vardon scoring 74 to Braid's 79. He was in better form in the afternoon, he and Woolley winning by two holes.

Woolley died in 1933, arthritis having curtailed his career after the First World War.

Edward Blackwell took the 1907 silver medal and another Kidderminster member, J.P. Humphries, the bronze. Humphries was patriarch of another prominent Worcestershire golfing family, he and his son G.N.P. becoming captains of Stourbridge in 1920-22 and 1923 respectively, while his other son R.P. won the gold medal in 1920 and 1922, having reached the semi-final of the Amateur Championship in 1914.

Modern club administrators frustrated by the ever increasing Health and Safety regulations may be interested to learn that two of the council's members, Rev. James and Mr. Bewlay, proposed that advice be sought from a solicitor regarding the liability of clubs for accidents to caddies under the Workmens' Compensation Act.

The five inter-county matches that year resulted in defeat against Gloucestershire at Rodway Hill but Worcestershire won the return match at Malvern, where they also beat Warwickshire and then defeated them again at Harborne. The match against Nottinghamshire was won at Kings Norton.

Readers familiar with the Old Testament will know that Jehu was noted for furious driving and "G. Hugh" appeared for Worcestershire in the top match. Another furious driver, Edward Blackwell, had accepted the invitation to play but clearly did not wish to be identified by his St Andrews cronies. Blackwell's pseudonym did not fool James Coventry, the *Birmingham Post*'s golf correspondent, however. Blackwell lost his match by 2 & 1 but the Worcestershire tail wagged and ensured a win by seven points to four.

Kings Norton hosted the match against Gloucestershire the following year and proved a happy venue for the home county, who also defeated Warwickshire at Malvern. Nottinghamshire were beaten at Hollinwell but the other two away matches, at Olton and Cheltenham, resulted in losses.

The Worcestershire "A" team won the Tomson-James Cup on their home course, despite the performances of Frank Woolley and a Kings Norton colleague who was also a member of The Worcestershire, Shirley Baldwin, who won the bronze medal. The silver went to W.W. Lowe, a home player with a good record in the event.

That golf was never considered an easy game was demonstrated by the council's rejection of a proposal that a local rule be recommended to all clubs, permitting a ball buried in its own loft through the green to be lifted and dropped without penalty and that a ball lying on the putting green having mud upon it might be lifted and cleaned. Now, of course, both these forms of relief are permissible; this and the subsequent abolition of the stymie may give the modern golfer some idea of the integrity and competitiveness of our predecessors and the condition of some of the golf courses on which they played. In these formative years, rules were regularly discussed at the council meetings, advice being taken from the R&A as and when necessary. This was not always a straightforward affair, as

Kidderminster Golf Club, 1893
Back row, left to right: Ellis Talbot, Spencer Thursfield, Mansfield Newcome, Rev. Wells, Sir Sydney Lee J. Humphries, A.V. Moore, Rev. R.S.T. Chesshire. Front row: Dr. O.C. Evans, G. Henderson A.H. Mayne, Dr. Waddell, C.N. Bass

the indifference of the seaside golfers and lawmakers to other governing bodies precluded a knowledge of hazards such as hedges and ponds on inland courses.

Worcester City staged the 1909 meeting, at which The Worcestershire "A" team retained the team championship. A local player, G.M. Archdale, won the gold medal, Woolley taking the silver and J.P. Humphries the bronze after a tie with J.Custance of the home club. However, there was controversy over the draw for starting times, prompting a letter to the committee from Mr. G.F. Ward, the captain of Kings Norton, claiming irregularities which were "unfair and against the spirit of the game" and an even more strongly worded protest from Frank Woolley. He would have preferred a later start on Wednesday rather than "having to get up in the middle of the night to be on the tee when it is my turn". He recommended the disqualification of both the teams from Malvern who had been granted the later starting times. Mr. Carr agreed to look up the conditions under which this would be possible. Mr. Burrow informed the committee that he would be tabling an amendment to the rules at the next council meeting. The controversy had arisen because four masters from Malvern College had been allowed to begin their first

The opening of Comberton Golf Club, October 23rd 1909

rounds at 1.30 p.m. A ruling was made saying that first rounds had to be commenced before 12.00 noon.

During this year the Comberton club was formed at Kidderminster. Comberton was further from the town centre than the club at Aggborough and opened on 23rd October with a match between Captain Eric A. Knight M.P. and George Law jun. Archie Compston, aged sixteen, was appointed the first professional at a salary of fifteen shillings per week earning an extra shilling for "keeping the closets clean". Archie learned the game at Penn Common, Wolverhampton, the original course of the South Staffordshire club. He went on to achieve considerable success, beating Walter Hagen by 18 and 17 in a seventy-two hole match in 1928. Hagen turned the tables in the Open Championship a few days later and Compston never won golf's greatest prize, his prime coinciding with that of Hagen and Bobby Jones. He played in the first three Ryder Cup matches, his best performance being a 6 and 4 defeat of Gene Sarazen in the thirty-six hole singles at Moortown in 1929, when Great Britain and Ireland won the trophy for the first time.

Comberton affiliated to the Union in 1913 and changed its name to Kidderminster Golf Club in 1921 as by this time the earlier Kidderminster club at Aggborough had ceased to exist.

The council meeting in February 1910 proved more contentious than normal, as a result of the protests about the draw for the previous year's county team championship. This became the chief item for debate: one proposal was that the competition be played in the afternoon only; another suggestion was that teams should consist of three instead of four members but that clubs could enter three teams. Both of these motions were defeated but a third suggestion met with more approval and it was agreed to circulate clubs to discover if they would be in favour of teams consisting of four players but only three scores counting. The majority of replies to this proposal was not in favour of change, so the rules and conditions remained the same as originally agreed and all four scores continued to count.

Stourbridge "A" won the Tomson-James Cup on their home green with a score of 338, F. Gordon Smith (Dudley) won the gold medal with a score of 161, with H.W. Pearce (Stourbridge) taking the silver and J.V. Humphries (Kidderminster) the bronze. Six inter-county matches were played, Somerset defeating us at Weston-Super-Mare. The home matches with Gloucestershire and Warwickshire were won but the returns lost, while Nottinghamshire were beaten at Hollinwell once again.

By 1911 Moseley had extended its course to eighteen holes and the county championship was held there, Kidderminster winning the team prize and Frank Woolley the amateur championship with a score of 146. H.W. Pearce was runner-up for the second year in succession, having tied with L.S. Ball from Worcester.

Leicestershire was added to the rota of inter-county matches, the first meeting, at Leicester, resulting in victory for the home team. Worcestershire's only other defeats were at the hands of Warwickshire, home and away, an ominous circumstance in view of the implementation of the 1888 Land Act which affected the county boundary between Worcestershire and Warwickshire. A survey by The Worcestershire's F.R. Burrow in the *Field* and reprinted in the *Midland Golfer* revealed that Worcestershire had the largest fixture list of the eleven county unions and were placed fourth in a league table of results. Yorkshire, who only played three matches, all successfully, were placed top.

In the meantime Burrow conducted a more detailed study which revealed that the southern counties had so far shown little interest in forming golfing unions, apart from Sussex (founded in 1899).The movement was based in the Midlands and the north. One purpose of the unions was to formulate local rules for situations not envisaged in the R&A rules, St Andrews apparently showing little interest in inland golf, a theme regularly explored by James Coventry in the *Birmingham Daily Post.*

At the council meeting of 1911 this was the main topic of discussion as five clubs were moved from the administrative county of Worcestershire into Warwickshire and that county union's secretary, as a result of a resolution passed by the Midland Golf Association, against the wishes of Worcestershire, was authorised to write to the five clubs, claiming them for Warwickshire. It was pointed out that the MCC, faced with a similar predicament in cricket, declared that the geographical boundaries of the counties were not affected by the Act and would remain as they were formerly. The suggestion that this procedure be followed by the golfing authorities was passed and Kings Norton, Moseley, North Worcestershire, Robin Hood and Edgbaston were cordially invited to remain within the Worcestershire Union. The Midland Golf Association's handbook marked the affected clubs with an asterisk but Mr. Bewlay was "glad to report that they (he and his fellow delegates) had succeeded in inducing Mr. A.M. Lee, honorary secretary of the MGA, to omit the objectionable asterisk and note in the year book referring to the clubs affected by the Greater Birmingham Act."

Robin Hood affiliated to the Warwickshire union in 1912 and shortly afterwards moved to a new course previously used by Olton Golf Club. Edgbaston remained with Worcestershire until 1921, eventually settling at Edgbaston Hall in 1936. Kings Norton's move in 1970 took them firmly back inside Worcestershire's boundaries.

It was at this club's original course that the 1912 county meeting was held, Frank Woolley collecting a third gold medal, Edward Blackwell coming second and J.P. Humphries third, Blackwell's performance assisting Kidderminster to victory in the Tomson-James Cup.

Another new county entered the fixture list, Yorkshire meeting and beating Worcestershire at the neutral venue of Hollinwell, where the county also lost to Nottinghamshire. Both matches with Warwickshire were lost and our only victory was over Gloucestershire at Malvern, though we lost the return at Minchinhampton.

Brand Hall, and the newly formed Gay Hill and Comberton Golf Clubs, joined the Union in 1913, as did Headley Heath but this club did not survive the First World War. Its course was on what is now the southern boundary of Birmingham, close to the present Gay Hill course and its first, and only, professional was Tom Lewis of the renowned Lewis family from Malvern. The county meeting was held at Malvern, The Worcestershire's "A" team winning the Tomson-James Cup once again, with Moseley second and Kidderminster third. J.P. Humphries won the gold medal after several worthy attempts with a score of 161. J.H. Baker of Evesham won the silver medal after tieing with Clifford Nicholls of Dudley.

The Clubhouse, North Worcestershire Golf Club

The county fared better in the inter-county matches, winning the home engagement with Gloucestershire but losing away. Similar results were recorded against Warwickshire but Yorkshire, undertaking a brief Midland tour with "an unrepresentative team" were beaten by six matches to four at Kings Norton and Leicestershire and Rutland suffered a defeat by ten matches to one.

The county's hard-working match secretary, F.R. Burrow, announced his retirement from the position at the end of the 1913 season and was asked to write about his experiences for the *Midland Golfer,* a short-lived but informative journal which first appeared in 1911. Burrow explained his role in assisting the formation of the Union, the liaison with other county unions and his pleasure in turning out successful teams. He joined The Worcestershire club in 1894, was a country member of Kings Norton for five or six years and joined Worcester City in 1907. He played, "or tried to play, every course in the county except one, and that one omission will, I hope, be rectified before another month is out." Although his retirement was occasioned by pressure of work, Burrow intimated in the article that he would be continuing as chairman of the Union. *Nisbet's Golf Year Book* for 1910 lists Mr. Burrow's address as 4, Harcourt Buildings, Temple, E.C., which explains his difficulties.

The North Worcestershire club's loyalty over the issue of boundary changes was rewarded with the allocation of the 1914 meeting, for which there was a record of fifteen entries for the team event. This was won by Kings Norton "A" with a score of 342, Kidderminster and Stourbridge "A" tieing for second place nineteen strokes further behind. Kings Norton's fine performance was due to the gold and silver medal winners, Frank Woolley and Rev. H. Pelham, while N.S. Howson of Moseley finished third after a tie with T.S. Hall of Evesham.

Two of the seven inter-county matches arranged were cancelled due to bad weather, but apart from defeat at the hands of Gloucestershire, the remainder were won, including a new fixture with Shropshire and a signal victory by seven matches to four over Yorkshire at Lindrick. It would appear our best players had no qualms about travelling to such distant venues.

Worcestershire's first decade as a county golf union ended with the outbreak of the First World War. The council, anticipating an early end to the hostilities, planned to hold the championship at Moseley in 1916, having abandoned the idea of such an event in 1915. The council also agreed to waive subscriptions for 1915 as the finances were in a healthy state, the balance at the end of 1914 being £19.2s.3d. It was reported at the meeting that no fewer than thirty of the Malvern Working Mens Club's one hundred members were serving in the army. The *Midland Golfer* published lists of the members who had enlisted from a number of Midland clubs. The sad evidence of other clubs' members' enlistment can be found on most of our country's golf clubs' memorials.

Many courses were turned over either completely or partially to agriculture, with the result that some did not survive the war.

Chapter Two

Transition & Triumph

WITH MANY courses still recovering from agricultural usage, golf was not an entirely normal feature of post-war life and the council did not meet again until 29th February 1920, five years and seventeen days after the last meeting.

The Earl of Plymouth was re-elected as president and G.D. Carr honorary secretary, though he pointed out that "he lived in the wrong part of the county to keep in touch with the best golf and that it would be well for the Union to find a younger man". Mr. G. Duncan Wright was appointed as match secretary to alleviate Mr. Carr's burden. Mr. N.S. Howson of Moseley became the first chairman.

The meeting decided to hold subscriptions at the pre-war level and to revive competitions as soon as possible. The annual meeting was arranged at Moseley, the home club winning the Tomson-James Cup with a score of 330. The gold and silver medals were won by R.P. Humphries, who entered from The Worcestershire club and set a new course record of 73, and J.L. Humphreys of Blackwell respectively, N.S. Howson taking the bronze medal after a play-off with S.C. Craven of Stourbridge and R. Green of Kings Norton.

One inter-county match was played in which we beat Warwickshire by six matches to five, a promising start to what was to prove Worcestershire's most successful era, in which the county would play a dominant part in English golf.

Just as 1920 had begun with the creation of the new position of chairman, the following year was the first for which a captain was elected. The first gentleman to receive that honour was J.P. Humphries. Under his guidance the county team beat Warwickshire at home and away, but lost to Yorkshire at Alwoodley, while both the matches against Gloucestershire were cancelled, one due to the coal strike, the other because the opposition failed to raise a team.

The 1921 annual meeting was held at Stourbridge and produced the largest entry to date, with sixteen teams contesting the Tomson-James Cup, which was won by Dudley with an excellent score of 327. The donors of the cup were elected vice-presidents of the Union at the council meeting, but sadly Mr. Tomson died during the year, while the Rev. James had become an Archdeacon.

S.C. Craven (Stourbridge) won the gold medal, after a tie with F. Gordon Smith on 160, who took the silver, while the newly appointed county captain, J.P. Humphries, took the bronze.

The captain's two sons, R.P. and G.N.P., in securing the gold and bronze medals in 1922 also ensured, with the assistance of their father and S.C. Craven, that Stourbridge won the Tomson-James Cup with a record score of 318 at Kings Norton. In the championship R.P. scored 153 and G.N.P. 158, separated by N.S. Howson who claimed the silver medal with 156.

As well as being re-elected as captain at the council meeting, J.P. Humphries was elected vice-president. His team enjoyed another successful season with wins over Gloucestershire at Stourbridge, Yorkshire, who lost $10\frac{1}{2}$-$7\frac{1}{2}$ at Moseley, and Warwickshire, beaten 7-6 at Olton. The only defeat was against Gloucestershire at Minchinhampton, by 5 matches to 6.

Between 1923 and 1938 the Tomson-James Cup commuted between Stourbridge and Moseley, both clubs making important contributions to Worcestershire's rising prominence nationally. This duopoly was broken by Blackwell in 1929, Moseley regaining the Cup in 1930, only to hand it back to Blackwell the following year. Brand Hall managed to win it for the only time in 1932. A year later Stourbridge won at Malvern. Moseley reclaimed the cup in 1934 and to show the rivalry was only friendly shared it with Stourbridge in 1936, but took sole possession again the next year. Kings Norton was the next club to have the temerity to break with tradition but Stourbridge laid claim to the trophy for the next two years and so held the cup until the resumption of golfing hostilities in 1946, when they proved worthy winners yet again.

The championship was also beginning to settle into a pattern, the new names on the medals becoming familiar in the higher ranks of the amateur game. Those who were to have a major impact also appeared in the county's administration; for example, Mr. Guy Bigwood of the Blackwell club, who in 1923 was elected chairman for the following season and remained in that position until his death in 1966. He had joined Blackwell in 1903, played for the county before the First World War, and afterwards served his club as honorary secretary. He became president of the club in 1944 and remained in that office until his death. He also played one match in 1929, against Warwickshire at Blackwell.

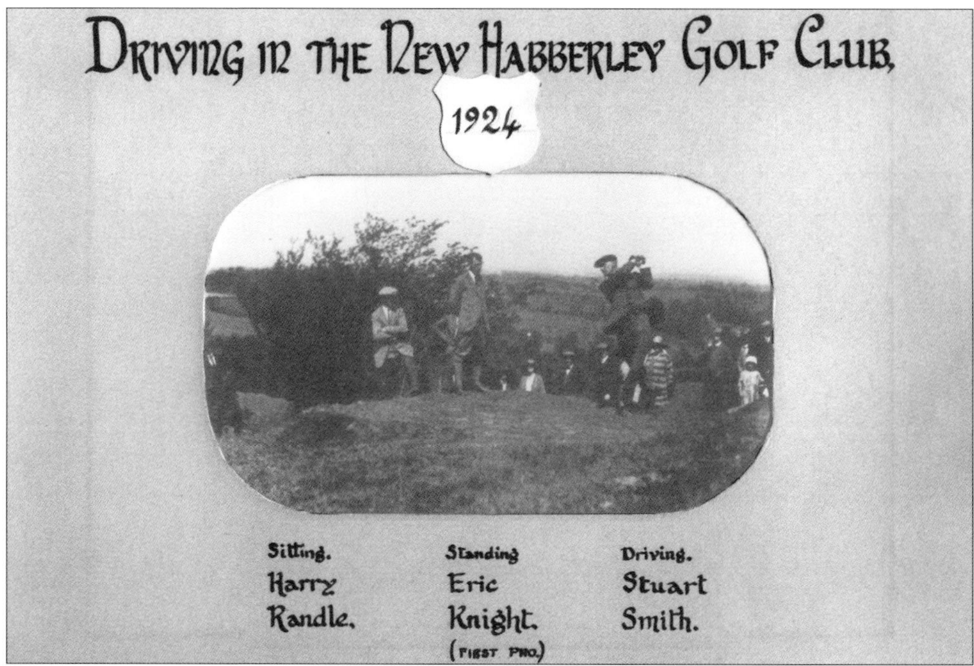

Habberley course opening 24th May 1924

Guy Bigwood was an all-round sportsman who played cricket for Barnt Green and football for Moseley before the war. He was a dominant character of firm opinions and a strong advocate of the amateur game. He became the senior partner in the estate agents, Edwards, Son, Bigwood and Matthews, a Justice of the Peace and also president of his professional association. The Worcestershire Union of Golf Clubs enjoyed its most successful years under his authority. So effective was his administration of Blackwell that it was regularly referred to as "Bigwood Golf Club".

The council sent two delegates, G.N.P. Humphries and E. Somers Smith, to a meeting in Manchester in February 1924 to assist in the arrangements for the formation of an English Golf Union, thirty years after Laidlaw Purves first perceived the need for such an organisation. Worcestershire resolved to support this Union from its inception and accordingly member clubs were asked to pay an extra guinea in addition to the annual subscription. E.Somers Smith and Duncan Wright were appointed the county's delegates to the Union, which began its operation in that year. One of its first tasks was issuing a new system of standard scratch scores which Worcestershire began implementing in 1925.

Habberley Golf Club joined the Union in 1924, when a record number of eighteen teams took part in the Tomson-James and fifty-five players entered the individual championship, E. Somers Smith winning the gold medal, R.P.Humphries the silver and W.W. Lowe reappearing among the winners to take the bronze.

Also appearing in 1924 were the first signs of the founding club's dissatisfaction with its course on the common. Voiced in the *Birmingham Gazette* in May, and echoed at a meeting held in the clubhouse a year later, the *Gazette's* correspondent wrote:

> The Malvern course possesses many peculiarities which, without in the least wishing to detract from its quality from a playing point of view, one can justly say have a somewhat disconcerting influence upon members of the majority of Midland clubs ... Many of the competitors found the traffic along the roads and the railways which intersect the course troublesome while few of them failed to negotiate the railway cutting from the 11th tee. It was the 12th where many found themselves in difficulties. Here not only has the roadway to be crossed, but a pulled tee shot usually finds the railway, which is, of course, out of bounds.

The Stourbridge/Moseley rivalry continued in 1925, when the meeting was held at Blackwell. In assisting Stourbridge to second place behind Moseley, Gerald Humphries broke the course record, scoring 73. This new record lasted one day, for Stanley Lunt of Moseley completed his second round in 72 strokes, giving him a total of 149 and the gold medal, Humphries coming second.

His brother R.P. "Percy", also had a fine season, winning the gold medal at the Midland Counties meeting at Olton and the amateur prize in the professional and amateur tournament at Copt Heath, finishing four shots behind the leading professional.

During the season the county team won three of the four matches played, losing to Gloucestershire at Cleeve Hill.

For the 1926 season the Union purchased the trophy known as the G.D. Carr Cup in recognition of that gentleman's continued service to the county as secretary. It was to be presented to the player returning the best scratch aggregate score in all three rounds of the county meeting and the first winner was J.L. Humphreys of Blackwell. He took the silver medal in the championship, second to Gerald Humphries. C.S. Buckley, also of Blackwell, won the bronze medal after a tie with C.J. Reece of Kings Norton. Mr. Carr was entertained to dinner by the Union and received a presentation in honour of his efforts on the Union's behalf.

J.L. Humphreys, CMG, CBE, was described as a brilliant golfer. The reason he did not figure more prominently in the county's golfing records is that he was only able to play golf when on leave from his position as Governor of British North Borneo. After gaining his Blue at Oxford in 1903-04, he entered the Civil Service, in which he had a brilliant career. He played rugby for the university and the Midland Counties, and golf for the Midlands and the Oxford and Cambridge Golfing Society as well

Dr. William Tweddell

as Worcestershire. He is listed in the "Who's Who" of golfers in *Nisbet's Golfing Year Book* of 1911, but was apparently not a member of a Worcestershire club at that time, although he did play for the county in 1910, his birth qualification rendering him eligible for selection. Blackwell granted him honorary membership in 1926.

The golf correspondent of the *Birmingham Gazette* described him thus: "Possessed of a good sound style, he played every shot with the firmness of the leading professionals. He was a fairly long driver, but straightness was his first consideration; and in approaching his shots invariably 'covered the pin' all the way." The writer considered that he would have earned national selection but for the fact that he spent most of his life in the Far East. He died in December 1929 on his way home from North Borneo.

Under the captaincy of William Pearson the county team beat Gloucestershire and Shropshire but lost to Warwickshire in a close match.

1927 heralded the emergence of Worcestershire as a major force in English golf. A young man named Eric Westwood Fiddian of the Stourbridge club won the Boys Amateur Championship at the Royal Burgess Club in Edinburgh, beating K. Forbes of Leven by 4 and 2 in the final, in a "sporting match". Earlier in the week he made his second appearance for the England Boys against Scotland, equalling the course record at Barnton. The *Birmingham Post* described the play thus:

> Splendid though McRuvie's golf was, it was eclipsed by Eric Fiddian's (Bromsgrove School), a finished and stylish golfer who played second for England as he did a year ago at Coombe Hill ... Fiddian went round in level fours and his score of 72 with everything holed out was all the more wonderful considering the course was soaked in many parts and very little run, if any, on the ball. Fiddian's figures made from the back tees equalled the record made for the course by W.B.Torrance, the British International player.
>
> Scotland won by seven matches to five despite Eric's play, and Eric McRuvie and he became very good friends.

Eric won the silver medal in the county championship, coming second to S.T. Matthews of Moseley, who also won the G.D. Carr Cup, while Stanley

Lunt took the bronze medal. Eric and his brother Douglas became key members of the county team, as did another Stourbridge member, Dr. William Tweddell. He bought a practice in the town after first inspecting the golf course and was invited to participate in the county trial on March 1st, when Mr. Pearson's team played Mr. J.P. Humphries' team at Blackwell. Tweddell holed in one on the fifteenth hole (now the sixth).

Dr. Tweddell took his annual holiday to coincide with the Amateur Championship, which in 1927 was held at the Royal Liverpool Golf Club, Hoylake. After a bye in the first round he had comfortable wins in the second and third rounds, before being taken to the 20th hole by J. Moir in the fourth round. His opponent in the next round was C.C. Aylmer, whom Dr. Tweddell disposed of by 4 and 3 with brilliant golf which took him to the turn in 33 shots. He won his next match against Len Nettlefold, a left-hander from Tasmania, by the same margin, thereby reaching the semi-final where his opponent was none other than Roger Wethered, the 1923 champion.

Dr. Tweddell continued his excellent form and was five up on Wethered after seven holes, eventually winning by 4 and 3. In his history of the championship, John Behrend recorded that the final was a disappointing affair, but not for Worcestershire. Dr. Tweddell beat the local favourite D.E. Landale 7 and 6, a margin that would have been greater had the doctor not twice been disturbed by newsreel cameras while putting for wins. The County Union celebrated his victory with a dinner and presentation in recognition of his achievement. During the year Tweddell also won the Midland Amateur Championship. As a result of these successes he was selected for the Walker Cup team which lost 11-1 to the United States in Chicago in 1928. He also served on the national selection committee during that year.

In the meantime the English County Championship was inaugurated in 1926. This involved teams of four players until 1938 when teams were reduced to three. The result was decided by stroke play until 1955 when the semi-final and final were settled by match play, four regions having been formed each sending a six-man team from the leading qualifying county. The current round robin system was instituted in 1982. Worcestershire qualified for the final in 1927 and came second to Surrey on so windy a day at Little Aston that only six players scored under 80 in the two rounds. One of these was Dr. Tweddell, whose total of 157 was the joint best score in the competition.

In the English Amateur Championship, which followed this event, Stanley Lunt lost to Warwickshire's Carl Bretherton by one hole in a memorable second round match, while Dr. Tweddell and Chris Buckley reached the sixth round. The winner was Phil Perkins, also of Warwickshire, and as a result an intriguing encounter was set up for later in the season.

The administration of the county's affairs in 1927 was placed jointly in the hands of Mr. Carr and Philip Padmore who was elected to assist him, an arrangement which continued until 1934 when Mr. Carr died. Padmore continued as secretary until 1948.

The rest of the season's matches are recorded in a match book: Eric Fiddian made his county debut against Gloucestershire on Saturday 25th June, losing to K.F. Tarrant. R.P. Humphries and his father, C.S. Buckley, N.S. Howson, William Pearson (the captain), G.P. Chamberlain, C.B. Kempson, C.R. Hough, R.C. East and E.A. Phipps made up the rest of the team, which won the match 11½-6½.

Fiddian did not play in the next match which was comfortably won against Staffordshire but he returned, along with Dr. Tweddell, for the match against Cheshire on 16th July at Hoylake, where the home team inflicted a most humiliating defeat upon our men, winning ten of the twelve singles and all six foursomes. Chris Buckley and Eric Fiddian scored Worcestershire's only points.

The season ended with a match against Warwickshire at Blackwell and was the cause of much interest because it brought Dr. Tweddell, the Amateur champion, head to head for the first time with the English Amateur champion and joint leading amateur in the Open Championship, Phil Perkins. A local paper reported:

> Dr. Tweddell did not open brilliantly. He was battling not only against a steadier opponent but against his own relatively poor form. His run-up to the second green was surprisingly short and a hooked shot from the third tee finished out of bounds …

Perkins went two up after seven holes but the doctor did not give up …

> Up to this point Mr. Perkins had a slight advantage in length, and it is no part of the plan of an experienced golfer such as Dr. Tweddell is, to strain to outdrive so prodigious an adversary … The match was too good to see, for both were fighting hard …

In the end Dr. Tweddell won by 2 and 1 and Worcestershire by 8 matches to 3.

Perkins was Dr. Tweddell's foursomes partner in the Walker Cup match in Chicago the following year and they were comfortably beaten by Jesse Sweetser and George von Elm, who also beat Tweddell in the singles, while Perkins played in the top match against Bobby Jones. Despite losing 13 and 12, Perkins was not disheartened, remained in the United States, turned professional and enjoyed some success, despite being accidentally shot in the leg by a gangster in 1932.

The rules of the Union were amended in 1928 to provide for an executive committee consisting of the officers of the Union together with the two delegates to the Midland Counties Golf Association. The notice required for a general meeting was reduced to fourteen days instead of thirty. These rule changes were the reason for the Union's issuing a booklet which also summarised the county's golfing history.

The county championship featured the same three winners as the previous year, but in a different order, for Eric Fiddian won his first gold medal, Stanley Lunt the silver and S.T. Matthews the bronze after tieing with Lunt. Eric won the G.D. Carr Cup, his third round being "an almost if not entirely impeccable 74", according to the *Birmingham Gazette.*

Dr. Tweddell entered the Open Championship but failed to qualify for the final rounds.

The county team put up a better showing against Cheshire at Blackwell, losing by the odd match although it was reported that we were not at our full strength. Dr. Tweddell played in the top match and Eric Fiddian in the second pairing, while Douglas Fiddian came into the team in twelfth position. It is interesting to see the name of one J. Braid jun. listed in the opposing team and he played again the following year when the match consisted of foursomes and fourballs, instead of the usual singles and foursomes format. He was the son of the great James Braid, five times Open champion and designer of over 300 golf courses in the British Isles, including a representative selection in Worcestershire. In the fourball match in 1929 he was partnered by the splendidly named Israel Sidebottom, and Eric Fiddian, who played against them in company with Chris Buckley, recalls that Braid, as well as being good company, was using his father's hickory shafted clubs. James jun. played against us twice more in the 1930s. The remaining results in 1928, apart from a convincing win over Gloucestershire, were disappointing, Staffordshire winning 11-7 and Warwickshire by one match.

Matters improved in 1929 when the only loss was to Cheshire at Stockport in the different format. Earlier, the council had decided only to play inter-county matches against counties having borders with Worcestershire. Staffordshire were beaten by 11-7, two of their points coming from the celebrated Charles Stowe in his first encounter with our team.

Blackwell interrupted the Moseley/Stourbridge domination of the Tomson-James Cup for that club's first victory.

Habberley had resigned from the Union in 1927 but by the end of 1929 there were eighteen member clubs, Rose Hill and Cocks Moors Woods having joined, although Brandwood House resigned, albeit temporarily, for they rejoined in 1930. Brintons Limited Golf Club and Malvern Common Golf Club further augmented the membership list.

The 1930 meeting was held at Stourbridge and resulted in an exciting tie between Eric Fiddian and Dr. Tweddell, on 143, with Stanley Lunt two shots

Dr. William Tweddell, Bobby Jones, Stanley Lunt and Eric Fiddian at Blackwell in 1930

behind. Eric won the play-off with a score of 146 to Tweddell's 155, and also the G.D. Carr Cup.

Both men entered the Amateur Championship at St Andrews and both reached the sixth round, when John de Forest eliminated Dr. Tweddell. Eric beat the well-known Tony Torrance of the R&A and so approached one of the most exciting and demanding matches of his career, for his opponent in the seventh round was none other than Robert Tyre Jones, popularly known as "Bobby". He remembers that the crowd was so dense he was unable to see Jones's approach to the first hole and it was his caddy who informed him that he had won the first hole with a four, after Jones had mishit his second shot. However, the American made few further errors and won the match 4 and 3. He went on to win the final against Roger Wethered, and the Open, and the Open and Amateur Championships of his own country, an achievement which can never be equalled. After his Open victory at Hoylake Bobby Jones honoured his earlier acceptance of an invitation to play at Blackwell the next day with Eric Fiddian, Stanley Lunt and Dr. Tweddell. He remained in touch with Tweddell for many years.

Although the match against Staffordshire resulted in an 11-7 defeat, the county won all its other encounters, beating Gloucestershire 14-4, Shropshire

Chris Buckley

10-8, having trailed by two points after the morning's singles, and getting the better of Cheshire at last when the normal format of singles and foursomes was used, although thirteen players participated in the singles matches. Another recovery was staged against Warwickshire, who lost all six foursomes matches after leading 7-5 at lunch.

The team had been strengthened by Dr. William Robb, a Scottish international. A general practitioner, he came to Birmingham in 1927, joined Moseley and became a leading figure in both the club and the county's activities. He participated in Moseley's success in the Tomson-James Cup in 1928 and the club's subsequent victories, but was not selected, or was not available for selection, until 1930 for the county team. He was the Highland Amateur champion in 1929 and 1930.

Blackwell won the Tomson-James Cup in 1931 when Worcester Golf and Country Club held the event at Boughton Park for the first time, the new course being reported as "in good order" in the county's minute book. Chris Buckley set a course record of 68 during the team event. He tied with Eric Fiddian for the bronze medal in the championship, but as the play-off did not take place within the stipulated time the medal was not awarded. The gold and silver medals, however, were won by Dr.Tweddell and Alan Newey of Moseley respectively.

Buckley had joined Blackwell in 1925 when he was already thirty-nine years old and a scratch player. Originally from Manchester, he moved south to play football for Brighton and Hove Albion in 1905, was transferred to Aston Villa the following year and joined Redditch Golf Club, of which he became captain in 1924. He became sales manager for the Austin Motor Company and chairman of Aston Villa. He played regularly for the county team from 1929 until 1935, and again after the Second World War. He became captain of Blackwell in 1948 and president of the club in succession to Guy Bigwood in 1967. Buckley and Eric Fiddian were involved in a memorable match at Handsworth after Eric had won that club's Open for the second time and been accorded honorary life membership. They were invited to play against the professionals Percy Alliss and Abe Mitchell. The organisers feared the worst for the amateurs and granted them a start of three holes up, which immediately became two when the professionals birdied the first hole. Eric heard a spectator mutter, "I told you so." He was not impressed and by the time he eagled the par 5 twenty-seventh hole he and Buckley had won the match 10 and 9.

Staffordshire were annihilated by seventeen matches to one in the first inter-county match of 1931 and Warwickshire and Gloucestershire were beaten in less spectacular fashion, while our only defeat was inflicted on us by Cheshire. Our four-man team of the Fiddian brothers, Stanley Lunt and Neville Seers finished second to Yorkshire in the English County Championship at Hunstanton, just two strokes behind the winners.

The increase in the number of affiliated clubs to twenty-three in 1932, with Warley and Churchill and Blakedown joining and Habberley resuming membership, and despite the Malvern Common club dropping out, was purely coincidental but nevertheless a reflection of the county's success. These clubs supplied eighteen teams for the Tomson-James Cup that year, when it was played at Brand Hall. The home club, represented by J.T. Mitchley, A. Lowe, E.W. Rigbey and L.N. Wilkes, won the event. Mitchley then won the gold medal and the G.D. Carr Cup and Wilkes tied with Stanley Lunt for the silver, Lunt winning the play-off. Before the Second World War Brand Hall was a private club and longer than its present yardage.

This was a vintage year for Worcestershire; not only was Spencer Newey of Moseley elected president of the English Golf Union, three of our players, Eric Fiddian, Stanley Lunt and Alan Newey, were selected for the Home Internationals at Troon, in which England beat Wales and Ireland and lost narrowly to Scotland. With the addition of Chris Buckley to these three, the county came third in the English County Championship at Royal St George's. Eric remained at the venue to compete in the English Amateur Championship and beat A.S. Bradshaw in the final. Later in the season he went to Muirfield to play in the Amateur Championship and reached the final, only to fall 3 and 1 to John de Forrest, the runner-up a year before. They became good friends and both were selected for the Walker Cup held that year in Brookline, Massachussets, when the Americans inflicted yet another heavy defeat on our team.

Back in the Midlands, the county team won three matches, halved one and lost 11-7 to Staffordshire after being all square after the morning's singles. The Moseley team of S.T. Matthews, Stanley Lunt and Alan Newey won the Midland team championship at Moseley with a record score of 223, Matthews winning the gold medal and the Frank Carr Cup, Lunt the silver medal and

J.T. Mitchley the bronze. S.T. Matthews continued his good form when he became leading amateur in the amateur and professional tournament at Sutton Coldfield.

At the end of this exciting year the council proposed that a second team match be arranged with Staffordshire for the following year. The players were all to be under thirty years old and not regular members of the county team. The fixture duly took place and was highly successful, the result being a halved match. This team subsequently beat the county ladies.

The team and individual championships were held at The Worcestershire in 1933 and Stourbridge reclaimed the Tomson-James Cup but a new name was engraved on the gold medal. John Fraser of the home club also won the G.D. Carr Cup, scoring 74 + 74 + 71 = 219. During a long career John won a multitude of trophies at his club but unfortunately a moment's indecision cost him international selection while still a boy. Apparently, he was eligible to play for both England and Scotland and, in the absence of his father, was unable to make up his mind quickly enough to satisfy the selectors.

John Fraser made his county debut in the match against Cheshire in July, when the county suffered a heavy defeat. We also lost to Staffordshire but beat Leicestershire and Rutland and Gloucestershire, both matches being played at Moseley.

Eric Fiddian, Chris Buckley, Dr. William Tweddell and Stanley Lunt travelled to Ganton for the English County Championship and put up yet another good performance, finishing second to Yorkshire. Moseley won the Midland Counties Championship for the second year in succession, Stanley Lunt setting a new record of 69 at Little Aston, which assisted his claiming the Frank Carr Cup. Eric Fiddian won the silver medal and two more of our players tied for the bronze, Dr. Tweddell beating Dr. Robb in the play-off.

Robb was involved in another tie when he and Chris Buckley recorded the same scores in the Howitt Bowl at Moseley. It took them 72 holes to reach a decision!

Having been eliminated in the second round of the Amateur Championship, Eric Fiddian entered the Irish Amateur Championship at Royal County Down. His brother Douglas had been runner-up in 1930 and Eric was fated to finish in a similar position, losing 3 and 2 to Jack McLean, despite scoring a hole in one in each round of the final.

By May 1933 the English Golf Union was implementing its standard scratch score and handicapping scheme and the county's clubs were assessed as follows: Blackwell 74, Brandwood House 71, Churchill and Blakedown 66, Droitwich 69, Evesham 72, Habberley 70, Kidderminster 73, Moseley 74, Redditch 67, Stourbridge 74, Worcester and County (sic) 74, Brand Hall 74, Brinton's Hall 68, Cocks Moors Woods 69, Dudley 73, Gay Hill 74,

Halesowen 71, Kings Norton 74, North Worcestershire 73, Rose Hill 69, Warley 69, and The Worcestershire 72. Redditch, Kings Norton and The Worcestershire were on their original courses; Brandwood House closed in 1936 and Brinton's did not survive the Second World War.

1934 began ominously when Guy Bigwood announced at the council meeting that Archdeacon James, one of the prime movers of the county Union and joint donor of the trophy that shares his name with J.J. Tomson, had recently died. He also reported the death after a long illness of Mr. G.D. Carr who had acted as secretary from the very beginning.

The Union adopted an idea already in use by Derbyshire and Warwickshire of the county individual membership scheme, whereby members of clubs within the county, upon payment of a fee, could enjoy the privilege of a free day's golf at other courses within the county. The advantage of the scheme was increased revenue for the county Union and it proved a popular idea.

This was the year when Worcestershire's promising performances finally bore fruit, when our team won the English County Championship at Formby on 21st April. Alan Newey 152, Eric Fiddian 152, Chris Buckley 152, and William Robb 154, set a new record score of 610, five lower than Cheshire and twelve ahead of Yorkshire – "a popular and decisive win" according to the *Birmingham Post*'s special correspondent. Newey was playing in place of Dr. Tweddell. Eric Fiddian had not entered the English Amateur Championship which followed this event but Stanley Lunt had and the *Post*'s correspondent was there to report on his success. After playing excellent golf all the way to the final against Leonard Crawley, an international at cricket as well as golf, Lunt made a poor start and was six holes down at lunchtime. It was Crawley who made mistakes in the second round, though, and Lunt pulled him back and eventually won on the 37th hole.

It was a great match, fought courageously and in a spirit of true sportsmanship. "He is one of the nicest men to play against you could possibly meet", said Stanley, referring to his opponent. "He is generous and sporting; he saw I was up against it this morning and tried to encourage me. I tried this afternoon to concentrate on getting my figures, rather than on any opponent."

Eric Fiddian did enter the Amateur Championship but was eliminated in the fourth round; had he beaten Wallace of Troon he would have met Jack McLean in the next round. Nevertheless he was selected for the Walker Cup again, held at St Andrews in that year. Once again Great Britain and Ireland were heavily beaten. He played in all the other international matches that year, as did Stanley Lunt.

Blackwell was the venue for the championships and Moseley won the Tomson-James Cup, represented by Stanley Lunt, William Robb, Alan Newey and J.W. Allen. The individual championship was won by a new arrival in the county, another Scottish doctor, G.H. Marshall, who had entered practice in Worcester and joined Worcester Golf and Country Club. Neville Seers of Kings Norton won the silver medal and Eric Fiddian the bronze, his third place tieing him with Seers for the G.D. Carr Cup, which he won in the play-off.

Dr. Marshall was immediately selected for the county team, and was one of the most successful players in what was a good season. Staffordshire were defeated 14½-3½, Gloucestershire 15-2 and Leicestershire 12-4, but we could only earn a half with Warwickshire and lost rather heavily to Cheshire.

Guy Bigwood, chairman of the Union, was elected president of the Midland Counties Golf Association and served on the English Golf Union's joint advisory committee.

Stanley Lunt replaced Eric Fiddian in the team selected to defend the English County Championship, which was held at Hollinwell in 1935. Chris Buckley returned the excellent score of 150 and the three Moseley players, Lunt, Newey and Robb, scored 151, 152 and 154 respectively to create a new record total of 607 and retain the title. The Worcestershire players all scored below 80 in each round, a feat achieved by no other team, on what the *Birmingham Post* described as "a day not too favourable for golf. The wind blew shrilly from the north-east and made things difficult at some of the outward holes." In contrast to Lunt's "steady, blameless kind of golf", Alan Newey's afternoon round was "a round of flaws and flashes".

Stanley Lunt carried on his steady form to reach the semi-final of the English Amateur Championship, losing to J. Woollam, another English international, who went on to beat Eric Fiddian in the final.

Later in the year Eric reached the sixth round of the Amateur Championship, losing to Dr.Tweddell, who proceeded to the final where he lost by one hole to the great American player, Lawson Little, who thereby retained the trophy. During the competition Little's caddie had to carry twenty-six clubs and this eventually led to the rule restricting players to fourteen being passed, after a suggestion from Dr. Tweddell. Little turned professional a year later and enjoyed some success in his native country.

This was the year Moseley and Stourbridge tied for the Tomson-James Cup and agreed to share it rather than arrange a play-off. However, Moseley won the Midland Counties team event, while Eric Fiddian won the silver medal and the Frank Carr Memorial Trophy and Alan Newey the bronze. The Worcestershire championship medals were won by J.T. Mitchley (Brand Hall) gold, W.M. Robb, silver, and J.T. Wheeler (North Worcestershire) bronze after a tie with W. Anderson (Stourbridge). Mitchley also took the G.D. Carr Cup.

Six inter-county matches were played in 1935, Worcestershire winning them all by impressive margins. Stanley Lunt played in all the Home

International matches as the England captain, supported by Eric Fiddian and, for the match against Ireland, Dr. Tweddell, who unfortunately sustained an injury and so missed the other two matches. Lunt also captained England in their victory against France.

1936 was the year in which the new terms of the individual championship were implemented: the leading eight players qualified to play off for the match play championship. Both Eric Fiddian and Stanley Lunt welcomed the idea, but only Lunt qualified for this after assisting Moseley to victory in the Tomson-James Cup. Eric missed a substantial part of the season as he had badly injured his back while working for the family business. The injury was sufficiently serious to terminate his international career but he continued to serve his country by acting as a selector. He was able to play in the Midland Counties Championship, winning the silver medal.

The leading qualifiers for the first match play championship were Stanley Lunt, William Robb, Neville Seers (Kings Norton), J.G. Allen (Moseley), W.C.I. Boulton (Stourbridge), G. Baynton (Blackwell), Dr. G. Marshall (Worcester) and K.C. Forbes (Dudley). An automatic draw saw the four leading qualifiers through to the semi-finals, Lunt and Robb proceeding to the thirty-six hole final which Lunt won 4 and 2. The first two rounds were covered extensively by the local press.

The English County Championship was played at Deal, Surrey taking first place while we finished a disappointing fourth, represented by Messrs. Robb, Lunt, Newey and Mitchley.

Probably the most exciting inter-county match was the halved one with Staffordshire when we earned 7½ points in the singles to draw level. The remaining matches were won with some ease, although the fixture against Yorkshire at Blackwell was abandoned after the visitors had taken a slight lead after the foursomes because of a torrential rainstorm.

During 1936 Fulford Heath and Tolladine Golf Clubs affiliated to the Union, followed later in the year by Malvern St Andrews. As Brandwood House had closed down there were twenty-five clubs in the Union.

Despite this increase, only fourteen clubs competed for the Tomson-James Cup in 1937 at Kings Norton. The home club's team of C.J. Reece, Stan Seymour, Neville Seers and D.W. Parker returned the lowest total recorded for this competition, 295, and Reece won the G.D. Carr Cup. The draw for the championship was different from the previous year, as Reece played and lost to Dr. Robb who had the second best score, 150, after Reece's 149. Dr. Robb beat Seymour in the semi-finals and E.W. Rigbey of Brand Hall beat Cyril Boulton. Five down at lunch time in the final Rigbey recovered slightly in the second round but failed to sustain the improvement and Robb won 5 and 3.

Three inter-county matches were won and two lost; interest in the county membership scheme remained at the same level as the previous year and Upton-on-Severn Golf Club became affiliated to the Union but did not enjoy a long existence.

During the year the Worcestershire Association of Professional Golfers was formed, with Guy Bigwood as its first president. The first committee members were Ernest Cawsey, W.R. Firkins, C. Hobley, K. Hooker, F. Larke, H.E. "Pop" Lewis, L. Matthews, H. Nash and A.R. "Dick" Wheildon. Wheildon was a prominent member of the Professional Golfers Association and in the previous decade had been part of a delegation led by J.H. Taylor which negotiated with the R&A the method by which professionals could qualify for the Open Championship.

This was the beginning of a long and happy connection between the professional and amateur players in the county and several of the latter have had the honour of serving as the Association's president. In 1978 the Association became the first such body to start a sponsorship scheme to provide pensions for the county's professionals.

Stourbridge reclaimed the Tomson-James Cup in 1938 on their own course, the venue having been moved from Kidderminster where a new clubhouse was being built and alterations made to the course. The club also did well in the individual championship, Eric Fiddian, Dr. Tweddell and Dr. W. Anderson coming second, third and fourth in the qualifying event behind Harley Roberts of Brand Hall. Eric beat Dr. Anderson and met Dr. Tweddell in the semi-final. The doctor prevailed in this encounter and beat E.W. Rigbey of Brand Hall in the final, one of three qualifiers from that club. William Robb took the other bronze medal.

Worcestershire players took all the medals in the Midland Counties competition at Beau Desert, J.S. Mitchley (Brand Hall) taking the gold, Dr. Anderson the silver and Dr. Robb the bronze. Harley Roberts won the West of England Open Amateur Championship at Burnham and Berrow, beating a local player in the final.

Four of the six inter-county matches were won, the Staffordshire match was halved but we lost to Cheshire.

In 1939 the English County Championship conditions were changed, teams being reduced to three players. Worcestershire was represented by Dr. W. Anderson, Stanley Lunt and J.S. Mitchley. In atrocious weather conditions at Birkdale our team prevailed over the opposition and the sixty miles an hour gale which blew away two marquees. Charlie Stowe of Staffordshire was the only player to break 80 in both rounds and helped his county to third place. Worcestershire's third victory in this event meant that they had equalled the achievement of Surrey and Lancashire. We also finished second twice and third once in the nine years from 1931. This "golden age" was brought to a harsh conclusion by the outbreak of the Second World War, but not before Stourbridge annexed the Tomson-James Cup "for the duration" and Dr. Anderson won the gold medal in the individual championship, defeating R.H. Crump of Blackwell in the final. The championships were held at Kidderminster, so one presumes the course alterations had been successful. Neville Seers would have thought so, for he set a new course record of 70 in a replay for the handicap prize, having already won the G.D. Carr Cup.

The previous year's success was repeated at the Midland Counties meeting, held at Castle Bromwich. Moseley won the team championship with the lowest score for forty years, Dr. Robb won the gold medal, the Spencer Newey Memorial Cup and the Frank Carr Memorial Trophy. Stanley Lunt won the silver medal and J.S. Doughty the bronze after a tie with Charlie Stowe and H.J. Hall. The county team won all the four matches played, including one against Glamorgan at Royal Porthcawl. The match against Leicestershire was cancelled as the opposition could not raise a team while the Warwickshire fixture, due to be played in October, was cancelled for more urgent reasons.

A council meeting was held on 25th January 1940 and Guy Bigwood expressed the view that the various national and area championships should not be played as too many potential winners would be unable to play in them. His view was forwarded to the English Golf Union, who obviously concurred as there was no more competitive golf until 1946. However, several professionals, organised by Henry Cotton, toured the country during the war playing exhibition matches to raise funds for various war charities. Realising that the county could play its part in raising funds for war charities, the executive arranged a number of winter competitions to this effect.

The prizes were of little value, following the credo of the English Golf Union, which maintained that "no amateur event should be financially worth winning". The competitions were foursomes – "a welcome variation from the widespread fourballer habit" according to the *Birmingham Post.* Professionals and ladies were entitled to play, the professionals being rated at plus 3, while the ladies added six strokes to their LGU handicaps. A meeting at Blackwell resulted in £50 being raised to "provide comforts for soldiers serving in the Worcestershire regiments".

The winners were W.C.I. Boulton and W.R. Firkins, the Stourbridge professional, while in third place were R.G.M. Morgan and J.G. Allen of Moseley. This represented Ronnie Morgan's last success for some time for not long afterwards his plane was shot down and he spent the remainder of the war in Stalag Luft III.

Gay Hill exhibition match opens the new course, 1922

A subsequent meeting at Stourbridge raised £150, a third of which was raised at an auction held at the meeting. Chris Buckley and A. Brack were the winners on this occasion.

Many clubs not completely turned over to agriculture devised local rules to cope with wartime conditions. However, some Worcestershire golf courses did not re-open after the war, echoing the fate of some in 1919. One such was Brintons Golf Club at Spennells, Kidderminster, where 114 acres were developed as a sports centre for the carpet factory's employees. As well as the nine hole golf course, there were a cricket pitch, three football pitches, hard tennis courts, a bowling green, swimming pool, a coarse fishing pond and an ornamental garden. The Georgian house was used as the clubhouse. The course was ploughed up for agricultural needs, despite an attempt to save the greens and plans to reopen it after the war were further dashed when a number of companies were evacuated from Birmingham and accommodated on the site. Spennells is now a housing estate, its last golfing link being that among the residences is the home of Will Painter, the Union's long-serving honorary secretary from 1984 until the appointment of Andrew Boyd in 1997.

Another casualty was a nine hole course at Hanbury.

Chapter Three

Fathers & Sons

As life began to return to normal after the war and golf courses began to resemble their pre-war appearance, the county Union resumed its activities. A meeting of the council was held at the Birmingham Chamber of Commerce on 24th January 1946, at which the accounts for the preceding six years were presented and adopted. The finances were in a sufficiently healthy state to preclude an increase in subscriptions, despite the number of affiliated clubs having fallen from twenty-six to nineteen. In addition to Brintons, Upton-on-Severn had ceased to exist; Malvern Working Men's Club and St Andrews club had fallen by the wayside and Habberley, Tolladine and Evesham had lapsed. Fortunately the last three clubs' fortunes subsequently revived. The chairman, Mr. Wilkes, standing in for Guy Bigwood, invited opinions on the resumption of competitions.

Stourbridge offered its course as the venue for the championship on 18th June, when the team competition for the Tomson-James Cup would also be played. This was won by the home club, but the gold medal and the G.D. Carr Cup were won by Bill Robb after a tie with Dr. Tweddell.

The only inter-county match resulted in defeat at the hands of Warwickshire at Robin Hood. Worcestershire fielded a strong team, but John Fraser's cousin, Duncan Sutherland, was in fine form and led his team to a four point victory, beating our county champion by 6 and 5. In addition to Dr. Robb, our team consisted of Stanley Lunt, J.T. Mitchley, Harley Roberts, Chris Buckley, now in his sixtieth year, Ken Frazier, Neville Seers, Stan Seymour, R.H. Crump, Ronnie Morgan, John Fraser and J.G. Allen.

Towards the end of the year a special meeting was convened at Blackwell to consider a request from the English Golf Union for an increase in subscriptions amounting to £4.6s. per affiliated club. This sum included a payment to the board of the Greenkeeping Research Office – now the Sports Turf Research Institute. The executive decided that each affiliated club would pay a subscription of one shilling per male member, based on membership numbers at 31st December. Members of municipal courses were to be charged nine pence per male member.

Harley Roberts

By this time Brand Hall had become a municipal club. The private club's lease had expired in 1940 and in 1945 Oldbury council purchased the course for £25,000, after the club had refused the offer to purchase the freehold. The club's most prestigious trophy, the Brand Hall Gold Vase, was presented to the Worcestershire Union for an annual competition. Over the years the club produced many fine golfers who represented the county and in 1947 a former member, Harley Roberts, was selected to play for England against France. He played sixteen matches for his country in 1947-48, and again in 1953, winning ten and halving one of them. He also finished runner-up in the English Amateur Championship in 1948. This tall, elegantly attired gentleman, an accomplished after-dinner speaker, died in 1989.

Other Brand Hall players to represent the county either side of the war were E.W. Rigbey and J.S. Mitchley. The municipal club also continued to figure prominently in county competitions. It was not too long before players from other municipal courses gained county recognition.

Guy Bigwood still ruled the Union with an iron hand. He signed two sets of minutes on 11th February 1947, but there are no minutes for a meeting on that date, presumably due to the illness of the secretary, Philip Padmore. He died early in 1948 and Derek Greey succeeded him as secretary, working from his office in his department store in Birmingham. Philip Padmore had completed twenty-one years of exceptional service to the county. Despite the firm control of the Union's affairs, results of the inter-county matches in 1947 were rather disappointing, apart from a four point victory over Warwickshire.

The championship was played at Halesowen for the first time and Moseley won the team event, while Harley Roberts, now a member of the host club, won the gold medal by nine strokes from Eric Fiddian. The *Birmingham Post*'s correspondent described his game as "precise, his strokes definite and his swing perfect. He is such an enthusiast for putting he has a plastic grip, with grooves to suit him placed on the handle. He began the day like a champion, driving prodigious distances and extraordinarily straight." This correspondent was the former Moseley professional, Dick Wheildon, and he provided lucid commentaries on, and analysis of, most important Midland tournaments. He was particularly interested in the way such expert players as Tweddell, Lunt and Robb had to "consider how to play their approach shots" on the tricky, banked greens. The answer was a run-up shot, not often called for on inland courses.

At the council meeting of 1948 it was proposed that £100 be authorised for the purchase of a trophy in memory of Philip Padmore, to be played for on the second day of the annual county meeting and awarded for the best nett score over thirty-six holes. It was decided to go ahead with the meeting despite the petrol rationing and this emergency does not appear to have affected the inter-county matches, as the furthest journey to an away fixture was to Enville, where we inflicted a heavy defeat on Staffordshire. Gloucestershire travelled to Worcester and lost at Boughton Park, while Cheshire were able to bring twelve men to Blackwell and suffered defeat by ten matches. The defeat at the hands of Warwickshire at Harborne completed a fairly successful season for the first team. The second team did not do quite so well, beating Staffordshire but losing narrowly to Warwickshire.

The team of Bill Robb, Stanley Lunt and Harley Roberts were runners-up in the English County Championship, held at Little Aston, where a week later Harley Roberts reached the final of the English Amateur Championship, in which he was beaten 2 and 1 by Alan Helm. Both were selected for England in the Home Internationals. Harley had tied with Stanley Elliott for the gold medal in the county meeting, in which Elliott had been a major participant in Blackwell's success in the team event, and lost the play-off over thirty-six holes, partly due to indifferent putting at a crucial stage.

The municipal club players did well in the Brand Hall Gold Vase in September, K. Jackson of Warley coming first, while three others took third, fourth and fifth places. These gentlemen were L.J. Davies of Cocks Moors Woods, A.C. Bedford, Warley and A. Morris from Rose Hill. Ronnie Morgan took the scratch prize with a 73 which included an eagle 3 at Gay Hill's 17th hole.

The first notable event of 1949 was a dinner given on 10th May at the Conservative Club, Birmingham, celebrating Guy Bigwood's election as president of the English Golf Union. Dr. Tweddell proposed the toast, pointing out that Mr. Bigwood had been the county's president for twenty-five years. Also in attendance were Major Laverack, the secretary of the English Golf Union, and Carl Bretherton, who was to the Warwickshire union what Guy Bigwood was to Worcestershire.

Despite E.W. Rigbey's score of 69 in the team championship, Blackwell retained the Tomson-James Cup at Stourbridge. Rigbey added 73 and 75 to this the next day, thereby tieing with Bill Robb for the G.D. Carr Cup. Robb, the county captain, had won the gold medal but lost the thirty-six hole play-off. His consolation was that he won the Philip Padmore Trophy. Later, Rigbey recorded the best scratch score in the Brand Hall Gold Vase.

Bill Robb led the first team to victory over Gloucestershire by 10 matches to 8, Staffordshire 10½-7½, Cheshire at Royal Liverpool 9½-8½, Warwickshire 11½-6½ and Glamorgan at Royal Porthcawl, by 4 foursomes matches to 2, the singles being abandoned because of bad weather. With three England internationals and one from Scotland in the side, this success is not surprising. The second team went down heavily to Staffordshire but managed to beat the ladies in an enjoyable fixture.

An innovation was the Worcestershire Open Championship which was sponsored by the *Birmingham Gazette*. The paper, a keen supporter of golf, having inaugurated their own open competition which became the Midland Open, put up £50 towards the prize fund of £150 for the professionals and assistants from twenty-one clubs in the county, who would compete with thirty amateurs for the Guy Bigwood Cup. It was won by an amateur, J.S. Mitchley of Stourbridge, who played "in his customary bold manner and scarcely made a weak stroke throughout". His rounds of 69 and 70 at Blackwell were four strokes fewer than those of the leading professional, G.F. Reynolds of Kidderminster. Stanley Seymour was two strokes further behind in third place, one shot ahead of his own club's professional, Bernard Preston.

At the dinner given by the *Gazette* after the competition in honour of the players, Guy Bigwood claimed that golfing history had been made. "It is the finest golf in the country to have amateurs and professionals playing together as they have done today."

Despite all this activity, it was realised that a number of courses in the county were still not fully restored after the wartime agricultural usage and it was proposed by the executive that the county membership scheme be held in abeyance for a time. This was agreed at the council meeting in January 1950.

Despite the cancellation of the English County Championship because of the petrol rationing, the county managed to fulfil an increased number of fixtures, the first of which was a match between the first and second teams at Moseley on 19th March. Despite being given two holes in both foursomes and singles the second team lost by three matches. They did better in May, beating Shropshire by the odd point at Kidderminster. A week later the first team squeezed home by one point against Gloucestershire at Boughton Park. They then challenged the Worcestershire professionals and emerged victorious, winning by four matches to three.

Michael Lunt, watched by his parents, Mr. and Mrs. Stanley Lunt

The team did not fare so well against Staffordshire, led by Charles Stowe. He won both his foursomes and singles and Worcestershire succumbed to a three points defeat, while the second team fell even more heavily at Dudley.

Although Moseley took the Tomson-James Cup in the team competition at Boughton Park, thanks to a fine 69 by Stanley Lunt, who was well supported by Bill Robb, Ronnie Morgan and Ken Frazier, the round of the day was played by Dr. Marshall, the 1934 champion, and a member of the host club. He set a new course record of 66, playing golf which was "well nigh perfect". He had had a long break from golf because of his wartime and other duties, but had returned "with greater strength and accuracy". Unfortunately he could not repeat that form in the individual championship, scoring 76 and 73 and finishing eleven strokes behind the winner, Eric Fiddian, whose scores of 67 and 71 in addition to his 72 of the previous day earned him the G.D. Carr Cup. D.W. Rigbey finished one stroke behind him to take the silver medal. Among the younger players to finish in the top ten was Roy Hobbis of Cocks Moors Woods.

One of the reasons that some clubs had not made a complete recovery from wartime conditions was the depleted number of their members. It was realised that younger players would have to be encouraged to join clubs, receive coaching and encouraged to compete. To this end Worcestershire, with the support of the *Birmingham Post and Mail* organised the Midland Boys Championship, which was held at Blackwell on 5th September, by which time our ageing first team had been beaten rather heavily by Cheshire at Stourbridge, but had managed to halve with Warwickshire at Olton two days before the boys' event, thanks to a spirited recovery in the singles after taking lunch down by four matches to two. The second team achieved the same score, in a less dramatic fashion at Gay Hill, Roy Hobbis marking his county debut by earning a valuable point in the foursomes.

Guy Bigwood and Harley Roberts organised the Boys Championship, which was won by John Brockway of Kidderminster, who greatly impressed Dick Wheildon, writing in the *Birmingham Post.* "His style and perfect control were a delight." Wheildon was less impressed with the boys taking spoons for their tee shots and with the deliberate pace of play, especially as they had played "carefree, happy golf" during their practice rounds. In third place was Michael Lunt, whose entry was listed as Uppingham, a number of other boys listing their public school on their entries. As this competition marked the beginning of the movement to encourage junior golf its history will be continued in a separate chapter.

The Brand Hall Gold Vase was played at Cocks Moors Woods and was won, appropriately, by a Brand Hall player, David Rees, playing off a handicap of 8, which Dick Wheildon predicted would soon be scratch. His nett score was 66.

The second Worcestershire Open Championship produced a different result from the inaugural event, professionals taking the first three places, Bill Firkins of Stourbridge returning 140 on his home course. Frank Miller of Brand Hall was second on 143 and Eric Booy of Fulford Heath tied with Dr. Tweddell on 145. Stanley Lunt was the second amateur and the assistants' prize was won by J. Common of Worcester Golf and Country Club.

Eric Fiddian accepted the invitation to become county captain for 1951 and a Union flag was designed and purchased for £7.1s.4d. The new standard scratch score scheme was proceeding successfully, although two clubs reported difficulties and Eric Fiddian, the English Golf Union's Midland advisor, was delegated to sort out the matter. At the council meeting clubs were asked to submit the names of players they considered worthy of a trial in the second team.

This does not appear to have been received with sufficient enthusiasm, for the only new name to appear in the opening match between the first and second teams was Jack Butterworth of Worcester, who played for the first team. He had recently moved to Worcester from Berkshire and was a scratch golfer. He had been an artisan member at Royal Lytham and St Annes before the war in which he fought in many campaigns. He remained in the army

Jack Butterworth

Roy Hobbis

until 1947 as a physical training instructor at RMA Sandhurst. The second team started two up in the foursomes and three up in the singles and the matches were played to the 18th, the score being calculated on holes up. After the foursomes the first team led by 11 holes to 6. The second team then made the most of their advantage and took the singles by 23 holes to 15, and so emerged victorious 29-26. It did not seem to make much difference to team selection, however.

Before the first match of the season the annual meeting was held at Kidderminster and on the first day Stourbridge won the team event. The highlights were scores of 69 by Roy Hobbis and Jack Butterworth. Neither could quite manage to reproduce that form in the individual event, Hobbis starting with an 80, improving to 75 in the second round, while Butterworth finished fourth with rounds of 76 and 73 to take the G.D. Carr Cup. J.T. Mitchley won the gold medal, Harley Roberts tied with Ken Frazier and took the silver medal in the play-off.

Roy Hobbis started playing golf in 1946 at Cocks Moors Woods, where he was taught by 'Pop' Lewis. He joined Kings Norton in 1951, when he earned selection for the Midland Counties team. He has continued to play a major part in the county's golfing history for over fifty years, being captain from 1977-79, finally becoming president of the Union in 2000-02.

Neither Butterworth nor Hobbis played in the opening inter-county match, which resulted in a narrow win over Staffordshire, our success being due to a fine foursomes performance in the afternoon which overturned a three point deficit after the singles. Butterworth, Hobbis and C.V. Grafton of Brand Hall were chosen for the next match against Gloucestershire, assisting the team to a win by three points.

On the same day the second team lost to Shropshire's first team, John Brockway earning a point in the singles on his debut.

The first team continued their successful run by defeating Cheshire 12-6 at Sandiway and Warwickshire by an even greater margin at Moseley. Stanley Lunt's son Michael joined Brockway in the second team for the match with Warwickshire and both won their singles but our lead after the singles was obliterated by a dismal performance in the foursomes. Neither boy was chosen for the match with Herefordshire which we won comfortably, nor for the Staffordshire match which resulted in a heavy loss.

Brand Hall Golf Club seemed reluctant to relinquish their Gold Vase, for A.E. Shaw of that club won it with a nett 68 playing off a handicap of 12. The club's professional, Frank Miller was the leading professional in the county Open but was beaten by one stroke by Bill Robb in a welcome return to form. Wheildon, who had employed Miller as an assistant while at Moseley, praised his play through the green but reported that Miller had difficulties with his putter, his last putt for a tie hanging on the lip of the hole. The veteran North Worcestershire professional, F.T. Sumner, tied with Ken Frazier in third place with scores of 140, two strokes behind Robb.

An unusual event took place in the summer of 1951, the year of the Festival of Britain. The previous year Stanley Lunt and Dr. Brown suggested a tournament be held to celebrate the end of the Second World War, the Festival and the start of a new era. They were entrusted with the organisation of the tournament, open to all Midland clubs, and with organisational assistance from Warwickshire. The three day event was held at Cocks Moors Woods and was a scratch competition comprising two rounds of stroke play for two-man teams on the first day, eighteen holes of foursomes the next day, followed by a foursomes match play final for the two leading teams.

After the first round Kings Norton, represented by Neville Seers and Stan Seymour, led by one stroke from Cocks Moors Woods and Moseley. They maintained their lead in the foursomes, in which Roy Hobbis and Stan Smith representing the municipal club managed a one stroke lead over Moseley's Bill Robb and Stanley Lunt. Roy and Stan then won the final in front of more than 500 spectators by one hole in a closely fought match. Also taking part were Harley Roberts and Jack Mitchley from Stourbridge, Ronnie Crump and Stanley Elliott from Blackwell and Jack

Butterworth and Alastair Shepherd representing The Worcestershire. Despite its success this event was not continued.

Stanley Lunt was appointed captain of the English team at the beginning of 1952, which was also his club, Moseley's, diamond jubilee year. Under his leadership England lost only to Scotland, the winners, in the Home Internationals, halving with Ireland and defeating Wales. They also beat France.

The first team, still made up of experienced players, administered a stern lesson to the second team who only earned two points in the singles in the opening match, J.H. Yardley beating Ronnie Morgan one up, while Dick Mirams and Michael Lunt earned halves. Playing with Yardley, Michael also halved his foursomes with Ken Frazier and Eric Fiddian. The ladies, who received twelve strokes, were beaten 4 – 3 at Stourbridge.

Moseley presented the Jubilee Shield for competition by the "B" teams at the annual meeting which was held at Kings Norton, also celebrating that club's diamond jubilee. Moseley won the Tomson-James Cup, Stanley Lunt producing the day's best round, 71. He was not in such good form the second day and a home player, Neville Seers, with two scores of 73 to add to the previous day's 74, won both the gold medal and the G.D. Carr Cup. Two Blackwell players, J.H. Bryant and A. Dawbarn, took the silver and bronze medals, Harley Roberts coming fourth and Roy Hobbis fifth.

The first team managed to retrieve a losing position against Cheshire at Moseley by a strong foursomes performance, in which Chris Buckley partnered Eric Fiddian. This was the last season for the sixty-six year old stalwart whose career had spanned twenty-three years of the county's history. Warwickshire won both the first and second team matches but the first team fared much better against Gloucestershire, winning by four points. They also subjected the professionals to a heavy defeat, prevailing in five of the six matches.

The success of players from municipal clubs continued in the Brand Hall Gold Vase, K. Jackson of Warley winning it for the second time. J. Jones of Brand Hall was second and two more Warley players, Jack Knight and A. Vaughan, third and fourth. The competition was held at Fulford Heath, described by Dick Wheildon as being in "splendid condition". He went on to describe it as one of the youngest clubs in Warwickshire! More accurately he stated that it was the longest course in the county at 6,448 yards.

Frank Miller played two steady rounds of 70 to win the Worcestershire Open once again, Harley Roberts coming second, four shots behind Miller and one ahead of Bill Robb. Bill Firkins was the second professional, in fourth place, and Ronnie Morgan was fifth. The event was held at Moseley and the dinner was attended by the Lord Mayor and Lady Mayoress of Birmingham, who presented the prizes.

The second team lost to Herefordshire but beat Shropshire. These two counties did not join forces until December 1956, by which time the Herefordshire ladies had thrown in their lot with Worcestershire ladies.

The county team returned to Moseley for another event on 5th October 1952. The club had challenged the county to a match as a part of the diamond jubilee celebrations. This was not a rash gesture – nine of the men in the Moseley team were either already county players or were soon to earn their colours; two of them were internationals. Even with Dr. Tweddell, Eric Fiddian and Harley Roberts in the team, along with Jack Butterworth who made his England debut two years later, the Worcestershire team could only manage 2½ to the club's 5½. The exercise was repeated on the occasion of the club's seventy-fifth anniversary and again in the centenary year, the latter event in a different format. The 1967 match was won 8-4 by Moseley, the club's team again containing county and international players.

The executive made some interesting decisions at the end of the year. The English Golf Union was moving towards new conditions for the county championship, regional qualifying, which we now have, being one suggestion. The executive seemed to prefer the framework in place at the time and regional qualifying did not come until 1955. Dr. J.L. Brown, of Kings Norton, seconded by Bill Robb, made a suggestion that would shock modern county players, namely that the match expenses should be paid by the players and not charged to county funds. The reasoning behind this became clearer when it was stated that if the county were to continue to support the Sports Turf Research Institute, an increase in subscriptions would be necessary. It was decided to recommend to the council meeting that clubs be responsible for paying this subscription directly to the institute and this was accepted by the council on 21st January 1953. The subscription paid by municipal golfers to the county was increased to one shilling. Despite the apparent financial constraints it was agreed to subscribe five guineas annually to the newly formed Golf Foundation. On the other hand, the executive had already rejected a request for support for the Walker Cup from the R&A, but had agreed to spend £20 on "suitable prizes" for a competition to mark Coronation year.

Stanley Lunt was re-appointed as England's captain and Dr. Tweddell took over the county captaincy, J.W. Allen of Moseley filling that position for the second team.

The 1953 season began with a match against the ladies, who were celebrating their fiftieth anniversary, and the gentlemen just managed to win. They also presented the ladies with prizes for annual competition to celebrate their jubilee. When the first team played the second team a week later on 7th April, the second team put up a good performance in the singles to trail by one point but, despite their start of two up, collapsed in the foursomes. The first team then lost by eight matches to ten against Gloucestershire, while the second team reasserted their supremacy over Herefordshire on the same day.

Moseley retained the Tomson-James Cup at Stourbridge, the home club becoming the first winners of the Jubilee Shield, fittingly, as the club shares the same foundation year as Moseley and Kings Norton. Jack Butterworth took all the trophies; the gold medal, the G.D. Carr Cup and the Philip Padmore trophy. Roy Hobbis was given two days leave from his National Service and his lack of practice was evident when he dropped six strokes in the last nine holes having had five birdies to the turn. Nonetheless he managed scores of 74, 76 and 74.

The first team travelled to Delamere Forest for the match against Cheshire and were beaten comprehensively but recovered to inflict similar embarrassment on Staffordshire. The Warwickshire match was closer but a superior foursomes performance saw Worcestershire home, four matches to the good. The second team did not fare so well against Staffordshire but managed a one point victory over Warwickshire and won by a larger margin against Shropshire.

The Brand Hall Gold Vase was played at Blackwell and there was a three-way tie between two North Worcestershire players, T.R. Cawthorn and A.C. Sparkes, and J. Colgan of Kings Norton, Cawthorn winning a three hole play-off. The Open was also held at Blackwell and Frank Miller once again took the title, despite his old trouble with the putter. He beat Jack Butterworth by two strokes, G.F. Reynolds of Kidderminster finishing in third place.

Worcestershire players featured prominently in Midland golf during the year; Bill Robb won the Midland Counties gold medal, Harley Roberts the Howitt Bowl and Stanley Elliott, in partnership with Frank Miller, won the Midland Amateur and Professional Foursomes. Stanley Lunt was elected to the England selection committee, while Dr. Brown was re-elected president of the Midland Golf Association.

Another happy event was the re-admission of Evesham into the Union.

Perhaps the most significant event in 1953, with the most long-lasting effect, did not occur on a golf course. The county's secretary, Derek Greey, managing director of Grey's department store in Birmingham, advertised for a secretary. The successful applicant was Brenda Smith. Twenty-five years later she admitted to Peter Ricketts in an interview for the *Worcester Evening News* that if the advertisement for the job had mentioned golf she would not have applied for it. She did not play golf and neither did her husband, Barry. Brenda took up her post at Grey's on 17th August and soon learned that

Greey was not only secretary and treasurer of the County Union, but also of the Wigorns Golfing Society, which was founded in 1950 by Greey, Guy Bigwood, Stanley Lunt and Bill Boulton.

Derek Greey soon set Brenda to work on the draw and starting times for the Midland Boys Championship. She was then involved in further fixtures and the accounts. Brenda did not visit a golf club until 1955, when she attended the county Open at Worcester Golf and Country Club, and she remembers the impression that the clubhouse made upon her. From then on she organised and attended every county event, continuing in this capacity after Derek Greey retired from business and resigned the secretaryship in 1975. David Rodway took over as secretary and Brenda worked from home, now an employee of the Union. Even when she and Barry moved to Ross-on-Wye to run a hotel for a year, she attended the events for which she was responsible. In addition to not playing golf, Brenda does not drive and Barry has acted as chauffeur from the beginning.

It is impossible to quantify what the county owes to this loyal, dedicated couple. Brenda's work has been recognised on a number of occasions – a silver candelabra on her silver jubilee with the Union, an impressive selection of Royal Worcester porcelain after forty years service and in 2001 she was made an Honorary Life Member, an honour she shares with Eric Fiddian.

The 1954 season began with a match between a Worcestershire men's team of sixteen players and the county ladies, who won five matches to the men's three. The second team also proved tougher opposition than in the past and only just lost the match. This result did not appear to influence selection but the first team performed impressively against Gloucestershire at Boughton Park to record a 12-6 victory, while the second team beat Herefordshire by two points, having won the singles 9-3.

Up until this time the Tomson-James Cup had been the preserve of a handful of clubs so it was refreshing to see the name of a new winning team on the trophy when the North Worcestershire club returned the best scores at Moseley. It was indeed a team effort: J.H. Greig scored 73 and each of his team-mates 76 for a total of 301. Despite Bill Robb's 69 and Ken Frazier's 72 the home club's other players were not on their best form. However, Stanley Lunt recovered the following day and took the bronze medal, two strokes behind Harley Roberts' 146. The gold medal was won, once again, by Jack Butterworth with rounds of 68, five below the scratch score, and 75. Added to his 75 of the previous day this score gave Butterworth the G.D. Carr Cup as well, but the Philip Padmore Trophy, which he had won in 1953, was won by D.E.Summers, the youngest player in the event.

Jack Butterworth missed the matches with Cheshire, which resulted in a heavy loss, and Staffordshire, which was a comfortable win. He was back in the team for the Warwickshire match which was another success, the score being 12-6.

North Worcestershire were to the fore again when one of the club's members, H. Forbes, won the Brand Hall Gold Vase after a tie with H. Thomas, a veteran with thirty years golfing experience, from Halesowen. There was no change in the result of the county Open, though, as Frank Miller completed his hat trick of titles. His score of 146 at Stourbridge was one better than the home professional, Bill Firkins, which in turn was one better than that of the leading amateur, Jack Butterworth. Bill Robb was fourth and Stanley Lunt fifth. *Berrows Worcester Journal* had taken over the sponsorship of this event from the *Birmingham Gazette* but this only lasted for two years.

1955 was the Union's jubilee year and a celebration dinner was planned to conclude the season, so it was up to our players to make it a memorable one. They did.

Delegates from fourteen of the twenty-two affiliated clubs attended the council meeting at Stourbridge Golf Club on 25th January and agreed that the individual membership scheme be resumed, Mr. W.O. Cooksey undertaking the management of the scheme. They also heard of the new qualifying system for the county championship.

After halving the opening match with the second team, a strong team defeated Gloucestershire 12-6 in the first inter-county match at Long Ashton in May. A set-back to the smooth running hoped for in this important year occurred when the team championship at Blackwell had to be postponed because of rain, wind and snow and eventually took place on 18th September. Conditions improved for the individual championship to go ahead on 18th May and, although Dick Wheildon reported that his putting was not so good, Jack Butterworth played beautifully from tee to green to win his third successive gold medal, one stroke ahead of F.L. Wilkinson of Rose Hill and two better than Stanley Lunt. Another municipal player, A. Holloway of Cocks Moors Woods, beat Wilkinson in a play-off for the Philip Padmore Trophy. As well as retaining the G.D. Carr Cup, Butterworth was awarded a special jubilee prize awarded by Guy Bigwood.

The second team's win over Herefordshire by seven points was an encouraging prelude to the important event one month later.

The new qualification process for the English County Championship, proposed by Guy Bigwood, divided England into four regions, each to hold its own qualifying tournament. Teams of six men from each county would play two medal rounds and the team with the lowest aggregate would represent the region in the national final. All six scores were to count. Selection for "The Six" became the highest honour the county could bestow.

A photograph taken before the final of the English County Golf Championship at Formby in 1955
Back row: E. Griffiths (press), Roy Hobbis, Neville Seers, Stanley Elliott, Ken Frazier
Seated: Dr. J.L. Brown (county president), Guy Bigwood (president, Blackwell Golf Club)
Derek Greey (county secretary), H. Hogg (press). In front: Lew Wilkinson, Jack Butterworth

The Worcestershire team travelled to Hollinwell for the Midland event. Their scores were: J.R. Butterworth 73+76=149; E.W. Fiddian 78+74=152; F.L. Wilkinson 83+77=160; S.L. Elliott 80+74=154; R. Hobbis 74+74=148; S. Lunt 85+82=167. This gave a total of 930, twelve strokes better than Staffordshire in second place. Roy Hobbis's score was the best individual performance of the tournament. He went on to be our most successful player in the finals.

Worcestershire beat Dorset in the semi-final at Formby by 6 matches to 3, Ken Frazier and Neville Seers having replaced Lunt and Fiddian in the team. The other finalists were Yorkshire, who had defeated Surrey by a similar score. Despite Roy Hobbis's continued good form Worcestershire lost heavily, by 7 matches to 2. Nevertheless, to have reached the finals in such an historic year was a fine achievement.

Dr. Tweddell turned out for the second team in the match against Staffordshire at Enville, which was won by the odd point, possibly one of the two his son Michael contributed to the score. The first team, without Hobbis, suffered heavily against Cheshire, losing 6-12 and on the same day Shropshire inflicted an even heavier defeat on the second team. Matters improved when the first team beat Warwickshire 11½-6½ at Moseley, although the second team lost by the same margin. Both Michaels, Lunt and Tweddell, played in this match, the former having just completed his National Service.

The Brand Hall Gold Vase was won by a municipal player once again, W.W. Southall of Rose Hill scoring 80-11 for a nett 69 at Halesowen, players from public courses filling the next five places.

Led by Jack Butterworth, Worcester Golf and Country Club won the rearranged team championship, while Michael Lunt's 69 assisted the Moseley "B" team's victory in the Jubilee Shield competition.

It had been decided as part of the initiative to develop juniors golf that as strong a county team as possible play a match against the best boys from the Midland Boys Championship. Butterworth, Hobbis, Wilkinson, both Lunts and Ronnie Morgan were members of the team which met the boys at Blackwell on 11th September. Among the boys were Ian Wheater and Tony Jowle, who became Worcestershire first team players. After the men had established a lead in the foursomes the boys, two of whom received a start, managed to halve the match, which therefore must be considered a highly successful venture.

The Worcestershire Open was won by Harley Roberts, with Ken Frazier second and Jack Butterworth third. The leading professional, in fourth place, was G.F. Reynolds of Kidderminster. Roberts' driving was described as "beautiful" and it was he who coped best with the torrential rain in the afternoon round.

The match against the ladies resulted in a heavy loss but the jubilee dinner was a huge success. Among the guests at Birmingham's Grand Hotel were Bernard Darwin, doyen of golf writers, Lord Bruce of Melbourne, the captain of the R&A, J.W. Manning, the president of the EGU and G.L.Q. Henriques, who had succeeded Guy Bigwood in that office in 1951.

Dr. Brown succeeded Neville Seers, another Kings Norton member, as captain for the 1956 season. He had an experienced core of players to call on and after a close match with the second team they annihilated Gloucestershire at Worcester in the first inter-county match, the visitors' only point coming from two halved matches.

Moseley claimed the Tomson-James Cup, with Stanley and Michael Lunt in the team, while Blackwell won the Jubilee Shield. F.L. Wilkinson was now a member of Blackwell and putted his way to victory in the individual championship, having fifteen single putts in the two rounds in amassing his scores of 73+74=147, to beat Jack Butterworth by three shots. Roy Hobbis won the bronze medal.

Golden Jubilee Dinner, 1954
Left to right: Lord Bruce of Melbourne (captain R&A)
E. Guy Bigwood (president W.U.G.C.)

Thanks to a superb 72 by Charlie Stowe in the second round, Staffordshire turned the tables on Worcestershire in the Midland qualifying event at Woodhall Spa. Only Michael Lunt played consistently and we finished second. We also came second to them in the county match three weeks later, losing by five points, and the second team could do no better. They also lost to Warwickshire but the first team recovered their form to win 12-6, then succumbed rather heavily to Cheshire. The second team performed better against Shropshire and reversed the previous year's result. Generous allowances enabled the Midland boys to beat the county team 10-8.

Yet again the Brand Hall Gold Vase was won by a player from a municipal club, this time the nineteen year old David Atherton from Warley, who scored a nett 67 playing off a handicap of 12. Another young player, T. Ward, playing on his home course, Stourbridge, came second and A. Holloway of Cocks Moors Woods, third equal with another home player, H.M. Smith, and D. Kelley of Kings Norton. The county Open championship was retained by Harley Roberts, playing very consistently, despite one unlucky bounce and two topped tee shots. His score of 144 was three shots better than that of G.F. Reynolds the Kidderminster professional, while Eric Fiddian came third on 148. In fourth place was a seventeen year old assistant from Cocks Moors Woods, M.H. Smith, who had a first round of 71, the best of the morning, but found one or two bunkers too many in the afternoon and finished with 78. Harley Roberts completed his season by winning the Howitt Bowl and the gold medal in the Midland Counties Championship.

While Guy Bigwood was president and chairman and Derek Greey the secretary, executive meetings were held in November at the Birmingham Conservative Club, a short walk from both these gentlemen's offices. A further meeting would precede the annual council meeting at the club hosting it. These January meetings were usually completed in under an hour.

Golden Jubilee Dinner, 1954
Left to right: G.L.Q. Henriques, Dr. W. Tweddell, E. Guy Bigwood (president W.U.G.C.)
Bernard Darwin, Lord Bruce of Melbourne (captain R&A), J.W. Manning (president E.G.U.)

The November meeting was different, for it was preceded by lunch. The minute book records a 12.45 p.m. start and Brenda Smith remembers the ensuing lunch and meeting being extremely convivial, the port continuing to circulate until the meetings closed sometime after 4 p.m.

In 1956 it continued until 4.45 p.m. Among the items covered was a letter from the secretary of Moseley regarding a proposal to adjust Michael Lunt's handicap to plus 1 and it was agreed to refer this to the English Golf Union.

A suggestion that ladies be permitted to have books of tickets for the individual membership scheme was favourably received and would be placed before the council meeting. W.C.I. Boulton proposed that a county foursomes knock-out be inaugurated in 1957 and a sub-committee was formed to prepare suggestions for the council. However, this sub-committee had not met by 22nd January the following year, the day of the council meeting. Another sub-committee was formed to discuss boys' golf and at the council meeting Dick Mirams was able to report on its activities; Harley Roberts, J. Conlon and A. Lloyd being Dick's colleagues on this committee. The matter of individual membership for Worcestershire lady golfers was carried, but the executive had still to consider the case of the municipal golfers and their green-fees.

The Union was accorded a further honour when W.C.I. Boulton was elected president of the English Golf Union in 1957, the third Worcestershire man to receive this honour. Only Stanley Lunt has filled this office since then as a representative of our county. Bill Robb took on a similar mantle for the Midland Counties Golf Association. They were congratulated at an extraordinary meeting of the executive on 8th April, when Guy Bigwood proposed and Dr. Tweddell seconded, that a dinner be arranged in Boulton's honour.

A request from the Midland Juniors Golfing Society for reduced green-fees for its members on Worcestershire courses was approved and forwarded to the clubs for their individual consideration.

In the meantime the county foursomes sub-committee had met and the inaugural event would be held at Stourbridge at the end of August.

Douglas Fiddian took over as captain in 1957 and cannot have been overjoyed at the result of the match between the first and second teams, the second team winning by one point. He was unable to call on Roy Hobbis who had emigrated to Canada to work as an electrician. Better news was the arrival of Welsh international Ian Hughes, who had joined Moseley, and he made his county debut for the second team against Herefordshire on 5th May, winning his foursomes 5 and 4 and singles 6 and 5. Ian Wheater also played an important part in the team's success. On the same day the first team had gone down to Gloucestershire after leading 4-2 at lunchtime. Hughes was duly selected for the match against Cheshire but lost both his matches in our heavy defeat. His form improved and he enjoyed a reasonably satisfactory season. Ian Wheater played for the county against the Midland boys this time and was partnered by John Brockway in the foursomes, in which they beat Malcolm Gregson, who played in the Ryder Cup ten years later, and Andrew Thomson, a future captain of Blackwell Golf Club.

The remaining first team matches resulted in a loss to Staffordshire and a half with Warwickshire. The second team did not have a happy season, losing to Staffordshire and being whitewashed in the foursomes by Warwickshire. Fortunately heavy rain prevented any further humiliation. Tony Jowle made his county debut in this match and playing for Warwickshire was one R. Baldwin. The Shropshire match suffered a similar fate, after the home team had taken a 4-2 lead at Ludlow.

Stanley Elliott had the best score in the team championship at North Worcestershire, but could not prevent Moseley winning the Tomson-James Cup once again, Blackwell finishing three shots behind. Harley Roberts could only manage a 77 on the first day but in the individual championship he "defied a testing wind" to score 71 and 67 to win the gold medal and the G.D. Carr Cup. N. Harley of Moseley won the silver medal and Eric Fiddian and F.L. Wilkinson tied for the bronze.

Ten teams contested the first match play foursomes on 31st August and 1st September at Stourbridge, Blackwell beating Moseley 5 and 3 in the final. Roy Chandler and R.H. Crump, a county veteran, represented Blackwell, while Tony Jowle was paired with T.P.S. Dunnett for Moseley.

The tenacity of the public course golfers was demonstrated yet again in the Brand Hall Gold Vase. This time a fourteen year old boy, who was recovering from two years in hospital with a dislocated hip, was the winner. D. Fereday was the son of the Warley professional and scored 79 off a handicap of 11 at Blackwell to win by two strokes from Andrew Thomson, then a member at Rose Hill, and A.E. Shaw of Brand Hall.

The county Open was held at Kings Norton and a home player, P.D. Kelley, a youth international, tied with the ever present G.F. Reynolds on 145. Frank Miller and Bill Firkins tied for third place. Maurice Woodbine attended the play-off and witnessed Reynolds finally claim the title by eight strokes, David Kelley's putting letting him down at crucial moments. According to Woodbine, Kelley "takes his golf seriously and is usually to be seen practising on the course early in the mornings before leaving for the office. On the day before the play-off he reported for a golf lesson at 7 a.m."

Kelley's dedication was rewarded eventually by his selection for the Home Internationals in 1965, 1966 and 1968, having made his county debut in 1957.

It was clear from the results of the first and second team matches that something had to be done to raise standards and at the executive meeting in November it was agreed to form a committee to assist the selection of the teams. The captain, second team captain and match secretary were to discuss this before bringing the matter to the council meeting, when other members would be co-opted. The council agreed to the co-option of newly elected vice-president Ronnie Morgan and Stanley Lunt to this sub-committee.

Further recognition of the improvement in boys' golf came in the form of permission for players under eighteen years of age to enter county competitions but not enter the sweepstakes.

When the 1958 season began with the traditional match between the first and second teams there were some new names among the players, but for the time being the first team relied on long-serving, experienced men. They beat the second team 9-6 and then achieved a very good win against Gloucestershire at Boughton Park. Warwickshire succumbed to us at Harborne and Cheshire were overthrown at Stourbridge. The only defeat was inflicted on us by Staffordshire, although Harley Roberts convincingly beat Charlie Stowe. Warwickshire won the Midland qualifying event at North Hants County, with Staffordshire second and Worcestershire third, eight strokes behind the winners.

The second team had a fine match against Warwickshire, emerging the winners by eleven matches to seven. In the team was Reg Newbitt, father of Neville, who was to follow him into the team in 1959. Shropshire and Herefordshire had combined by this time and even with Hughes and Wheater in our team they proved too strong for us. The Staffordshire match was abandoned due to flooding after we had taken a one point lead in the foursomes.

Tony Jowle

Hughes was a member of the Moseley team alongside Michael Lunt, Ken Frazier and Tony Jowle and they had a comfortable win in the team championship. The next day the "superbly consistent" Harley Roberts added yet another gold medal to his trophy cabinet, while Tony Jowle beat Michael Tweddell in the play-off for the silver medal. Tweddell was more successful in another play-off, however, when he beat Harley Roberts by one shot for the Philip Padmore Trophy.

The club match play foursomes had now become the Boulton Salver, thanks to the generous benefactor, and was won by Kings Norton "A", Neville Seers and David Kelley, who were taken to the twenty-first hole by two other county players, A. Dawbarn and M. Ireland of Blackwell's "B" team. Fourteen teams entered the tournament this year, Redditch and Rose Hill being given byes in the first round. However, the latter team failed to turn up and Stourbridge proceeded to the next round, represented by the Fiddian brothers, who were eliminated by the runners-up. It was significant, and a tribute to Mr. Boulton, that a very large proportion of the field consisted of county golfers.

In July a representative county team enjoyed a halved match with the Midland Juniors Golfing Society, whose team included Michael Lunt, Michael Tweddell, John Beharrell, Martin Ireland and David Kelley. With the obvious exception of Beharrell these young men all represented the county first team during the season. In September a mixed match was arranged with the society and a strong Worcestershire team emphasised the value of experience by beating, by six matches to nil, a team which included Kelley,

Jowle, Bridget Jackson and two of Warwickshire's best lady players, Sheila Armstrong and Gillian Carvill.

Kelley and Jowle then played for a full strength county team against the Midland boys, whose team included Bill Firkins jun. and Richard Livingston, later a successful professional at Midland clubs. The boys received three holes up in both foursomes and singles but lost narrowly by the odd match.

Jack Butterworth won the Howitt Bowl for the third time in four years, while Frank Miller, now Moseley's professional, returned to his best form in winning the county Open at his home course. Runner-up was another home player, Tony Jowle, with Butterworth third after a play-off and Harley Roberts fourth. Miller's first round of 68 was compiled in terrible, wet conditions but the rain abated in the afternoon. The correspondent of the *Birmingham Post* concluded, "There can be nothing but congratulations for the young Jowle, whose rounds of 72 and 73 were models of consistency … One can only say that his day will come. He is certainly a golfer to watch in the future." The paper's accompanying photographs demonstrate just what the players had to contend with.

Tony also enjoyed success in the British Youths Championship at Dumfries and County, where he was leading amateur, tied with Brian Huggett, and was runner-up in the Boyd Quaich at St Andrews.

When the executive met in November it was decided that, because green-fees had to be paid, the municipal courses would be excluded from the individual membership scheme. Club members' subscriptions to the Union were increased to 2s.6d. which included one shilling to assist the English Golf Union, of which Stanley Lunt had just been nominated deputy president. He had also been honoured by the Worcestershire Professional Golfers Association as their president. His son, Michael, was congratulated for winning the Golf Illustrated Gold Vase with a record score of 65 over the New Course at Sunningdale during the previous season and for having played for England for the third year in succession.

Mr. Cooksey reported a successful year in which 447 books of tickets had been sold for the county individual membership scheme. £42.15s.6d. accrued to the county's funds and £128.6s.7d. was distributed to the twenty-two clubs in the county. Modern golfers paying subscriptions around the £1,000 mark may well wonder at these sums.

Ronnie Morgan was elected captain for the 1959 season and immediately set an example to his team by gaining maximum points in the opening match with the second team, who won by four matches, having received a two holes up start.

As some of his younger players were playing against the county for the Midland Juniors Golfing Society's team which also included John Beharrell once again, Ronnie was probably not too disappointed at losing by one match. Neville Newbitt played for the society in this match and made a sufficiently good impression to earn selection for the second team against Warwickshire, his father accompanying him in the team. Later in the season Stanley Elliott's son Ian appeared for the team, continuing the family theme in Worcestershire golf. It should not be forgotten that two dynasties of golfing professionals, the Cawseys and the Lewises, have given the county sterling service since the introduction of the game within our boundaries and other professionals such as Bill Firkins have been followed by their sons.

Ronnie Morgan would have been much happier after the team event at the county meeting; Moseley "A" won the Tomson-James Cup at Worcester, Tony Jowle returning a score of 68 and Morgan himself was a member of the club's team which won the Jubilee Shield. He then tied with Mike Herman-Smith for the bronze medal, which he won in the play-off. There was also a play-off for the gold medal, Harley Roberts prevailing over Roy Hobbis, who had come home on holiday from Winnipeg. A third play-off was necessary for the Philip Padmore Trophy and Morgan was not quite so successful, for a 6 handicap player from Redditch, A. Mutton, beat him and Herman-Smith quite convincingly.

A stiff breeze sprang up in the afternoon of the Midland qualifying event at Sutton Coldfield, affecting Tony Jowle's club selection. Morgan had included two other Moseley players in his team, the others being Michael Lunt and N. Harley. B. Pitchford, F.L. Wilkinson and R. Sandilands made up the team which finished first and so qualified for the final at Ganton.

Having beaten Somerset in the semi-final, Worcestershire faced Yorkshire in the final once again. Of the team which qualified only Lunt, Jowle and Pitchford remained, Jack Butterworth, Ian Wheater and Ian Hughes replacing the other three. Lunt and Hughes won their foursomes 2 and 1, Butterworth and Wheater won one up but Jowle and Pitchford finished two holes down. John Stobbs described our performance as "tenacious". Jack Butterworth covered the seventeen holes of his match in five under fours and lost 2 and 1. Michael Lunt scored our only point in the singles. Nevertheless, it was a fine performance, an improvement on the previous final against Yorkshire and a good way to end the decade.

Twelve strong pairs met at Kings Norton for the Boulton Salver and North Worcestershire emerged the winners, C.V. Grafton, a long-serving first team player and B. Pitchford, fresh from the national finals, beating Stanley and Michael Lunt 2 and 1.

The first team now had a different look, younger players taking the places of the seasoned veterans, and after halving the foursomes with Warwickshire, put in a strong performance in the singles to win by three points. The second team also managed a win by the odd match. Shropshire and Herefordshire were now considered worthy of a first team fixture but in the event fell short and lost rather heavily. The Cheshire fixture was played at Prestbury and Worcestershire were just successful; having taken the foursomes five matches to one, our men experienced the type of fight back Yorkshire had mounted at Ganton and one point separated the teams at the close. Staffordshire were defeated far more convincingly at Stourbridge, although the second team lost at Bloxwich and also to Gloucestershire at Worcester. The first team match at Stinchcombe Hill was abandoned at lunchtime when low cloud reduced the visibility to twenty yards, by which time Worcestershire were leading by four matches to two.

The Brand Hall Gold Vase had a fairy-tale quality on this occasion. It was won by a local player, J.L. Dale, a 7 handicapper who worked on a night shift and therefore had not been to bed the night before the competition. In addition to that he used ladies clubs because of a weak wrist. J. Kilshaw, another Rose Hill player who subsequently graduated to Blackwell, was second and J.H. Ward of Cocks Moors Woods finished third, so the municipal club's monopoly of this event was not completely broken. It appears from the press cutting that a new qualification process was in operation, the competition now being open to medal winners in Worcestershire clubs during July and August.

Stan Seymour of Kings Norton, with "two model rounds of 71", won the county Open, the next two places also being taken by amateurs, R.H. Crump and R.W. Sandilands, both of Blackwell, the venue for the tournament. The leading professionals were Eric Booy of Fulford Heath and G.F. Reynolds. Booy had shared the lead with Bernard Preston after the first round but fell away in the afternoon while Preston "threw his chance away over the last nine holes in a manner little short of tragic". Frank Miller also had his problems, hitting two shots out of bounds and lipping out with the third putt on the 9th hole.

To complete what must be regarded as an important year, Michael Lunt represented Great Britain and Ireland in the Walker Cup at Muirfield and England in the Home Internationals. Ian Wheater won the President's Putter in the Oxford and Cambridge Golfing Society meeting at Rye, while Tony Jowle won the British Universities Championship at Moortown and the British Youths Championship at Pannal. Finally, Jack Butterworth won the Howitt Bowl for the third year in succession with two rounds of 68.

Worcestershire at the end of the 1950s was still at the forefront of English golf, with every prospect of remaining there for some time.

Chapter Four

Never So Good – Almost

As BRITAIN entered the 1960s prime minister Harold MacMillan, himself a golfer, told the nation that they "had never had it so good". This was almost true of Worcestershire county golf at the beginning of the decade. Among the effects of this apparent prosperity were the increasing number of new golfers and more disposable income for a wider choice of leisure pursuits involving the whole family. This may have been partly responsible for a problem which was to arise during the season.

In November 1959 county officials were reminded of their duty to attend county matches. Despite its success the first team was not always as well supported as it deserved to be. Then at the council meeting in January two gentlemen suggested, from the floor, "the desirability of revising the rules to provide for some individual members other than officers to be appointed to the executive committee. It was suggested that this would be a more democratic arrangement than exists at the present time." The executive committee, which had changed very little over the preceding years, agreed to consider the proposal, and were then re-elected en bloc. Guy Bigwood felt that as there were so few meetings during the year, most of which were concerned with the playing of the game, a larger executive committee would be unwieldy. However, he was prepared to accept the co-option of three elected members to the executive. This was agreed at the council meeting a year later,

The conditions of the Brand Hall Gold Vase, for a trial period of two years, were altered so that it became a club team competition. Six players with handicaps of 12 and below would represent each club, four scores counting over eighteen holes.

Stanley Lunt took office as president of the English Golf Union and Ronnie Morgan continued as county captain.

The 1960 annual match between the first and second teams was tied, David Rodway and Andrew Thomson making their debuts for the second

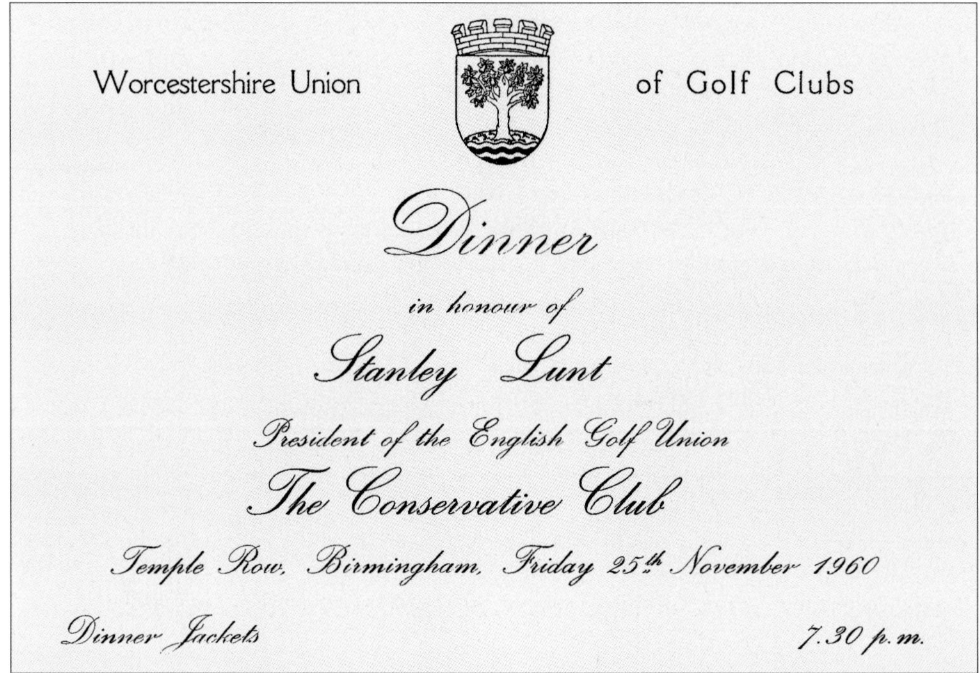
Worcestershire Union of Golf Clubs

Dinner

in honour of

Stanley Lunt

President of the English Golf Union

The Conservative Club

Temple Row, Birmingham, Friday 25th November 1960

Dinner Jackets 7.30 p.m.

team. A fortnight later the first team beat Gloucestershire by five points. They subsequently lost to Warwickshire by a similar margin, which coincidentally was the score by which the second team defeated their opposition. Shropshire and Herefordshire had the better of the match at Shrewsbury, despite a slight Worcestershire recovery in the singles. The $8\frac{1}{2}$- $9\frac{1}{2}$ score was repeated when Cheshire came to Blackwell and took the foursomes 5-1, before the home team rallied to win the singles, but by an insufficient amount.

A much better performance resulted in a two point win against Staffordshire at Enville but the second team failed at Kings Norton. Denis Hayes made his county debut in this match, beginning a career in which he distinguished himself by his major contributions to the administration of the game. Another player new to the county colours was David Lait, who a few weeks previously had won the Midland Boys Championship. At the end of the year the match secretary, Roy Chandler, reported that he had difficulty in getting a second team together and that he intended writing to all potential team members giving details of fixtures and asking them to indicate their availability. As a result Stanley Lunt and Bill Boulton offered to turn out for the second team at short notice if required.

The annual meeting was held at Kings Norton and the home club won both team prizes, snatching the Tomson-James Cup from Moseley's grasp when H. Bayley staged a brilliant recovery and Moseley's last man struggled to an 80. They improved on this one stroke victory in the Jubilee Shield, in which they were five strokes clear of Moseley. Jack Butterworth and Ken Frazier both scored 72 to take the lead in the G.D. Carr Cup. Neither man could reproduce this form the following day, when Harley Roberts, who had taken 76 strokes in the team event, returned a card of 68 in the morning. Having played "magnificently in conditions which made the course most difficult", according to Maurice Woodbine in the *Birmingham Post*, he began the second round comfortably. Then disaster struck: a three putt, followed by a pitch shot dragged into a bunker where it settled under the lip, led to one of Harley's two worst rounds in competitive golf. His 81 gave him a total of 149 which was matched by David Kelley and Bob Sandilands. Sandilands won the play-off, with Roberts second, and the former tied with Jack Butterworth for the G.D. Carr Cup, for which they played off in the Open in September, Sandilands emerging the victor.

Both were selected for "The Six", joining Ian Wheater, Tony Jowle, Michael Lunt and David Kelley in the team which travelled to Luffenham Heath. Sandilands and Butterworth had poor first rounds but recovered in the afternoon, while Tony Jowle returned two 73s to produce the best individual score. As a result Worcestershire qualified once again for the semi-finals. Alistair Sheppard replaced Butterworth for this event, which was held at Seacroft. We were drawn against a strong Surrey team containing four internationals, two of whom, Ian Caldwell and David Frame, either had been or would be Walker Cup players. We led 2-1 after the foursomes and were unfortunate not to win the third, a brilliant Surrey recovery being countered with three putts from our men who eventually lost on the 20th green. The singles were disappointing, only Lunt and Sheppard winning, resulting in Surrey's victory by one point. The next day they were defeated by Northumberland, by the same margin.

Only ten teams entered the Boulton Salver, Bob Sandilands and R.H. Crump of Blackwell winning the final one up on David Kelley and Stan Seymour of Kings Norton's "A" team. This club was more successful in the new format for the Brand Hall Gold Vase, their best four scores totalling 299, eight ahead of Halesowen. Brand Hall finished third and Warley fourth, so the municipal clubs maintained their excellent record in this competition.

The county Open was won by Bill Firkins jun., aged nineteen, with scores of 73 and 68 at his home course, Stourbridge. John Wiggett of Kings Norton was the runner-up, while the leading amateur in third place was Harley Roberts, Bob Sandilands tieing with Tony Jowle for fourth.

Other successes by our players were recorded by Michael Lunt, who won the Midland Amateur Championship and continued his international career,

J.S. Mitchley (Brand Hall) putting on the 18th green, watched by F. Bartlam (Worcester) during the Worcestershire Open Championship at Stourbridge, 1960

and David Rodway, who won the Howitt Bowl. Dick Mirams requested financial assistance for the junior golfers at the beginning of 1961 and the council voted in favour of a donation of £20, which was supplemented by donations of 5 guineas each from Mr. W.J. Lamb of Droitwich and Mr. J.H. Buckley of Halesowen.

The price of a book of tickets for the individual membership scheme was increased to £1 and it was agreed that no member could buy more than one book. Some clubs were already becoming concerned at the number of visitors using the scheme, which caused some problems later on.

Stan Seymour took over the captaincy from Ronnie Morgan. He gave the second team a start of two up in the foursomes and the singles in the opening match, the result of which was a win by thirteen matches to five for the second team. Despite that no one from the second team was selected for the first inter-county match with Gloucestershire, which Worcestershire won by two points. The second team were on the wrong side of the same score when they played Gloucestershire for the first time, Fred Savage making his first appearance for the county.

The first team was strengthened in July by the return of Roy Hobbis. He arrived home in time for the annual meeting, scored 73 in the team event, which was won by Blackwell on their own course, but could only manage two scores of 80 in the individual championship. This was won by Tony Jowle, who did not play in the Moseley "A" team, with a score of 151. He had to play off for the Philip Padmore Trophy and beat J. Duggan of Droitwich fairly comfortably. The winning Blackwell team included Ian Wheater, whose 72 was the best of the day, F.L. Wilkinson, Stanley Elliott and Bob Sandilands. These last two were involved in a four-way tie for second place the following day, along with Harley Roberts and C.V. Grafton. Alistair Sheppard of The Worcestershire was also involved in the play-off as he had tied for the G.D. Carr Cup with Sandilands. The outcome was that Elliott took the silver medal, Grafton the bronze and Sheppard the G.D. Carr Cup. Had Grafton not over-clubbed on the 18th hole of his morning round he might well have been involved in a different play-off. His second shot bounced on the green, rolled past the clubhouse and finished in the car park. His 6 on this hole resulted in a score of 77.

Roy Hobbis was in better form for the Boulton Salver, which he and Stan Seymour won for Kings Norton "A", beating Stourbridge "B" one up, the runners-up being represented by Dr. Tweddell and P.H. Plant. Only eleven teams from six clubs entered this event, but nearly all the players involved had represented the county at one time or another.

Roy joined Michael Lunt, Ian Wheater, Tony Jowle, Alistair Sheppard and Bob Sandilands at Chesterfield for "The Six" on 24th June. The full field was a representative "Who's Who" of Midland golf and Worcestershire's winning margin was just one stroke, compared with eight the previous year. It was a tense affair and mistakes by contenders from other counties saw us home. The semi-finals were at the magnificent links of Saunton. Jack Butterworth and David Kelley replaced Hobbis and Sandilands for the match against Middlesex. Only Jowle and Kelley succeeded in the foursomes but our team fought back in the singles and had Ian Wheater's new clubs been more familiar he, too, might have won. His left-handed clubs had been stolen one month before and he had received the new set only a few days before the tournament. In fact they had been stolen from the boot of Alistair Sheppard's car at Chesterfield the night before the qualifying round, in which Wheater contributed more than might have been expected with a mixture of hastily borrowed clubs. Perhaps he should have retained them for the final! The next day Lancashire claimed the championship by beating Middlesex by seven matches to two.

The inter-county matches continued with a halved match against Warwickshire, the second team losing their match by four points. Shropshire and Herefordshire were soundly despatched by a difference of seven points, so to fall by an even greater margin to Cheshire was something of a setback.

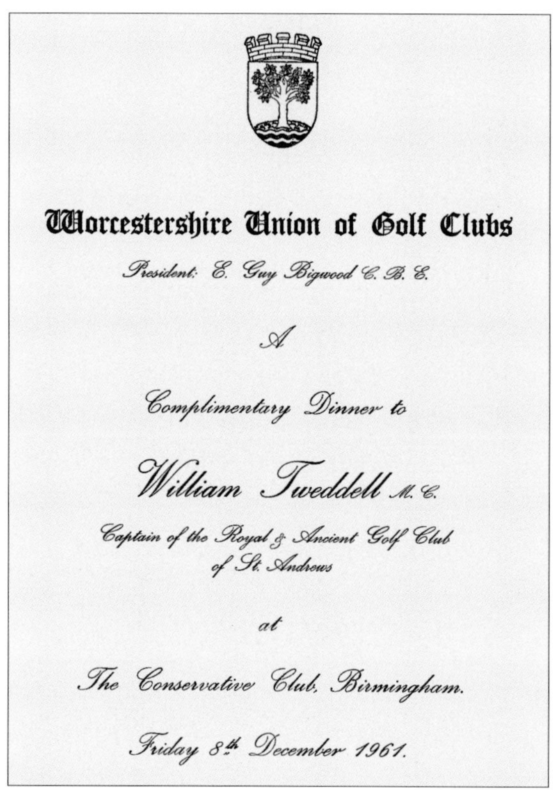

Worcestershire Union of Golf Clubs

President: E. Guy Bigwood C.B.E.

A

Complimentary Dinner to

William Tweddell M.C.

Captain of the Royal & Ancient Golf Club
of St. Andrews

at

The Conservative Club, Birmingham.

Friday 8th December 1961.

The first team recovered by defeating Staffordshire, Harley Roberts and A. Sheppard beating Charlie Stowe and Howard Thirlby by 7 and 6, but Charlie had his revenge on Harley in the singles. The second team were not so successful against that county, losing by 12 matches to 6.

Droitwich managed to finish ahead of Kings Norton on the latter club's course in the Brand Hall Gold Vase, Roy Green, a tall, willowy 3 handicapper returning a gross 71. Dudley finished in third place, one stroke ahead of Warley.

Tony Jowle, when interviewed by the *Birmingham Post*'s special correspondent, said he "had never putted better", when he broke the Kidderminster course record by four shots in the county Open. His round of 67 added to his first round of 71 made him champion by two strokes from the leading professional, Bernard Preston. Stan Seymour finished third on 141.

As the season drew to a close the county Union celebrated two happy events, both given ample coverage in the local press. Guy Bigwood celebrated his golden wedding and Dr. William Tweddell was elected captain of the Royal and Ancient Golf Club of St Andrews. Among those sending good wishes was his old friend Bobby Jones who recalled that "he had spent many enjoyable golfing occasions with Dr. Tweddell", among them the fourball match at Blackwell in 1930 the day after Jones had won the Open Championship. A happy coincidence was the winning of the Glennie Medal by Dr. Tweddell's son Michael.

Other memorable feats achieved by Worcestershire players were the selection of Michael Lunt for the Walker Cup matches, Tony Jowle's successes in the Midland Amateur Championship and the inaugural Leicestershire Fox, Ian Wheater's second victory in the President's Putter of the Oxford and Cambridge Golfing Society and David Rodway's retention of the Howitt Bowl. David was also elected a member of the Society, having gained his Blue the previous year.

In view of the poor response to the Boulton Salver the executive agreed that a change of format was required. Earlier in the year Stan Seymour had written to clubs to encourage more entries, to no avail. It was decided to hold the competition on one day only and that it would consist of a thirty-six hole medal, with a handicap limit of 6 and a maximum entry of fifty pairs. This was later modified to twenty-four pairs. "A" teams entered by the closing date would all be accepted, the "B" teams selected by ballot.

Moseley announced that the club wished to withdraw from the individual membership scheme because of the amount of play on the course. The club was asked to reconsider in the light of the extra revenue generated by increasing the price of ticket booklets to £1, and it agreed to remain in the scheme during 1962.

This became the main topic of discussion at the council meeting in January 1962. In addition to Moseley, other clubs were beginning to be disenchanted with the scheme. The original purposes of the scheme had been to allow members of the smaller clubs to have a cheap day out on the courses of the more important clubs, and to raise funds for the county Union. Clearly if two or three of the "more important clubs" dropped out the scheme would lose its popularity.

Once again it was Guy Bigwood who came up with a possible solution, outlining a scheme which had worked successfully in Yorkshire and other counties. For a subscription of one guinea per annum, every member of every club in the county was entitled to become a county member. This would entitle him to a copy of a year book relating to the Union's affairs and to buy a specially designed tie. Two competitions per year, in the spring and the autumn, would be held on the best courses in the county, with no entry fee, but good prizes. Those members keen on competitions would "get plenty for their money" while the senior golfers no longer interested in competitions would hopefully still be "only too happy to be associated with the county Union".

The existing scheme would continue in 1962 but every club was asked to consider the alternative and inform the honorary secretary of their opinions. These were duly voiced at a brief meeting in August. Three clubs had made it clear that they were withdrawing from the scheme at the end of the year. As well as the additional wear and tear on the course, "some individual members were inclined to endeavour to take possession of the whole club, and did not enter their names in the visitors' book before playing". Clubs were slow in paying the money taken for the ticket booklets to the county.

What promised to be an exciting season began disappointingly with the second team losing heavily to Gloucestershire at Henbury. Their first team came to Stourbridge a week later and beat us by two points after we had led after the foursomes.

John Preston

Stanley Lunt marked the passing of forty years participation in the county team championship by scoring 75 round his own course in assisting Moseley's winning the Tomson-James Cup by twelve shots fewer than Stourbridge. Nineteen year old David Allen also played his part in this by scoring 71. Blackwell won the Jubilee Shield. Squalls affected play in the individual championship, Tony Jowle being among those who suffered. The weather did not seem to affect Jack Butterworth, who had missed the previous two meetings. He opened with 75 in the morning and began his afternoon round with an eagle 3 (Moseley was played in a different order in 1962, the first being the present 16th and a par 5.) A second eagle at the 6th (now the 3rd) helped him to a score of 72 for a total of 147, five better than Tony Jowle who recovered his form somewhat in the afternoon. Harley Roberts came third, and David Kelley, now a member of Blackwell, and Roy Hobbis finished on 155, Hobbis regretting two shots out of bounds. This put him into third place for the G.D. Carr Cup, which Butterworth won, Harley Roberts separating them.

Worcestershire came second to Staffordshire in the Midland qualifying event at Whittington Barracks. Our neighbours lost the final to Northumberland at Sunningdale.

Despite the new format, the Boulton Salver only attracted fifteen pairs, from eight clubs, including Rose Hill, who entered two teams. David Kelley and R.H. Crump, playing off scratch, recorded the best gross score as well as the winning nett to take the trophy for Blackwell. Kelley then combined well with Michael Lunt in the foursomes in the match against Warwickshire, beating Alex Holmes and John Leach by 5 and 4. The morning session finished all square but Warwickshire outplayed us in the afternoon to win by three points. The second team lost by the same total despite leading after the foursomes.

A better performance against Shropshire and Herefordshire was more encouraging but the Cheshire match at Kidderminster was won decisively by the visitors after we had taken a lead in the foursomes, only

Butterworth, Hobbis and Thomson winning their singles. A fortnight later a slightly changed team recorded a very welcome win against Staffordshire at South Staffs.

Denis Hayes was largely responsible for Stourbridge's success in the Brand Hall Gold Vase, returning a nett 69 off a handicap of 3 on his home green. He was abetted by Michael Tweddell, John Preston, who had become Midland Boys champion just one week previously, and W.H. Oliver. Droitwich and Kidderminster tied in second place on 302, two strokes in arrears.

The county Open was a triumph for the amateurs. Harley Roberts and David Kelley both equalled the amateur course record at Boughton Park with scores of 65. As Roberts had also played well in the morning for 71 to lead Kelley by a stroke, he became the champion. Kelley finished second, Tony Jowle third, Jack Butterworth joint fourth with Michael Lunt and B.W. Cullimore of Droitwich. Bernard Preston was the leading professional and a young assistant, Nick Underwood from Blackwell, had a second round of 67.

The *Birmingham Post* ran a series entitled "Midland Portrait Gallery" during the year and featured both Dr. Tweddell, smiling brightly, and Guy Bigwood, whose smile was a little grimmer. Maurice Woodbine, the golf correspondent, profiled Dr. Tweddell, who admitted that before he accepted his medical practice in Stourbridge he went along to examine the golf course.

He was born in Whickham, County Durham in 1897. On leaving school he went straight into the army and was sent to France with the Royal Fusiliers in 1915. He returned to England in 1916 to be commissioned and was back in France in 1916. He was wounded twice and was awarded the Military Cross and Bar at Paschendale in 1917. After the war he studied medicine at Aberdeen University and played for the university golf team from 1922-24. He had started to play golf on a nine hole course close to his home before he was seven years old.

Bill Tweddell came to Stourbridge with a handicap of plus 3, which the club did not recognise and put him off scratch until he had won five successive competitions. He was the first Midland golfer to win the Amateur Championship. Visitors to Stourbridge Golf Club see his portrait as they enter the club, a fitting tribute to a fine golfer.

Guy Bigwood was profiled by a staff reporter who was obviously more interested in our president's achievements in his career as a chartered surveyor which also included a great deal of public service, administering charities and dispensing justice as a magistrate. He was awarded the CBE in 1958.

He was educated at Shrewsbury, a "soccer" school, and followed that game in the winter, although cricket was more important to him and he captained Barnt Green for a number of years. He also attained a handicap of 4 in his golfing prime but admitted to the interviewer that it was now 18, with which most seventy-six year olds would be satisfied. Like Dr. Tweddell, his portrait, subscribed by the members, hangs in his club. As well as the highest honours golf can bestow, Guy Bigwood was also accorded many professional laurels. There is no doubt that much of the county's golfing success from the late 1920s until the mid-1960s was due to the drive and influence of these two gentlemen.

Guy Bigwood opened the council meeting of 1963 by explaining why the individual membership scheme was to be discontinued, giving the reasons propounded at the August meeting of the executive. He received strong support from most clubs, but there were dissenters and the proposal was carried by ten votes to four. He then re-iterated the details of the scheme operated by Yorkshire and other counties which he had described at the previous council meeting. Mr. Cooksey would continue to run the scheme, which would commence in March, but a sponsor would be required in each club to recruit members, a £10 life membership being on offer as one incentive to join.

More disturbing news was the fact that Jack Butterworth was leaving the county and moving to Kent for business reasons. He was to have been captain for the new season. John Fraser accepted the office instead, thirty years after he had made his debut for the county. Thirty years later he was to become president.

His season began with a win against the second team at Blackwell. Undeterred, the second team played Gloucestershire at Kidderminster two weeks later and turned a two point deficit after the foursomes into a two point victory by virtue of a gritty singles performance. The first team achieved a similar result against Gloucestershire in much the same way, although the Gloucester tail put up spirited resistance to restrict our advantage to just one point.

Kings Norton's "A" and "B" teams took the Tomson-James Cup and the Jubilee Shield at Stourbridge in the county meeting, Roy Hobbis playing a major part in the "A" team's victory by ten strokes from Worcester Golf and Country Club, by taking 71 shots. He was less effective in the individual championship, slipping to 78 and 79. Harley Roberts, nearing the end of his fifty-first year, took the gold medal with scores of 72 and 73 to add to the previous day's 72. He finished five shots clear of Michael Tweddell, while David Kelley took the bronze medal. Harley's performance made him an undisputed winner of the G.D. Carr Cup.

Michael Lunt did not play in this meeting: he was preparing for the Amateur Championship at St Andrews, having played in the losing Walker Cup team. The American team remained in Britain and entered the championship. Michael progressed comfortably to the fourth round, in which he eliminated G. Blocker jun. from the United States, the second

American to fall to him, won 3 and 2 in the fifth round to knock out J. Boston from Ireland and faced Richard Davies, the holder and another American, in the sixth round. Michael emerged victorious after a close and exciting match and went on to meet Ed Updegraff, yet another American, in the semi-finals. Michael was three up with three to play and a "haar" was developing over the course. Updegraff birdied the 16th and won the Road Hole with a four. Both players were on the home green in two shots, but a long way from the hole. Michael's putt stopped two yards short on the damp green and Updegraff's putt finished closer. After a long careful look, Michael Lunt holed the putt.

Michael Lunt
with the Amateur Championship trophy

In the meantime another British player, John Blackwell, was having a battle with Ed Luceti, the final member of the American team. Blackwell had been playing carefully, allowing the American to make the mistakes, but, two up with five to play, he drove out of bounds. Luceti, unbelievably, followed him and lost the hole.

Both John Behrend, in his history of the competition, and Henry Longhurst described the final. The players were all square after the first round, then Blackwell took the lead with a birdie at the first hole of the afternoon round. Michael soon brought him back to level and by the turn he was two up, Blackwell having hit his drive into the bushes and then taken three putts at the 7th. A birdie at the 12th after a long putt unnerved Blackwell, who missed from five feet, but he hung on until the 17th.

Longhurst described Blackwell as an eccentric. He wore a tie while playing and had an unmatched set of clubs. He putted with his left hand below the right, which was less common then than it is now, to prevent "the twitch". Longhurst wrote: "He is in fact, at forty-nine, what the amateur golfer used to be – a relic, and a very welcome one, of the past."

Longhurst recalled Michael's father recovering from five down to win the English Amateur a year before the new champion was born. He wrote: "The son is a more worthy winner. He has a beautiful 'lazy' action, especially with his irons, and is a smooth putter." Michael's fiancée, Vicky Macdonald, pulled his trolley for him; they were married the following month.

Maurice Woodbine added Michael to the pantheon of the "Midland Portrait Gallery" in The *Birmingham Post,* pointing out as the other writers had done that Michael had achieved his championship against the full American Walker Cup team.

Perhaps adjustment to married life accounted for his taking 80 in the first round of "The Six", although he improved by four shots in the afternoon. David Rodway had been called in at short notice to replace a sick Harley Roberts and join Jack Butterworth, Tony Jowle, Ian Wheater and David Kelley in the team. A short missed putt in the tense closing stages meant that Worcestershire had tied with Nottinghamshire, who had the better score over the second eighteen holes and so qualified for the semi-finals.

Jimmy Duggan, a former West Bromwich Albion footballer, and his partner Roy Green, his cousin, won the Boulton Salver for Droitwich at Boughton Park, with a score of 141. Roy Hobbis and Neville Seers won the scratch prize.

The first team put up a tremendous performance against Warwickshire at Moseley, winning 13½-4½, but the second team almost reversed that result in their match, losing 12-6. The first team then inflicted an even heavier defeat on Shropshire and Herefordshire. This run of success came to an end at Warrington, where Cheshire, after halving the foursomes, just managed to outplay us in the singles which they won by two points. The Staffordshire match was halved but the second team experienced another heavy defeat at Beau Desert.

The professionals did much better than usual in the county Open, Frank Miller becoming champion for the fifth time. Nick Underwood came second, having shown such promise the previous year, and set a record of 65 for the reconstructed North Worcestershire course. Miller's score consisted of two 68s, Underwood having slipped to a 72 in the afternoon. The leading amateur was John Kilshaw of Blackwell, five strokes behind Underwood on 142 and tied with another professional, Ron Moses. The county's leading amateurs all appear to have had bad days.

As well as playing in the Walker Cup, Michael Lunt played in the other international matches and in the Commonwealth matches in Australia. He also won the Howitt Bowl. David Kelley was a reserve for the English team in the Home Internationals and won the Gleneagles Foursomes with Peter Butler as his partner. Harley Roberts was elected president of the Midland Counties Golf Association for the following year and The Worcestershire won that organisation's team competition.

Guy Bigwood was taken ill in November and Bill Boulton took the chair at the executive meeting, proposing a toast to Bigwood's speedy recovery. It was decided that the annual match between the first and second teams should be replaced by a trial, to be held at Malvern. A meeting was arranged with the intention of co-ordinating second team golf with that of the junior golfers, a commendable notion after the previous season's results.

The first suggestion of forming a league for county matches was placed before the executive, who felt that this was not desirable.

Guy Bigwood had recovered in time for the council meeting in January 1964 and opened the meeting by congratulating Michael Lunt on being named the Golf Writers' Golfer of the Year. Mr. Cooksey urged more clubs to take part in the county membership scheme, reminding delegates of the success of the meetings held the year before.

John Fraser's team opened their season at Blackwell on 5th April by routing Gloucestershire in the singles after halving the foursomes. The second team played Gloucester later that month, losing narrowly at Bristol and Clifton; they also lost their other two matches. The first team continued to win their matches until the final fixture, losing by a large deficit to Staffordshire at Little Aston in September, after an equally disappointing visit there in July. Norman Bolton made his first appearance for the county during this season.

Reference has been made throughout these pages to the ability of the members of the municipal clubs, which have produced many fine players for the county's teams. That many of these go on to join private clubs when invited to do so is not surprising but the opportunities given to them by the public courses should never be underrated or dismissed lightly. One such player was Neville Newbitt, twenty-one years old in 1964, a scratch golfer since he was sixteen and a member of Brand Hall. He became assistant to Frank Miller and worked at Moseley for eighteen months before being re-instated as an amateur. On 2nd and 3rd May he became the youngest player since Eric Fiddian, and the first player to enter from a public course, to win the Midland Amateur Championship. He had rounds of 73+75+76=224 at Harborne to beat Michael Lunt and Harley Roberts, no less, by one stroke.

Newbitt was also a member of Sandwell Park by this time, but retained his Brand Hall membership in order to retain his Worcestershire qualification.

He finished sixth in the individual championship at the annual county meeting at Kidderminster ten days later, after Roy Hobbis had led Kings Norton to victory in the Tomson-James Cup, with a score of 74. Dr. Tweddell played for the Stourbridge "B" team which took the Jubilee Shield. Hobbis continued to play sound golf in the first round of the championship, his 70 being equalled by Bob Sandilands, who then dropped shots at four of the first five holes in the afternoon, while Hobbis continued steadily, eventually winning the gold medal by three strokes from Sandilands and the G.D. Carr Cup, which he won by five strokes. Roy had come close on several occasions in the past, so once again a worthy winner emerged as champion.

Needless to say he was in "The Six", which also included the new Midland Amateur champion Neville Newbitt, Michael Lunt, David Kelley, Tony Jowle and Harley Roberts. The event was held at Moseley on 20th June. Worcestershire finished first, eight shots clear of Nottinghamshire and twenty better than Staffordshire who came third.

The finals were at Little Aston and our old rivals Surrey were the opposition for the semi-final. Andrew Thomson and Ian Wheater had replaced Hobbis and Roberts and beat Dudley Millenstead and Reg Glading, two noted players, in the foursomes, which finished 3-0 in our favour. They both earned points in the singles as well and Surrey were demolished 7½-1½. In the meantime Northumberland, who had become as dominant in the competition in the 1960s as Worcestershire had been in the 1930s, scored half a point less than us in eliminating Somerset, setting up a tense final. Lunt and Kelley were sent out third in the foursomes to ensure a point, but it was the only one we gained in the morning. Worcestershire put up strong resistance in the singles but could not prevent Northumberland winning their third title in five years. Just two points separated the teams at the close.

In the meantime North Worcestershire "B" won the Boulton Salver at Kidderminster with a score of 140, seven strokes better than Brand Hall in second place. Blackwell "A" and "B" were third and fourth respectively. Kidderminster won the Brand Hall Gold Vase despite a strong challenge from Droitwich and The Worcestershire, one stroke separating the three teams. Frank Miller retained the county Open title with 141, two shots ahead of John Wiggett, Ron Moses and David Kelley, the leading amateur. Nick Underwood was next, his afternoon round improving on his morning score by five strokes.

Worcestershire players continued to do well in other events, the most notable being a second appearance in the final of the Amateur Championship by Michael Lunt. Though there were a number of Americans in the field, all Michael's opponents were members of British clubs, including the great Irish golfer Joe Carr, whom Michael beat in the sixth round on the 19th green. John Behrend recalled that this was the match which excited most of the spectators. The two players had met at a party the night before and Carr had told Michael that he should not let him get three up, or Michael would never get them back. In the event Carr did go three up at the 5th, but Michael recovered to become one up at the 15th. He then three-putted the 16th, recovered after a wild tee shot on the 17th and when Carr missed a short putt on the 19th progressed to the final. His opponent in the final was Gordon Clark from Northumberland, our nemesis in the English County Championship. The match swayed one way and another, but there was to be no sweet revenge, Clark winning on the 39th hole.

Tony Jowle reached the fourth round and found himself up against another Northumbrian, Alan Thirlwell, whom he took to the 19th, but could not save the match.

Michael also represented Great Britain and Ireland in the Eisenhower Trophy in Rome and was on the winning team, as he was in the Home Internationals in which he was joined by David Kelley. Tony Jowle won the Howitt Bowl and David Rodway became the third Worcestershire player to win the Leicestershire Fox. Blackwell won the team championship in the Midland Counties Championship after a tie with Moseley. The final honour went to our long-serving secretary, Derek Greey, who was elected president of the Worcestershire PGA.

The executive met in November and thanked Mr. Cooksey for all his efforts on behalf of the county membership scheme, which had attracted more members during the year. The proceeds were all paid into one account and the Union was able to purchase a further £400 War Loan at 3½%, for the sum of £237.2s.0d., leaving the county's finances in a healthy state.

Brand Hall Golf Club had written to propose that Neville Newbitt's handicap be reduced to plus 1, but the executive did not agree to this. They also disagreed with a suggestion from Dr. R.J. Henderson that the Union should sponsor a competition for golfers over the age of fifty, but said they would have no objection if he wished to support it himself. They also found a request from the Worcestershire PGA for an alliance competition unacceptable, as was that body's secretary's request that the Union should endeavour to increase the retaining fees paid by clubs to their professionals. It was felt that, as the Union had no jurisdiction over such matters, no action could be taken.

The idea of blazer badges for players qualified to play for the county was more favourable received.

At the next meeting, which preceded the council meeting, a letter from Dick Mirams was read, suggesting that the juniors golf sub-committee should be replaced as it had been in office for the last ten years. As a result one of the county's most popular characters, Dr. Bill Cunningham, was proposed as chairman, assisted by Bill Byard of Gay Hill and Andrew Mirams of Moseley, Bill's own club. Bill Cunningham is still remembered with great affection by all the players who passed through his teams.

It was agreed to arrange a fixture with a group of golfers from the Brigham Young University of Utah. The executive also agreed that an honorarium should be paid to Brenda Smith, "as an expression of our appreciation for all she does for the Union".

With Michael Lunt as county captain in 1965 the team had a convincing win against Gloucester in the first match, Harley Roberts contributing two points. The second team, having halved the foursomes, stumbled again in the singles and lost by three points. They eventually improved on the previous season by defeating Staffordshire, but lost to Warwickshire. The first team also beat Warwickshire and Shropshire and Herefordshire, but lost to Cheshire and Staffordshire, for whom Trevor Homer was making his first appearance against us. Partly because of his international commitments, Michael Lunt did not play in any of these matches. He played in the halved Walker Cup match at Five Farms, Maryland, a rare near-success for Great Britain and Ireland, and won the Leicestershire Fox and the Howitt Bowl.

Stourbridge won the Tomson-James Cup for the tenth time. It was held at Boughton Park and the home team won the Jubilee Shield. Roy Hobbis had the best round of the day, a 72, but had two poor rounds in the individual championship, which was won by David Kelley, six strokes ahead of his nearest rivals, Dr. Henderson of Worcester Golf and Country Club, David Rodway, representing The Worcestershire, and Harley Roberts, all on 145. Having scored 74 in the team event, Kelley's aggregate of 213 gave him the G.D. Carr Cup by four shots over Dr. Henderson.

Four days later, Kelley won the Midland Amateur Championship at Northants County, returning a score of 215, playing "steady, unspectacular golf".

David Kelley was an obvious selection for "The Six" and joined Michael Lunt, Andrew Thomson, Ian Wheater, Neville Newbitt and David Rodway at Woodhall Spa. We put up a good performance but it was not good enough to prevent Warwickshire pushing us into second place by a difference of four strokes. Kelley also played for England during this exceptional season.

Michael Tweddell and the young John Preston won the Boulton Salver for Stourbridge with a magnificent first round of 67–2=65, to which they added 76 nett in the afternoon. Kidderminster came second, two shots in arrears, and later in the season tied with North Worcestershire for the Brand Hall Gold Vase.

When the county Open finally took place on 18th November at Moseley, fog on the original date having prevented any play, Kings Norton had a field day. The competition was reduced to 18 holes and John Wiggett scored 71 to tie with his assistant, Tony Mutton. Roy Hobbis was the leading amateur, tied on 72 with Frank Miller. The play-off was arranged for 22nd December and despite being inconvenienced late in the round when a small piece of flint flew off his lighter and struck him in the eye, Wiggett was in total command, winning by five clear shots.

The Open was actually held one day after the November executive meeting. Ominously, Guy Bigwood was not in attendance. Further hints of change became evident when Roy Chandler, the match secretary, reported that Cheshire wished to abandon our long-standing fixture with them. The chairman, Bill Boulton, proposed to discuss this with the Cheshire president when next they met, but any discussion which may have taken place was obviously fruitless. We also refused Gloucestershire's request to alter the second team fixture with them to a colts' match. In fact, Chandler was attempting to arrange more matches for the second team.

It was proposed to celebrate the Union's sixtieth birthday with a dinner at the Raven Hotel in Droitwich during March.

Another decision was that the chairman and honorary secretary should visit clubs holding county competitions a few days before the event to discuss the arrangements for the day. These were given the following priority: an extension of the bar licence to cover the whole day; a good, comprehensive snack bar rather than a set lunch; a starter, who might also act as a marker for a competitor without a partner; control of caddies; availability of coffee; good car parking facilities and finally, arrangements for the clubhouse to be adequate and clean.

Some new faces appeared in the county teams during 1966 alongside many familiar figures, some of whom faded from the scene during the season. Both teams lost to Gloucestershire in the opening matches and then narrowly to Warwickshire. The first team lost to Nottinghamshire, while the second team's match was abandoned when the Blackwell course became unfit for play, with the home county holding a slender lead after the foursomes. Matters improved with victories over Shropshire and Herefordshire by both teams and the first team finished the season with a close win against Staffordshire, while the second team lost to them by a narrow margin.

Kings Norton won both team competitions on their own course but none of their players could match the lowest round of the day, a new amateur record of 69 for the newly constructed course by the twenty-three year old Andrew Thomson, now a member of Blackwell. Another young player did even better the following day when Andrew Forrester of Brand Hall became the youngest player since Eric Fiddian to win the gold medal, with rounds of 71 and 75. Neville Newbitt was second, making it a memorable day for Brand Hall, while W.B. Owen of the home club, in third place, took the G.D. Carr Cup. Unfortunately the field was slightly diminished by the absences of Michael Lunt, Ian Wheater and David Kelley, who, having played in the Brabazon Trophy the previous week, were unable to sacrifice a second week of work.

They were able to take time off for the Midland "Six", though, and joined Forrester, Newbitt and Thomson at Olton. In a desperately tense finish David Kelley, our last man on the course, needed to beat Charlie Stowe's score by eight shots to give Worcestershire a chance of qualifying. He made a good start, faltered, but recovered, while the fifty-seven year old Staffordshire

The Executive Committee of the
Worcestershire Union of Golf Clubs
request the pleasure of the company of

....

at a Dinner to
Honour the 1966 English Amateur Champion
Michael Lunt
the Conservative Club, Ethel Street, Birmingham
on Friday, 20th January 1967

R.S.V.P.
D. E. GREEY
THE BRIDGES.
ALVECHURCH. WORCS.

RED COATS OR
DINNER JACKETS
RECEPTION 7P.M.

veteran stumbled, almost unbelievably, to a tired 82, giving Worcestershire the difference they needed. A three-putt on the 18th by another Worcestershire team member created a tie, but we were declared the winners by virtue of our better second eighteen holes, the precise condition which reduced us to second place in 1963.

J.R. Higson replaced Forrester for the finals, which were held at the Royal Cinque Ports. After beating Devon 6-3 in the semi-finals we faced our old rivals Surrey in the final. Michael Lunt and David Kelley had the distinction of beating Dudley Millenstead and Peter Oosterhuis in the foursomes by one hole. Newbitt and Wheater also won in the morning to set up a tight finish. Kelley halved his match and Newbitt won the last singles 7 and 6. Unfortunately these were our only successes and Surrey won 5 matches to 3, the halved match not being added to the score. This was the last time that Worcestershire contested the national final.

Bernard Cullimore and Norman Bolton won the Boulton Salver for The Worcestershire, the first time a team from this club had done so. Fifteen clubs entered teams for the Brand Hall Gold Vase, which was held at Halesowen, and it was won by the home club, with Droitwich second.

The county Open resulted in a tie for two men from Kings Norton; the holder, John Wiggett, and the amateur, John Ward, Wiggett winning the play-off by one stroke.

The Old Clubhouse, Kings Norton

In the meantime Derek Greey and the Warwickshire secretary, Bill Dudley-Evans, who was also president of the Midland Counties Golf Association called a meeting to discuss the congested fixture card which had resulted in leading players becoming unavailable for county matches. This was to have a more positive outcome a year later.

Perhaps symptomatic of this situation was that, during the season, Michael Lunt won the English Amateur Championship, to follow his father's achievement, represented his country, won the Harlech Gold Cross, the Leicestershire Fox (for the second time), the Mere Trophy, the Whitchurch Dragon and the Whittington Trophy. David Kelley also played in the International matches and won the Howitt Bowl, while Andrew Forrester won the West of England Open Championship.

The county Union suffered an immense blow at the end of the year when Guy Bigwood died. His influence on golf, not only in Worcestershire, but on a national level, had been enormous. The annual report stated: "The loss to us and indeed to the world of golf is irreplaceable." So, with his passing and our last appearance to date in the county finals, the second great era of Worcestershire golf drew to its close.

Worcestershire Seniors 1998

Kings Norton Golf Club, 1996

Left to right: R.V. Mirams (past president), D.T. Humphries (president), J.R. Fraser (immediate past president)

Courtesy: Peter Ricketts

Two Champions – Eric Fiddian (1928, 1930, 1950) and Mike Reynard (1981, 1992, 1993, 1995 1996, 2001) – Stourbridge, 2001

Courtesy: Peter Ricketts

Richard Wassell (Kidderminster), County Amateur Champion, Youths Champion, G.D. Carr Cup, 2000

The Worcestershire Boys Team which won the first English Boys County Championship, 1986
Back row, left to right: Spencer Edwards (Kings Norton), John Bickerton (Droitwich)
Jonathon Reid (Kings Norton), Darren Prosser, captain (Moseley), Glen Lowe (Kings Norton)
Neil Swaffield (Stourbridge), Craig Clarke (Moseley). Front row: John Scott, joint junior organiser
Roy Chandler, president, Jim Gray, joint junior organiser

Courtesy: J. Moreton

First time winners of the Severnside Tournament 1994. Left to right: Lee Priddey (Droitwich)
J. Moreton, James Toman (Worcester), Austin Russell (Stourbridge), Chris Heeley (Moseley)
Oliver Darby, captain (Little Lakes), Simon Deakin (Kings Norton)
Robert Hough (North Worcestershire), Richard Copsey (Kidderminster)

The County First Team 1990
Left to right, back row: Matthew Houghton, David Eddiford, Rob Stevens, David Rodway (captain) Simon Timmins, Alan Robinson, Peter Swinburne. Front row: Mick Daw, Neil Swaffield Andrew Terry, Simon Braithwaite

Courtesy: J. Moreton

John Fraser presenting Craig Moss with John Fraser Cup, 1999

Chapter Five

Into the League

After the death of Guy Bigwood, Dr. William Tweddell was elected president of the county Union, a fitting recognition of his achievements within the county and nationally.

1967 was a year of changes: alliances were started, something Bigwood had resisted, and, arising from the Midland Counties Golf Association meeting, it was proposed to form a league of the Midland counties on the model of the one formed in the south-east. As the second team would also be involved eventually, the match secretary, Roy Chandler, wrote to the twenty-two clubs in the Union requesting the names of young golfers worthy of a trial in the second team. The second team captain, Dick Mirams, requested that second team matches should comprise twelve players per side. The first teams would field ten players. The other four counties were the ones against whom the county already played friendly matches, Warwickshire, Staffordshire, Nottinghamshire and the combined Shropshire and Herefordshire team.

The match with Gloucestershire was retained as a friendly match at the beginning of the season. This took place on 9th April at Cirencester and resulted in a win for the home team, by one point, after the foursomes had been shared. The second team did better, winning 11-7 at Worcester.

The executive was not happy with the arrangements the professionals had made for the alliances, but agreed to give them time to sort matters out and showed willingness to "give them a boost" if necessary. The council meeting stood for a few moments in silence in memory of Guy Bigwood and learnt that a cup had been purchased to commemorate his dedication to the county. This was to be played for at the meetings of the membership scheme.

The meeting also discussed the request of the English Golf Union that all county championships be held on the same weekend to avoid clashes with important open events. This would entail clubs closing their course for a full

The Worcestershire County Team

Celebrating the 75th anniversary of Moseley Golf Club, 1967

weekend and it was hoped that the members of the club holding the event would be granted the courtesy of other courses within the county. This change would take effect in 1968.

Another idea which did not materialise was the writing of a brief history of the Union. Brenda Smith recalls that this was eventually delegated to her but pressure of work with Derek Greey, in addition to the normal county work, prevented this.

Harley Roberts was in good form once again in the Tomson-James Cup, assisting Michael Tweddell, John Preston and J.L. Longmore in winning the trophy for Stourbridge at North Worcestershire. Kings Norton won the Jubilee Shield, Ben Owen returning the lowest score of the day, 70.

The gold medal was won by a re-instated amateur. The thirty-one year old Malcolm Hampton had his amateur status restored twelve months before the championship, having held professional posts in Sweden and Norway in 1962, before attempting the tournament circuit in 1964. He left Worcestershire sometime in 1971 and moved south. His subsequent activities included teaching juniors in the emergent Slovenia in the late 1990s. He equalled the course record in miserable conditions with a 68 and added 70 in the second round to win by five shots from Andrew Forrester. Alan Guest won the bronze medal.

The first league match was played on 4th June against Nottinghamshire at Hollinwell. After leading by the odd match at lunchtime we only managed three and a half points in the singles and lost by two points. The second team shared the foursomes at Stourbridge and fared only a little better in the singles, losing the match by one point.

Despite a course record of 66 at North Hants County by Michael Lunt, recovering from a serious loss of form, Worcestershire could only come second to a consistent Staffordshire team in the Midland "Six". The Boulton Salver was won by Ben Owen and Terry Kilshaw of Kings Norton, with Norman Bolton and Bernard Cullimore in second place.

The county then fielded a team against Moseley to celebrate the club's seventy-fifth anniversary, the club winning again as they had fifteen years before.

The first team then returned to more serious golf and beat the powerful Staffordshire side by ten matches to five in the league. The second team also enjoyed a narrow victory. The next encounter, with Warwickshire, resulted in a tie, but the second team lost heavily. The final league match produced an emphatic win over Shropshire and Herefordshire and put the county in second place in the table. The second team also had a successful game at Kidderminster, winning all the foursomes. The visitors' fight back resulted in their winning five of the singles to go down 13-5.

Denis Hayes

After the start of the Brand Hall Gold Vase had been delayed by fog Blackwell managed to hold off a strong challenge from Kings Norton to win by a single stroke at Gay Hill. One unfortunate gentleman from Moseley suffered the indignity of taking eight putts on the 12th hole. He elected to putt up the slope in front of the green and only the fifth attempt remained on the putting surface. He completed the 120 yards par 3 in 11 strokes.

Frank Miller won the county Open for the seventh time. It was played at Stourbridge and Michael Tweddell and Andrew Forrester were the leading amateurs, tied in second place with an assistant at Cocks Moors Woods, John Roach, who had returned a score of 70 to equal Miller's morning round, but he unfortunately dropped three shots from the 15th to the 17th in the afternoon, while Michael Tweddell followed a new record of 67 for the recently lengthened course with a disastrous 76.

Once again our players featured in events outside the county. Michael Lunt, in a quiet year for him, won the Harlech Gold Cross; Andrew Forrester won the West of England Open Championship and the Howitt Bowl, while Tony Jowle won the Leicestershire Fox for the second time. Roy Hobbis and Ben Owen won the Finney Shield, the annual foursomes tournament at Harborne.

Sadly, the year ended with the death of Bill Boulton on the course at Aberdovey while playing in the Wigorns' annual match. He had been a founder member of this society but will be best remembered for his work for the English Golf Union, which he served as president in 1957 and then as chairman of the championship committee. He had only recently been appointed to the committee of the Senior Golfers Society. His contribution to the county was second only to that of Guy Bigwood.

Denis Hayes, who had been the captain of Stourbridge in 1963-64 and had been elected to the Royal and Ancient Golf Club of St Andrews, joined the Implements and Ball Committee of the ruling body in 1967 and became its chairman. In 1980 he became the chairman of the Rules of Golf Committee, and it is to him we owe the clarity of the present book of rules. He also served as chairman of the General Committee in 1976 and from 1984 to 1988, during which period he was also joint chairman of the World Amateur Golf Council. In these various capacities, Denis was active on the course in the Open Championship and the Masters. His stories of how Augusta is prepared for the Masters are interesting, to say the least. Once he had relinquished these globe-trotting commitments Denis became the chairman, and then the president, of our county Union. Worcestershire's role in the wider world of the game continued to be an influential one.

The executive decided that players representing the county teams could purchase a sweater and after playing ten matches would receive a county badge. Such had been the success of the league in 1967 that it was decided that the second teams would also compete in a league during the coming season. One benefit was that it had become easier to raise teams for the matches.

The 1968 season began on 21st April when the first team recovered from a slight deficit to defeat Shropshire and Herefordshire by nine matches to six at Worcester. The second team travelled to The Herefordshire at Wormsley, more picturesquely known as Ravens Causeway, and inflicted a humiliating defeat on the opposition by eleven points.

The customary friendly with Gloucestershire produced an encouraging victory by twelve points to six, but the second team could only win one foursomes match and five singles, with one halved match, to lose rather severely.

The disqualification of a Moseley player when his team was in contention for the Tomson-James Cup meant that Blackwell had a comfortable twelve stroke win, while Stourbridge won the Jubilee Shield. Andrew Thomson had played a large part in Blackwell's performance, scoring 74. It has been shown that a good round in the team event is often the prelude to a serious loss of form in the individual championship. This was not the case this time, as Thomson had rounds of 71 and 67 on his home course at Blackwell to take the gold medal and the G.D. Carr Cup, while his nett score gained him the Philip Padmore Trophy.

He continued his good form in the league match against Warwickshire, who were annihilated at Olton, Ronnie Hiatt scoring their only point playing against Michael Lunt. The second team added to our neighbours' discomfort at Gay Hill, never a happy venue for Warwickshire, a fact that has been duly noted by our fixtures secretaries. Nevertheless it was Warwickshire who won the Midland "Six" at Kedleston Park, thirteen shots clear of Worcestershire in third place.

Thomson continued his excellent season by winning the Boulton Salver in partnership with Paul Muddyman.

The Nottinghamshire fixtures were held at Moseley and Sherwood Forest respectively and resulted in two excellent victories for Worcestershire, so the Staffordshire match would settle the league title. The first team's one point deficit in the foursomes represented Staffordshire's winning margin after we had halved the singles. The second team retrieved some pride by winning 10-8 at Kings Norton and thereby won the new second team league in its inaugural year, the first team finishing second to Staffordshire.

David Kelley, playing in the 1968 final of the English Amateur Championship at Ganton

The Brand Hall Gold Vase was played at North Worcestershire and was won by Moseley, for the first time since it had become a team competition. Peter Ricketts reported on the success of the county membership scheme which had grown to 650 members. The season ended with the county Open which was won by David Kelley with a score of 140. Another amateur, Roy Green of Droitwich, was second and the leading professionals, tied on 142, were Frank Miller and Bill Firkins.

Earlier in the year Kelley had reached the final of the English Amateur which he lost rather heavily to Michael Bonnallack, who retained the trophy. Yet another Worcestershire player, Roger Chalkley of Moseley, won the Howitt Bowl and Malcolm Hampton won the Public Golf Courses Championship.

The November executive meeting had much to discuss. Progress on the alliances was pronounced satisfactory. It was agreed a minimum of £50 be given to junior golf and that Dr. Cunningham be asked to attend the next executive meeting in January 1969. As a result £75 was made available and the president suggested that to increase the support for the juniors and be "as generous as possible", £250 worth of shares be purchased, on the advice of the county's stockbroker. Dr. Cunningham also proposed the inauguration of a colts section for youths over the age of eighteen, which was agreed.

A further innovation was suggested by Harley Roberts who thought that a pre-season match against the county's professionals would provide good training for potential team members. It was agreed that the arrangements be left to Mr. Roberts but nothing further seems to have transpired.

One possible reason for the professionals' indifference may have been the low value of prize money they could win in their competitions and Dr. Tweddell, as president, suggested at the council meeting that each club be asked for a donation to boost the prize funds.

At the same meeting Stanley Lunt drew attention to an English Golf Union circular regarding the handicapping of category one golfers, then comprising plus to 3 handicaps. These handicaps, previously fixed by the clubs, would now be ratified by the county. Therefore standard scratch scores for competitions would have to be calculated very strictly by a "responsible and knowledgeable person".

It was at this meeting that Derek Greey was elected honorary secretary and treasurer of the county for the twenty-first time and the following week a dinner attended by 120 people was held in his honour. In his weekly column Peter Ricketts quoted the comments about Greey from Dr. Tweddell and Roy Chandler, the former stating, "he exudes bonhomie", while the latter concurred with,"he is always a source of infinite goodwill". One of Derek Greey's more unusual golfing exploits was holing out through the two shilling tote window at Ludlow racecourse.

Derek Greey was elected president of the Worcestershire Professional Golfers Association and a cup for competition in the alliances was purchased and named in his honour at the suggestion of Frank Miller. This was won by the Blackwell "A" team led by Simon Fogarty in the winter of 1968-69, playing in a twenty-seven hole format in which each professional had three partners. George Waddington and Douglas Stevenson were the two partners tieing with Fogarty for first place. He also returned the best professional score.

The first team began their 1969 season with a 10-8 victory over Gloucestershire at Cotswold Hills, losing the first three foursomes but winning the second three and taking the singles 7-5. The second team lost at Stourbridge by the same score.

Moseley dominated the team and individual championships on their own course, Andrew Forrester, a British youth international, leading the way in the Tomson-James Cup with a 70, well supported by Roger Chalkley 75 and Tony Jowle 76, although Michael Lunt was not on form and returned 81. The club also won the Jubilee Shield and the next day Andrew Forrester, 6'6" tall and weighing 14 stones, broke the course record with 64, adding a 70 in the second round to win the gold medal six strokes ahead of David Kelley. He also won the G.D. Carr Cup.

The match against Staffordshire was won comfortably at Blackwell, although the second team lost by the odd point at Enville. They improved considerably in their next match, trouncing Nottinghamshire 13-5, while the first team managed to win at Sherwood Forest after being a point behind at lunchtime. They maintained a one hundred per cent record and won the league by beating Warwickshire 9-6, the same total by which they disposed of Shropshire and Herefordshire a fortnight later. The second team also prevailed over them in their match, but had to wait until September before their encounter with Warwickshire, whom they defeated 11-7. The defeat against Staffordshire consigned them to second place in their league. In their first match the colts' team enjoyed a victory by four points over Gloucestershire.

Despite their success in the Midland league, our team could only manage fourth place in the English Counties qualifying event at Willesley Park.

In June Blackwell's pair of Terry Shingler and G.G. Checkley won the Boulton Salver by one stroke from Malcolm Hampton and Neville Newbitt of Brand Hall, while the Brand Hall Gold Vase produced a tie between the same two clubs. Terry Shingler and Andrew Thomson both returned gross scores of 72.

Brand Hall's leading player was Neville Newbitt and he tied with Hamish Macdonald, the Droitwich professional, in the county Open at Worcester, both scoring 136. Newbitt was less successful in the play-off, encountering rather too many trees, and failed to complete the second round of the thirty-six hole play-off when he hit his ball into bushes on the final hole. Macdonald returned scores of 67 and 72.

A seventeen year old assistant from Moseley, Bob Cameron, won the Derek Greey Cup with Vernon Green in the Worcestershire Alliance. He and Roy Dunnett also shared second place with three other pairs at Blackwell.

As well as playing in the youths' international matches, Andrew Forrester won the West of England Championship and Ian Hughes of Moseley won the Howitt Bowl.

The January council meeting of 1970 was the last to be held at the old Kings Norton club. The new course at Weatheroak was under construction and opened on 1st November that year.

The meeting was informed of a renewed drive to recruit members for the county membership scheme and make club members more aware of its existence. Bill Cunningham had had a better response from eighteen out of the twenty-two clubs regarding entries for junior competitions and Frank Miller, Ron Moses and Simon Fogarty were providing regular coaching for the boys.

Harley Roberts stated that the formation of the Midland league had been a "wonderful shot in the arm" for county golf, which had been "literally dying on its feet" a few years previously. He hoped that every player would make an effort to play for the county rather than in individual events.

The honorary secretary informed the meeting that the executive felt that it would be strengthened by an infusion of new blood and two new members would be elected from the floor of the house. Nominations were to be forwarded to the secretary. As a result of this it was agreed in November to invite E.J. Vickerstaff of Fulford Heath and Jeffrey Adams of Gay Hill to join the executive. Jeff was still in office as manager of the county membership scheme in 2005!

Both the first and second teams made excellent starts to their seasons with convincing wins over Gloucestershire and a fortnight later the first team continued this good form by beating Warwickshire 9-6. The second team was less successful, losing rather heavily, 13-5, at Moseley.

The championship was held for the last time on Kings Norton's original course and Roy Hobbis celebrated by setting a new amateur course record of 66, ensuring the club of victory in the Tomson-James Cup. Moseley retained the Jubilee Shield.

Roy could not quite repeat such a performance the following day, returning 74 and 71 to take the silver medal. The gold medal was won by thirty-six year old John Toddington, 3 handicap, who had not played for the county's second team, much less the first, and had not won his club, Gay Hill's, championship, although he had previously qualified for the Brabazon Trophy. On a parched course he had rounds of 74 and 70 and attributed his success to an alteration in his swing plane to cure a shank.

A special event was held at Blackwell in May to mark the retirement of the doyen of Worcestershire professionals, 'Pop' Lewis, after his thirty-four years at Cocks Moors Woods. 51 professionals and 102 amateurs from Worcestershire, Warwickshire and Staffordshire competed for the Pop Lewis Cup. Although the day was marred by rain and thundery weather over £200 was raised on Pop's behalf. The event was won by Jim Rhodes, then at Walsall, and his 4 handicap partner, John Smith, who returned an amazing score of 61.

The county colts played Warwickshire colts at Moseley on 17th May and lost by three points, two future professionals, David Russell and Pip Elson, representing their respective counties.

The Boulton Salver resulted in a tie between Moseley, represented by Tony Jowle and Clive Nickless, and Gay Hill, Jeff Adams being partnered by P.J. Cassidy. Both pairs had their good and bad moments, Tony having trouble on the greens and Jeff chipping into a bunker, although the Moseley pair did have a run of three birdies to take them to the turn in the second round.

The next round of league matches brought an impressive victory over Shropshire and Herefordshire, sadly not matched by the second team, but what appeared to have been a strong team submitted rather tamely to Staffordshire, while the second team could do no better.

John Toddington was picked for the match against Nottinghamshire but did not score a point. However, the remainder of the team displayed a return to form and recorded an 11-4 victory. The second team also managed to improve sufficiently to win 12-6. The first team result put them into second place in the league.

The Brand Hall Gold Vase was held at Brand Hall, but the home team could only manage second place behind Moseley, Clive Nickless returning a score of nett 63 off a handicap of 7, his best competitive round.

David Kelley won the Midland Counties Amateur Stroke Play Championship at Stourbridge.

The county Open at Moseley came to a dramatic climax when Malcolm Hampton threw away a comfortable lead by driving out of bounds on the final hole. He tied with Terry Shingler, who went on to win an eighteen hole play-off by a single shot. Even then there was a tense climax when Shingler three-putted the 16th and the 18th greens, while Hampton dropped a shot on the par 3 17th and could only make par on the final hole.

Perhaps not quite as dramatic an event, but still something of a surprise, came at the council meeting on 12th January 1971, when it was announced that Warwickshire had set up a county membership scheme similar to ours and after only one year had attracted a larger membership than that of the Worcestershire scheme. The newly co-opted executive members, Messrs. Adams and Vickerstaff, were given the task of visiting our clubs and drumming up more support for the scheme. The recruitment drive was a success, for they reported at the next meeting that the membership scheme had reached saturation point.

Bill Cunningham had some success with a plan to increase juniors funds by asking supporters to make a donation of £1 on a bankers order form. Some readers may be surprised to know that over thirty years later their donations are still most welcome and gratefully received!

On the golf course, the first team could only manage a halved match with Gloucestershire, although the second team performed well in the singles after halving the foursomes to emerge winners 11-7. Both teams beat Shropshire and Herefordshire in the opening league games.

Blackwell won the Tomson-James Cup in an exciting finish, their last player requiring no worse than 84 to put host club Stourbridge in second place. Using new clubs which replaced recently stolen ones Rod Chantrill just managed to return the necessary score. Kings Norton won the Jubilee Shield.

The next day John Toddington, now playing off a handicap of 1, won the gold medal with a score of 142. In second place was fourteen year old David Russell, one stroke behind, while David Kelley won the bronze medal with 144, which added to his 69 the previous day earned him the G.D. Carr Cup.

Blackwell also enjoyed success in the Boulton Salver when Paul Muddyman and John Driver returned two nett rounds of 72 at Gay Hill. Later in the season Moseley retained the Brand Hall Gold Vase on their own course.

A determined foursomes performance against Staffordshire placed the first team in a good position and they built on this in the singles to win 10½-4½. The second team also scraped home by the odd point. The first team's victory over Nottinghamshire was much narrower, and the second team only managed a half. In the final league match Warwickshire fought back fiercely after trailing 4-1 in the foursomes and took six of the singles matches, restricting our winning score to just one match. This meant that Worcestershire had won all their matches, and therefore the league, for the third time in the five years of its existence. It was fitting that the putt which won the final match was struck by fifty-nine year old Harley Roberts, our captain, who had so warmly welcomed the idea of league golf. The executive agreed in November to hold a dinner to celebrate the county's victory.

Two Blackwell members, David Kelley and Terry Shingler, tied for the county Open on 142, professionals Richard Livingston and Alan Roach tieing for third place on 144. In an exciting play-off Kelley hit a fine 4-wood over 200 yards to within ten feet of the 16th hole, while Shingler's approach found a bunker. Kelley won the play-off by two strokes. Shingler had the consolation of being elected captain of the Midland Counties Golf Association, while David Russell played for England boys against Scotland at Barassie.

The November executive meeting in this memorable year was a long affair. A disturbing communication came from the captain of Stourbridge, at which the county championship had been held in May over a weekend, as requested by the English Golf Union. This had caused a financial loss to the club and inconvenience to the members. The club felt that it would be reluctant to accept the fixture in the future if it were to be held at the weekend. The executive decided to revert to the original Tuesday and Wednesday dates, double the entry fee to £1, and explained the reasons to the ensuing council meeting. Stourbridge was not the only club in the county to hold strong feelings about this.

John Fraser proposed that a Worcestershire Senior Golfers Society be formed for golfers over the age of fifty-five. "The Executive Committee gave their unofficial blessing to this proposal, but stressed the fact that such a society could not be affiliated to the Worcestershire Union of Golf Clubs, or run by them."

The executive and council meetings in January 1972 both concluded with a vote of thanks to the retiring president, Dr. Tweddell. He was succeeded by Harley Roberts, who handed over the captaincy to Dick Mirams, saying that there was no reason why Worcestershire could not continue to win the Midland league, "or perhaps occasionally being runners-up", thanks to the work of Dick and Bill Cunningham.

His prophecy was accurate in its second prediction; losses against Warwickshire and Staffordshire placed Worcestershire runners-up to the former, despite emphatic wins over Nottinghamshire and Shropshire and Herefordshire, for whom a young man called Sandy Lyle was making one of his first appearances. The only improvement the second team made on this performance was earning a tie with Nottinghamshire.

Only eight clubs entered teams for the Tomson-James Cup, which Blackwell won thanks to a last minute replacement, the sixty-four year old chairman of the club's green committee, Bob Wright. He had been due to start the competitors but David Kelley was obliged to withdraw the evening before the meeting because of a business commitment. After several fruitless telephone calls, Andrew Thomson remembered that Wright would be on the first tee at Gay Hill. Wright, holding a handicap of 8, eventually agreed to play and his score of 91 compared very favourably with many lower handicapped players, for only twenty of the sixty players broke 80. This was good enough for Blackwell to win by five strokes from Kings Norton, Terry Shingler, David Russell and Andrew Thomson all having produced good scores.

The next day Terry Shingler, who according to the *Birmingham Post* said he had "never struck the ball so well and scored so badly", produced rounds of 74 and 76 to win the gold medal and the G.D. Carr Cup. M. Wrigglesworth of Kidderminster took the silver medal and the Philip Padmore Trophy. David Russell tied for the bronze with John Wharrad and David Rodway.

Worcestershire finished in third place in "The Six", Trevor Homer ensuring that Staffordshire qualified two strokes ahead of Warwickshire, Moseley being the venue for the event.

Kidderminster and Fulford Heath tied for the Brand Hall Gold Vase and agreed to share it for six months each.

Kevin Bayliss, Bernard Preston's assistant at Lickey Hills, won the county Open at Stourbridge, having already won the Assistants Championship. David Russell tied with Simon Fogarty for second place, bringing a year of near misses to a conclusion: he had been runner-up in the Carris Trophy and was first reserve for England in the youth internationals.

Michael Lunt was appointed captain of England for the international matches; Terry Shingler won the Homer Salver; Andrew Thomson won the Carl Bretherton Bowl and Roy Hobbis the Hollinwell Trophy. Worcestershire was still a prominent force in English golf. The question was, how long would we remain so?

Chapter Six

Change & Expansion

ALTHOUGH Bill Cunningham and Dick Mirams had been praised for their efforts in introducing younger players into county golf, other counties were also moving in the same direction. We were no longer assured of first or even second place in the Midland league, which had been joined by Derbyshire for the 1973 season. These younger players included golfers of the calibre of Peter McEvoy and Sandy Lyle.

The executive agreed that the county would pay for overnight hotel expenses prior to away matches, to enable our teams to play a practice round on Saturday, if they so wished. It was not obligatory for those who would find an overnight stay difficult. Bill Cunningham proposed that team members should wear blazers, with the opportunity to earn badges after ten appearances. However, the president thought that this might be expensive, because of the rising price of wool.

Until this time clubs holding the annual council meeting met the expenses of meals and drinks. It was suggested that this was too great a burden upon them and that either the county fund the meeting or those attending pay for their meals.

The 1973 meeting began rather ominously, for Chris Buckley had died during the winter and Derek Greey was in hospital, so missing any meeting for the first time. He received a telegram from the president wishing him a speedy recovery and the meeting stood in silence in memory of Chris Buckley.

Dick Mirams asked for more support for county matches; with a little more enthusiasm the county could reclaim its winning position in the league.

During the year the newly formed Redditch Kingfisher Golf Club, playing over Redditch Golf Club's former course at Plymouth Road, became affiliated to the Union. The course had been taken over by the local council and part of it was sold to permit the intricate network of roads in the town to expand, reducing the course to nine holes.

Despite the influx of junior talent, Harley Roberts played in the opening match, the friendly with Gloucestershire, which resulted in a half. The second team managed a win, however.

Blackwell retained the Tomson-James Cup, thanks to Terry Shingler, David Russell, Andrew Thomson and David Kelley. Shingler, after a tip from David Russell regarding his swing, won the gold medal, Russell tieing with Kevin Harbun and Michael Lunt two strokes behind Shingler's 144. These three had to play off for the silver and bronze medals, and Russell scored 65 to win the silver medal, Harbun taking the bronze and the Philip Padmore Trophy.

The league results were disappointing: a win over Warwickshire and a tie with Nottinghamshire being outweighed by losses against Staffordshire, Derbyshire and Shropshire and Herefordshire. The second team did slightly better, winning three matches and losing three. Making his county debut during this season was Peter Adams of Gay Hill, who went on to become a loyal, popular and long-serving member of both teams and the executive.

Although we finished second in "The Six" we were fifteen strokes behind Staffordshire, whose team included future professional Pip Hinton, Geoff Marks and Trevor Homer. Our team could not have been stronger: David Russell, Terry Shingler, Richard Langridge, Andrew Thomson, David Kelley and Roy Hobbis.

The Brand Hall Gold Vase produced a tie between Kings Norton and Droitwich, one of whose players, Jimmie Gray, subsequently had a major part to play in our Union's history.

The county Open was won by Hamish Macdonald, the Droitwich professional, with a score of 138, one ahead of Bill Firkins of Stourbridge and two better than Ron Moses and the two leading amateurs, Neil McClean of Worcester and Harley Roberts. McClean won the gold medal by just one stroke in the play-off.

This competition was the cause of consternation for the executive when it met in November. The prize money, provided by the county Union, amounted to £100, contrasting with the £350 Staffordshire was able to offer through their sponsors. Harley Roberts said it was time for Worcestershire to find sponsors and several firms were mentioned as possible sources of funds. When the two principal companies approached declined to offer assistance, it was suggested that an approach be made to John Jacobs of the Professional Golfers Association. This was not done immediately and the issue became a tiresome and long-running problem.

It also highlighted the fact, explained to the council meeting by Dick Mirams, that it was impossible to make important decisions when there were only two executive meetings a year. More frequent meetings were needed, involving fewer officers, if the county's golf was to be run efficiently. The council approved the proposal, the management of the Union remaining vested within it.

The new officers comprised the president, vice-presidents, a chairman, a secretary who would also act as treasurer, the captain, second team captain, match secretary, the two English Golf Union delegates and the two delegates appointed to the Midland Counties Golf Association. An auditor would be appointed but not act as an official of the executive, which in its turn included the above with the exception of the vice-presidents. This committee "shall have the power to carry out the day-to-day running of the Union and to perform such other functions as shall from time to time be allotted to it by the general committee or by the council. The executive committee shall meet at least twice a year and shall have power to co-opt one or two additional members and the persons so co-opted shall serve until the next Annual General Meeting."

In 1974, for the first time in many years, it was found impossible to have a pre-season friendly match with Gloucestershire as a date convenient for both counties could not be agreed. The season therefore began with a halved league match with Shropshire and Herefordshire, the most encouraging feature being Terry Shingler's win by 8 and 7 over Sandy Lyle in the singles, although the future Open Champion and his partner had a comfortable win over Terry and Charles Richmond in the foursomes.

The match with Warwickshire was also tied but the remaining matches were lost, Nottinghamshire inflicting the heaviest defeat by a six point margin. The second team managed to beat Nottinghamshire and Warwickshire but lost to Staffordshire and Shropshire and Herefordshire. The match with Derbyshire at Burton-on-Trent was abandoned when the course flooded after Worcestershire had established a 4-2 lead in the foursomes.

Richard Langridge helped Worcester win the Tomson-James Cup and then went on to win the gold medal and G.D. Carr Cup. The former champion of Kent and South Africa had rounds of 67, 69 and 70 over his own club's course, while team-mate Simon Pimley took the silver medal and Michael Lunt the bronze. Graham Fidoe of Moseley won the Philip Padmore Trophy after finishing in fourth place.

Langridge then went on to win the Boulton Salver in partnership with Charles Richmond, again on the course at Boughton Park. These two joined Terry Shingler, Roy Hobbis, Michael Lunt and David Kelley for "The Six" at Torksey. Worcestershire finished in third place, ten strokes behind Lincolnshire, the host county, and Staffordshire. Despite his commitment to the national team Michael Lunt made himself available for the county as often as possible and was seen as an inspiration to others.

Birmingham Post photograph from county archives

Presentation to Derek Greey by Harley Roberts, 1975

Blackwell won the Brand Hall Gold Vase, largely due to a nett 67 by Terry Kilshaw, who had won the Second City Pro-Am tournament the previous day. His club-mate Terry Shingler won the county Open at Kings Norton in October, when the competition was reduced to one round because of heavy rain. His score of 71, one under par, was remarkable in the conditions and five strokes better than that of the leading professional Alan Roach, an assistant at Fulford Heath. Kevin Bayliss, now at Churchill and Blakedown, and Ron Moses of Redditch municipal shared third place on 77.

Under Michael Lunt's captaincy England won the Home Internationals. Terry Shingler won the Formby Hare, and tied for the Leicestershire Fox and the Homer Salver. Roy Hobbis won the Hollinwell Trophy for the second time.

The year ended with the retirement of Derek Greey from the secretary's post after twenty-seven years of what he described as "just mucking along". His modest assessment does not do justice to all his hard work, which was duly recognised by the inauguration of the Derek Greey Trophy for the match play championship. A dinner was held at Moseley in his honour on 19th February 1975 and he was presented with a painting of his favourite race horse, the Grand National winner, Red Rum.

At the council meeting in January Greey was thanked for "the many acts of kindness and generosity he had performed over and above his normal official duties". Telegrams wishing him a happy retirement came from Pop Lewis and Bernard Preston. After a standing ovation, Derek Greey proposed David Rodway as his successor.

David won his Blue at Oxford in 1960 and was duly elected to the Oxford and Cambridge Golfing Society the following year, during which he won the Howitt Bowl. He was one of a number of Worcestershire players to win the Leicestershire Fox, played for annually at Willesley Park, Ashby-de-la-Zouch. He also won the Royal Mid-Surrey Antlers and played regularly in the British and English Amateur Championships. David began his long association with the county in the 1960s, remaining in the secretary's position until 1977, by which time he had been elected a member of the Royal and Ancient Golf Club of St Andrews.

Dick Mirams stood down as captain and Terry Shingler was elected in his place, while Fred Savage took over the second team captaincy from John Fraser. In thanking Dick, Harley Roberts said that no captain had worked harder to ensure success and it was not his fault that the team had not done better in the last few years. In reply Dick hoped that more settled pairings could be found for the foursomes and wished Terry success.

It was proposed that the annual club subscription to the Union be increased from 25p to 35p per member from January 1976, but Frank Reilly of Cocks Moors Woods stated that the municipal clubs might find it difficult to pay this increase out of their small funds. The president pointed out that this increase was payable by members through their subscriptions, not from club funds. The sum involved included 10p per head payable to the English Golf Union.

The Gloucestershire fixture was re-instated but the first team lost heavily, twelve matches to six, at Cirencester. The second team did much better at Worcester and won by a three match margin.

The 1975 county meeting was held at North Worcestershire and the Tomson-James Cup was won by Blackwell, of which club Michael Lunt was now a member, his score of 72 combining with Andrew Thomson's 69, Terry Shingler's 76 and Nick Wase-Rogers' 77. Stourbridge won the Jubilee Shield. This was but a prelude to an eventful individual championship.

An Australian company, Precision Golf Forgings, had set up business in Kings Heath, half a mile from Moseley Golf Club. It was natural that their manager, Des Turner, join the club. He had captained the New South Wales team of which Jack Newton had been a member and won the Australian Foursomes Championship on three successive occasions. Moseley immediately awarded him a scratch handicap and he entered the county championship. His scores of 74 and 67 meant that he won the gold medal by five shots from Simon Pimley and Alan Price of Halesowen, the latter winning the play-off for the silver medal. Unfortunately, residential qualifications meant that Turner would not be eligible to play county golf for Worcestershire for several weeks.

Terry Shingler managed to beat Peter McEvoy by one hole in his singles against Warwickshire, Simon Pimley beat Paul Downes, Alan Pugh beat Tony Allen, Mike Harris beat Ronnie Hiatt and Andrew Thomson defeated John Mayell 5 and 4. Our five points shared the singles, but sadly a one point deficit in the foursomes meant that Warwickshire won the first league encounter of the season. The second team lost heavily. This set a pattern for the season, the first team's best result coming against Derbyshire with a win by two points. The other matches were lost by embarrassing margins, even though Des Turner had completed his residential qualification by September and won his singles against Nottinghamshire. The younger players had not played to expectations and the more experienced players found themselves back in favour.

The second team enjoyed a convincing win over Shropshire and Herefordshire, tied with Derbyshire and lost the remaining matches.

Alan Price and Mike Harris won the Boulton Salver for Halesowen at Worcester by three strokes. Price was also in form for the Brand Hall Gold Vase at Dudley, which his club won by five strokes from Gay Hill. The county team finished seventh in "The Six" at Shifnal, our worst performance up to this time, although David Kelley tied on 140 for the best individual score with Geoff Marks and Sandy Lyle.

The first match play championship for the Derek Greey Trophy took place on 23rd and 24th August at Blackwell, the best sixteen finishers in the individual championship competing. Terry Shingler beat Des Turner in the first round, Fred Savage in the second by a substantial margin, and David Rodway by the same score, 6 and 5, in the semi-final. In the first flight Mike Wrigglesworth of Kidderminster progressed to the final at the expense of Alan Guest, Simon Pimley and Alan Price. Wrigglesworth's putting let him down in the final and Shingler, eleven under par for his four rounds, won by 5 and 4 and received the trophy from the ever jovial Derek Greey.

The county Open championship was held at Kidderminster, where the members had generously raised the sponsorship necessary to provide a suitable prize fund of over £600 for the professionals. Ian Richardson of The Worcestershire won the event with a score of 67+71=138, eight strokes better than Hamish Macdonald, while the leading amateur was Terry Shingler on 148, a score equalled by four professionals.

Outside the county, the only major successes recorded by Worcestershire players were the ten shot victory of Harley Roberts in the Seniors Open

Derek Greey (left) presents the Worcestershire Match Play Cup to Terry Shingler Watching are the 1975 county secretary, David Rodway, and Mike Wrigglesworth, beaten by Shingler in the final at Blackwell

Championship at Turnberry and the winning of the Winchelsea Foursomes at Harlech by Michael Lunt and Terry Shingler.

When the newly constituted general committee met in October, it was informed that the membership scheme had increased to 1,122 members. It expressed its thanks to David Rodway's father for running the Boulton Salver so efficiently and increased the indispensable Brenda Smith's honorarium to £500.

Droitwich Golf Club wrote to the secretary suggesting that the county levy be increased to 50p. For this to be ratified, a special general meeting of the council would be required and it was suggested that if Droitwich had the support of three or four more clubs, the council could vote on the proposal.

During 1976 Little Lakes Golf Club became affiliated to the Union, bringing the number of member clubs to twenty-four. Although it then had a nine hole course, the club did not join the newly formed Small Clubs league, consisting of Tolladine, Evesham, Warley and Habberley. This competition was for two teams from each club playing an alliance fourball medal off handicap. The first winner of both "A" and "B" team leagues was Tolladine.

The first team's season began in 1976 with a narrow win over Glamorgan by one point, the second team enjoying the same result. Then the disappointing run of results experienced the previous year repeated itself, the first team beating only Shropshire and Herefordshire. The second team fared little better, tieing with Derbyshire and Shropshire and Herefordshire and losing the remaining matches.

The captain of the county boys' team, Philip Marshall, led Stourbridge to victory in the Tomson-James Cup on the club's own course, scoring an excellent 69. It was a more experienced player who won the gold medal, though. Roy Hobbis finished one over par to beat Simon Pimley by four strokes and David Kelley by nine, and claim the G.D. Carr and Philip Padmore Trophies as well. This was the sixtieth anniversary of the county meeting.

When "The Six" played at Northants County Golf Club on 26th June, so many players complained of the intense heat that seven of the ten captains agreed that the competition be reduced to twenty-seven holes. Despite three good rounds by the new champion, Terry Shingler, and Simon Pimley, this did not help Worcestershire who repeated the disappointing seventh place they had occupied a year before.

Paul Muddyman and Ian Wade, the Blackwell "B" team, won the Boulton Salver at Halesowen and it was another Blackwell player who won the match play championship at Kidderminster. Terry Shingler beat Roy Hobbis at the 19th hole in an exciting final, having eliminated Des Turner in the semi-final. Hobbis, having won his first round match at the 24th, had a slightly easier win over David Rodway and beat Simon Pimley 5 and 4 in his semi-final.

The county Open was sponsored by two factory owners, David Fabb and Stephen Neal, both handicap golfers at Stourbridge. Their generous support of £500 enabled the previous year's figure of £605 prize money to be maintained when the tournament was held at Moseley. Although the *Birmingham Evening Mail*'s reporter stated that the winner Ian Richardson's round was free of errors, in fact Richardson pulled his tee shot into deep rough on the par 3 17th where his ball was located by none other than the author! Richardson then played a superb shot which resulted in his saving his par and finishing on 143, two strokes better than David Kelley, the leading amateur. Terry Shingler finished third.

At a subsequent general committee meeting Michael Lunt suggested a sub-committee be formed to formulate rules for the organisation of the county Open, as at the time the professionals had little involvement with its running. This sub-committee met in January 1977, chaired by Harley Roberts and attended by Nick Underwood, Arthur Ashford and Eric Booy representing the professionals.

The winter of 1976-77 saw the institution of an inter-club foursomes knock-out tournament upon the suggestion of Ray Baldwin. This became the Droitwich Shield, presented by Ray and Mr. A.C. Ives. Nine clubs entered the initial competition, which was considered a most satisfactory beginning. Halesowen beat Moseley in the final at Kings Norton.

Terry Shingler rounded off a frustrating year's golf by winning the Champion of Champions Tournament and the Finney Shield at Harborne, partnered by A. Smith of Walsall. He handed over the captaincy to Roy Hobbis and Norman Bolton took over the second team. Relieved of the cares of captaincy he was able to concentrate more on his own game and was duly rewarded later in 1977.

This was the year of the Queen's Silver Jubilee and it was decided to mark the occasion by arranging a competition in which every golfer in the county could participate, if he so desired. This competition would also serve as a fund-raising event for the Silver Jubilee Fund, to which the Union had been asked to contribute. It was to be administered by the Prince of Wales, its aim being to "promote the efforts of young people to develop themselves and help others of all ages, both inside and outside sport."

Qualifying rounds in two divisions were held at each club, for an entry fee of 50p. The winners and runners-up in both divisions then played a greensomes stableford at Kings Norton. The outcome was a donation of £250 to the fund. The Silver Jubilee Trophy was won by Kidderminster and fifteen clubs participated in the event.

The inter-county matches followed the dismal pattern of preceding years. After beating Gloucestershire by the odd point at Kidderminster the first team did not win again until September, when they beat Shropshire and Herefordshire. The Nottinghamshire match was halved but the rest of the league matches were lost by distressing margins. Roy Hobbis, in his captain's report at the council meeting in December, said that "at least we did not finish wooden-spoonists". The younger players had come up against some first class golfers and Roy believed that did them no harm at all.

The second team managed to beat Nottinghamshire, tied with Glamorgan and lost their other matches. Among the players who made their county debuts during the season were Steve Carpenter of Brand Hall, a re-instated amateur, who had a memorable summer, and Will Painter of Kidderminster, thus beginning his long association with the county. In the second team match against Shropshire and Herefordshire in September another young player, Michael Reynard, recorded his first point for the county, earning a half in his singles.

The performances by Carpenter and Painter earned them selection for "The Six", which was held at Olton, the other members of the team being Terry Shingler, Tony Jowle, Alan Pugh and David Kelley. Worcestershire finished in second place, fifteen strokes behind Warwickshire. Our closest neighbours were now enjoying a period of success similar to that which Worcestershire experienced in the 1930s and 1950s.

Michael Lunt, Terry Shingler and Stanley Lunt with the English Amateur Championship Trophy, 1977

Simon Pimley, matchplay champion 1977

Blackwell won the Tomson-James Cup on their own course and the club's "B" team secured the Jubilee Shield. The club was also well represented in the individual championship; Simon Pimley won the gold medal and David Kelley the silver. The bronze medal was won by Steve Carpenter after a play-off with a fellow member of Brand Hall, Michael Curry. Carpenter took the G.D. Carr Cup and Pimley the Philip Padmore Trophy. The Boulton Salver was also held at Blackwell but on this occasion the winners were Stourbridge, represented by none other than Harley Roberts and Philip Marshall.

Kings Norton won the Brand Hall Gold Vase at Gay Hill thanks to consistent scoring from B. Jackson, A.M. Guest, P. Swinburne and D. Brander.

Simon Pimley beat Andrew Thomson on the 19th green at Redditch to win the Derek Greey Trophy for the match play championship and Steve Carpenter won the county Open with a score of 139, two shots better than the leading professionals, Nigel Blake and Chris Thompson. Ian Richardson was one stroke further behind.

While these results offered hope for the future the chief honours were reserved for Terry Shingler, who had entered the English Amateur Championship at Walton Heath. He won his first round match and went out to watch his friend, John Mayell of Warwickshire. Mayell was two down with

Courtesy: Brenda Smith

Ray Baldwin giving Brenda Smith her first golf lesson, Worcester, August 1978

four to play when Terry sportingly shouldered his bag and offered words of encouragement, saying that a birdie was needed. Mayell responded by making three and won his match against Michael Hughesdon on the 20th. He went on to reach the final, where his opponent was Terry Shingler. After a good start by Shingler, Mayell began a fight back and mistakes by both players produced an exciting match which finished on the 15th hole when Mayell missed a crucial putt. As a result, Terry Shingler was selected to play for his country in the Home Internationals and participated in a victory for England. The county Union duly celebrated by holding a dinner in Terry's honour at Kings Norton on 30th November.

The year ended with the resignation of David Rodway as secretary, due to his business commitments. His place was taken by Ray Baldwin, secretary of Droitwich Golf Club at the time, having switched his allegiance from Warwickshire where his previous employment had been as secretary at Harborne Golf Club. Ray had taken up golf after injury had ended his rugby career and soon attained a single figure handicap and represented Warwickshire, becoming a vice-president of that county's union.

Although Ray had accepted the position in a "caretaker" capacity, it was not until 1982 that he handed over to his understudy, Will Painter. Ray then took on the secretaryship of the Midland Golf Union, acted as Worcestershire's development officer and travelled many thousands of miles advising clubs on matters ranging from the constitution of their management to safety on the course, and even designing new courses.

Ray had already acknowledged that with such an able assistant as Brenda Smith the task would not be too burdensome and Brenda was duly voted an increase in her honorarium at the next council meeting. The following year Ray gave Brenda her first putting lesson and a very complimentary profile of her appeared in the *Worcester Evening News*.

Results in 1978 showed a slight improvement to justify Roy Hobbis's optimism, despite heavy losses by both teams to Gloucestershire in the opening friendly matches. The league matches with Warwickshire and Derbyshire were both won, the latter by a commendable margin, but the remainder and the friendly match with Glamorgan were all lost. The second team beat Nottinghamshire and Derbyshire, which was the sum total of their success. Younger players were still being given the opportunity to play county golf but the seasoned veterans were the men who gained the points. Nevertheless Roy Hobbis was full of praise for them when he presented his report to the council in December, as some performances had been most encouraging. He re-iterated previous pleas for more support for the county matches.

Dr. Bill Cunningham

The county meeting was held at Kings Norton and Blackwell retained the Tomson-James Cup. The gold medal was won by a municipal player, Michael Curry of Brand Hall, with Alan Price of Halesowen in second place, while the twenty year old Alan Robinson of Blackwell won the bronze medal, having played the lowest round, 70, of the championship. Terry Shingler won the G.D. Carr Cup by virtue of his 71 in the team event, while the Philip Padmore Trophy was claimed by Norman Evans of the home club.

Warwickshire qualified for the third time running in "The Six" but did not repeat their previous successes in the finals. Their qualifying score was twenty-one shots better than our second place finish.

Terry Shingler had a series of tough matches in the matchplay championship at Gay Hill, and reached the final having played fourteen more holes than his opponent Will Painter, who prevailed by one hole.

Will also began the county Open at Moseley in excellent form, returning 69 in the first round to lead the field but sadly he fell away in the second round and Tony Jowle with 73 and 70 won the day, with Terry Shingler second. Ian Richardson was a shot further behind Terry to finish as leading professional. Sponsorship for this event was raised by Alan Pugh of the home club and the county expressed their indebtedness to him. His generosity enabled prize money for both amateurs and professionals to be increased. A tankard was presented to Richardson for the best seventy-two hole aggregate in the Open and the professionals own championship, while Tony Jowle became the first holder of the Secretaries Bowl for his scores in the championship and the Open. This trophy was donated by the secretaries of the Union.

Moseley Clubhouse, 1926

In the other county competitions Moseley won the Brand Hall Gold Vase, Kidderminster "B" the Boulton Salver and The Worcestershire "A" team beat Worcester "A" in the second Droitwich Shield final. Roy Hobbis won the EGU Individual Members' Trophy and Michael Curry was runner-up in the Champion of Champions Tournament.

At the annual council meeting Dr. Cunningham announced his retirement as chairman of the juniors sub-committee. He had worked diligently for eighteen years recruiting players, organising matches and competitions and raising funds to supplement the amount provided by the Union. Norman Bolton took over from Bill, who wished him the best of luck!

Chapter Seven

Play for Pay – Pay and Play

THE LAST two decades of the twentieth century brought major changes to the world of golf. The European Tour was expanding after some years of uneven progress and young men were attracted to the idea of playing for pay rather than the honour of representing country or county. In 1990 the R&A calculated that 700 new golf courses were required within ten years to accommodate the converts.

At the same time farmers were being encouraged to set aside land because of over production, oblivious of the fact that in the past the best courses had been laid out on land suitable for little else. Many new clubs soon found themselves in administration, but some developers managed to get it right and Worcestershire is fortunate that at least two new clubs did just that.

In 1979 Kings Norton won the Tomson-James Cup, Peter Swinburne returning a fine score of 70 at The Worcestershire. Unfortunately he could not reproduce this form the following day and David Kelley took all the major prizes. Terry Shingler won the silver medal and Alan Price the bronze, one stroke ahead of the eighteen year old Mike Reynard, who was about to have a memorable year, earning selection for the England Boys team.

Excellent putting was the reason that Terry Shingler, abetted by Fred Parkes, won the Boulton Salver at Kidderminster. Fulford Heath won the Brand Hall Gold Vase on their own course, beating Stourbridge by one shot. Droitwich "A" won the Droitwich Shield, beating Halesowen "B" in the final at Kidderminster.

Shingler then added to his laurels by winning the match play championship at The Worcestershire, defeating Paul Daniels of Worcester 5 and 4, while Ian Richardson added a third county Open title to his tally. Charles Smith of North Worcestershire was the leading amateur.

The first team beat Staffordshire and Derbyshire but lost their other matches, while the second team fared little better, beating Shropshire and Herefordshire and Glamorgan, tieing with Nottinghamshire but losing the other four matches. Roy Hobbis reported that the league had been very close until the last match and although we had not won the league he was not unduly disappointed. The first team, including some past players, had a very enjoyable match with The Worcestershire to celebrate the club's centenary.

Two county stalwarts died during the year; Derek Greey, the popular former secretary, and one of his close friends and fellow Blackwell member, Stanley Elliott, who was the county champion in 1948.

Harley Roberts, the president of the Union, and Ray Baldwin, the secretary, were concerned at the lack of knowledge clubs showed of the county's affairs and the lack of participation in events. They proposed a change in the regulations which would involve dissolving the general committee and replacing it with a council consisting of one representative from each club and the officers. This council would hold two meetings a year. In March officers would be elected, accounts approved and items normally dealt with at the December meeting would be discussed. The second meeting in October would deal with fixtures and subscriptions, giving clubs time to inform members of any proposed increases. This was timely as an increase of the subscription to the county had been suggested, bringing it up to £1 per member, further exacerbated by the implementation of VAT. The council meeting approved the new structure, which then had to be passed at an extraordinary general meeting. The aim was to allay the feelings of some clubs that the county Union was "a closed shop". The new scheme came into operation in October 1980.

The effects of the county's scheme for juniors and colts were highlighted in that year's annual meeting, Peter Swinburne winning the gold medal and the Philip Padmore Trophy, while Mike Reynard took the silver medal and the G.D. Carr Cup, having assisted Moseley's "A" Team in winning the Tomson-James Cup with a score of 70 at Fulford Heath. Moseley's "B" Team won the Jubilee Shield. Later in the year Mike won the youths' championship and the match play title, defeating Andrew Thomson in the final.

Gay Hill's team of Alan Guest, Malcolm Duggan, Colin Clarke and Reg Godfrey won the Brand Hall Gold Vase and discovered that the cup had been erroneously engraved, crediting them with a win in 1979.

The county Open was played at Redditch and produced a tie between Tony Jowle and Terry Shingler. The play-off over a wet course produced problems for Shingler, who failed to escape first time from bunkers on three occasions, giving Jowle the title. The Secretaries Bowl was won by Mike Reynard. Five professionals tied for third place, including Mike Deeley and Chris Thompson from Droitwich and Kevin Hayward of Fulford Heath. As no sponsor had come forward an entry fee was imposed for the first time and the costs of running the event were shared by the county PGA and the Union.

With only two wins in the Midland league, Worcestershire was placed last. The second team did better, winning three of their five matches. Sixth place in the county "Six" was also a grave disappointment. There were some successes to report, however: Tony Jowle, the county captain, won the Bretherton Bowl, Terry Shingler and Michael Lunt won the Winchelsea Foursomes and Philip Guest of The Worcestershire was selected for England Boys and England Schoolboys.

The fourth Droitwich Shield competition was won by The Worcestershire "A", who beat Kings Norton "B" at Droitwich.

Stanley Lunt celebrated his eightieth birthday during the year and was the subject of a short profile by David Davies in the *Birmingham Post.* In it he revealed that he had broken his age three times, "but never in a medal".

The annual meeting in 1981 was held at Moseley and the home club, led by Tony Jowle, whose 67 was described by David Davies as "a round of considerable character", retained both the Tomson-James Cup and the Jubilee Shield. His team included Mike Reynard, Alan Pugh and Roy Hobbis, who had recently moved from Kings Norton. Tony had to dig even deeper the following day in the individual championship.

Incessant rain reduced the morning round to eight holes. Ray Baldwin had to cast his mind back to 1955 to recall similar conditions. He defended his decision to continue with the tournament because the greens steadfastly refused to become waterlogged and the fixture list had become so congested that an alternative date would have been impossible to arrange. In the event Tony Jowle took the G.D. Carr cup, but the gold medal was won by Mike Reynard, Roy Hobbis was second and another Moseley player, Graham Jones, was third and won the Philip Padmore Trophy. Reynard told the *Post*'s reporter that he had been hitting at least 600 practice shots a day, having been warned by his father that if he did not improve he would have to find himself "one of the dreaded nine to five jobs".

Richard Lane and Tim Pickering of Stourbridge beat Will Painter and Steve Gough by one stroke in the Boulton Salver at Blackwell. Gay Hill retained the Brand Hall Gold Vase but lost the final of the Droitwich Shield to The Worcestershire "A" team.

Charles Smith was an unexpected finalist in the match play championship, never having played for the county, and he took Tony Jowle to the 21st hole, never having led, but regularly pulling back to all square, before Jowle finally prevailed. Tony had in fact been the first reserve, having finished seventeenth in the championship. On the way to the final he eliminated Roy Hobbis 5 and 4, while Smith beat Mike Reynard by two holes in the semi-final.

Smith's performance put some established players under pressure to perform better and, at the council meeting, Tony Jowle reported a more successful season in which the first team finished third in the Midland league, one reason being more consistent availability of players.

At the same meeting Hagley Golf and Country Club was welcomed into the Union and Jeff Adams reported a successful year for the membership scheme, prompting a gentleman from Habberley to suggest that a third meeting be held each year. Jeff replied that this had been discussed but it was felt a third meeting would have to be held in July, not a good month for competitions, and pointed out that players applying unsuccessfully for the first event were given priority for the second meeting.

The captain of Stourbridge then suggested that competitors in the scheme's events should be charged half the club's normal green fee, while the secretary of the Union suggested that members of county associations, such as the captains and seniors, should pay a fee of £2 to play on other courses. Jeff then proposed a green fee of £1 per member of the scheme. However, Will Painter, speaking on behalf of the Kidderminster committee, said they would strongly resist any attempt by the county to dictate to whom they should charge green-fees or give courtesies, and Mr. Buggins of North Worcestershire proposed that no green-fee charges be made. When it came to the vote, his proposal was carried.

This particularly lively meeting continued with a letter from Rose Hill asking why the club's members were not invited to play in other clubs' opens. The president pointed out that they had supported the county's events on a regular basis and should be borne in mind in the future.

When the executive met in March the matter of green-fees for county membership scheme meetings was raised again, as the result of letters from five clubs, who felt a fee should be paid. If clubs withdrew from the scheme it would collapse, as it had in its previous form. The council meeting immediately after this voted against the proposal to charge a green-fee of £1.

At the same meeting Will Painter took over from Ray Baldwin as secretary. Ray had first taken the position seven years previously in a "caretaker" capacity, which he had intended to last one year. He was elected a vice-president of the county but was still to give the Union much hard work and good advice, as development officer, secretary of the Midland Golf Union and, for the remainder of the year, our representative to the EGU.

Another new appointment in 1982 was that of Andrew Thomson in place of Tony Jowle as captain. His first season, despite the promise Tony Jowle had alluded to the previous November, was a disappointing one, the best result in 1982 being a halved match with Warwickshire, who won the league. The losses to Derbyshire and Shropshire and Herefordshire were particularly distressing, but the team suffered from both injuries and lack of availability of key players. The second team, led by Fred Wortley, fared little better with one win, one tied match and three losses. As many as forty players had been contacted to raise the twenty-two players required for the teams, including forty-three year old Alan Price of Halesowen who wrote a heart-felt letter to the president which was read at the subsequent council meeting. Mr. Price was duly elected second team captain at that meeting. Sixth position in "The Six" was also disappointing, being two places lower than the previous year. Even so, Andrew Thomson led by example, finishing the season runner-up to Will Painter for the President's Shield.

Kidderminster had last won the Tomson-James Cup seventy years previously at Kings Norton. They had their third victory at Droitwich, who were staging the championship for the first time, in an exciting finish when their last player, Paul Denston, who did not know that he needed a par 3 to seal victory for his team, bunkered his tee shot. He recovered to eight feet, sank the putt and Will Painter's 71 and Nick Hunter's 70 had not been in vain. Droitwich were second, their best score, 74, being returned by seventeen year old David Eddiford, playing off a handicap of 3, who continued the next day with 72 and 71 to win the gold medal, the G.D. Carr Cup, the Philip Padmore Trophy and the colts' championship which was now incorporated into the main meeting. By the time of the match play championship in August David had turned eighteen and reduced his handicap to 2. He beat another Droitwich player, Nigel Perry, in the final by 5 and 4.

Rose Hill demonstrated their support for the county, noted at the previous council meeting by the president, by winning the Boulton Salver, David Glover and Colin Warburton returning a score of 142 at Stourbridge. This created a problem, as the winning club stages this competition the following year. Birmingham council was very concerned at the potential loss of a day's green-fees on one of its most popular courses. A compromise was reached and the council agreed to the Union's holding the Salver at Rose Hill the following year, but the problem did not end there.

They were not the only municipal club to feature in county competitions, for Redditch Kingfisher reached the final of the Droitwich Shield which they lost to Kings Norton's "A" team by the odd match. The Brand Hall Gold Vase was won by The Worcestershire on their own course.

Mike Reynard completed a frustrating season, in which he had come second in two national tournaments and three others, by winning the county Open by seven strokes from Bill Firkins, this over twenty-seven holes as the start had been delayed by fog. Mike's first round score of 62 comfortably broke the course record at Worcester. He was not the only man to produce memorable golf, though, as Colin Colenso and Graeme Harris of The Worcestershire both had holes in one. By finishing fifth David Eddiford completed his haul of trophies by winning the Secretaries Bowl. The event was sponsored by Mr. Roger Hamilton-Brown of Officescapes, who donated £500 towards the prizes.

1983 began with a new handicapping system, most club golfers finding their handicaps increased, and a ruling by the EGU that in future the 1.68" ball would be used in all county matches and competitions.

The council meeting stood in silence to the memory of two men who had served the county in preceding years, Charles Shaw, who had assisted Jeff Adams with the membership scheme and had been a vice-president, and Eric Stuart, a former county player. Charles Shaw had no such ambitions as a player but had recruited a number of members to the scheme. His company donated a cup to Charles' club, Moseley, which became the trophy for a unique competition in greensomes format, for which players enter individually and a low handicap player is drawn to play with a higher handicapper. This has become a popular event which fosters excellent club spirit.

This was also the year in which the Midland Golf Union was formed, uniting the Midland Counties Golf Association with the Midland group of the EGU. This meant that all golfing matters in the Midlands would be under one jurisdiction and Worcestershire supported this important development.

Norman Bolton was obliged to stand down as chairman of the juniors sub-committee due to business commitments and the indefatigable Bill Cunningham agreed to take up the reins once again.

The annual meeting was postponed due to the wet condition of the course at Redditch and took place in July. Nigel Perry and David Eddiford led Droitwich to a successful retention of the Tomson-James Cup, Moseley coming second, while their club's "B" team won the Jubilee Shield. Terry Shingler returned a disappointing 82 in the team competition and that evening struck a bet at odds of 20-1 against that he could not play the course in level par. By dint of eagling the 18th hole in the morning round he won his bet and was £100 better off. By adding 75 to the first round of 72 he also won the gold medal, four strokes ahead of Mike Reynard, who took the G.D. Carr Cup. A three-way tie for the silver medal between Andrew Terry, Tony Jowle and Craig Pates was resolved when Pates won the play-off, while Terry won the Philip Padmore Trophy.

The problem over the venue for the Boulton Salver was solved for the time being by the members of Rose Hill who offered the council £450 to compensate them for the loss of revenue. The council insisted that this did not set a precedent. Little did they know what was about to ensue. Club member and greenkeeper Clive Marsh had been at the course at 4.00 a.m., raking the bunkers and setting up a starter's hut. Then with his partner Tom Doyle he went out and won the event with a score of 140. To complicate matters further, another municipal club, Cocks Moors Woods, finished second. Nor was this the end of a developing saga.

The qualifiers for the match play championship returned to Redditch in August. Chris Norman, a re-instated amateur in 1979, and now eligible to compete, had booked a holiday and told his wife to expect him home at lunchtime on Saturday as he did not expect to survive the first round, in which he met Gordon Bailey. Not only did he survive the first round, he got through the second, beat Mike Reynard in the semi-final and met David Eddiford in the final. Eddiford had eliminated Terry Shingler in his semi-final and led almost all the way over the first nine holes. Norman, feeling a win was needed to keep some semblance of domestic harmony, fought back against the less accurate Eddiford and eventually won on the 19th hole.

Terry Shingler's consolation was the invitation to become an England selector, which he gratefully accepted. At the time he was the only scratch golfer in the county.

Earlier in the year The Worcestershire "A" won the Droitwich Shield, while Gay Hill won the Brand Hall Gold Vase. The county Open champion was Andy Hill, an assistant at Fulford Heath, who beat Mike Reynard in a play-off. Mike won the Secretaries Bowl as a result of his performance, and was selected as reserve for the England Youths team. This year the event was sponsored by Alan Pugh of Ceramic Art (Dental).

The county teams both improved on the previous year's performances, the first team finishing joint third in the league, having defeated Derbyshire and Staffordshire but losing the remaining three matches. The second team also won two matches, beating Derbyshire 12½-5½ and Shropshire and Herefordshire 10-8. The losses were less severe than those of 1982, perhaps because first team availabilities had improved. Tony Jowle played in all five matches and accumulated five and half points out of a possible ten and won the President's Shield, for which Andrew Thomson, the captain, was once again the runner-up. At the council meeting he reported that, although our team had finished eighth in "The Six", it was the youngest team the county had ever fielded and, indeed, the youngest in the tournament.

Once again the president appealed for more support for the county teams and Mr. J. Wright of North Worcestershire suggested that clubs be notified when one of their players was selected for the county so that a notice could be posted to that effect and that the results of matches be circulated to the clubs for similar display. Harley Roberts, the president, recalled that the *Birmingham Post* used to publish reports on all the matches but "now, unfortunately there is only an occasional mention".

Roy Chandler announced his retirement after twenty-six years as match secretary at the beginning of 1984 and requested that something be given to

Will Painter with the Guy Bigwood Cup

the county rather than to himself, as had been suggested. As there was no trophy for the most successful second team player it was decided that the Chandler Shield would be a fitting memorial to Roy's work and a suitable reward for its recipient, who would also be presented with a voucher and a replica. It was felt, though, that Roy should receive some sort of memento and "a rather unusual glass decanter" was purchased and engraved "Roy, for your services to Worcestershire Golf". Simon Pimley took over the vacant position on the executive.

A new appointment was made at this meeting, that of first team captain elect and that honour fell upon Will Painter, the honorary secretary of the Union. He had been a regular member of the team for some time and played a vital part in Kidderminster's success in the Tomson-James Cup in 1982.

New handicap limits were set for county competitions, 8 for the county championship, 12 for the Brand Hall Gold Vase and 10 for the Boulton Salver. Boys under sixteen could qualify for the Midland Boys Championship with a handicap of 10, while the older entrants needed to play off a maximum of 8.

Weather once again caused a postponement of the annual meeting, this time because the Gay Hill course was too dry. The championship was rearranged for July and eighteen teams competed for the Tomson-James Cup, while fifteen contested the Jubilee Shield. Moseley won the former and the host club's "B" team the latter. This was Moseley's third victory in five years.

The municipal clubs received great encouragement in the individual championship, for the gold medal was won by a recently re-instated amateur, Terry Martin of Rose Hill. David Eddiford won the silver medal and the colts' championship while the only scratch player in the field, Mike Reynard, won the bronze medal and the G.D. Carr Cup. Terry Martin and Simon Pimley tied for the Philip Padmore Trophy.

Terry was also in contention when the Boulton Salver returned to Rose Hill, the council having accepted similar terms to those of the previous year. That he and his partner S. Green were placed second because of a higher second round than the winners did not solve the problem that had arisen in the last two years, because Michael Daw and Gary Green were members of Warley, the nine hole municipal course. Their two rounds were 68, 67, against 66, 69 by Martin and Green. Rose Hill's winning team from the previous year finished in third place.

Warley felt that their club would be unable to stage the event the following year, so their winning team was invited to choose a course for the 1985 competition. Even this proved not to be easy, as the original date and venue were both altered and the Boulton Salver was played at Kings Norton.

Moseley won the Brand Hall Gold Vase on their own course, beating Gay Hill by one stroke. The nett scores were Alan Boden 69, Mike Reynard, Chris Norman and Craig Pates 70 each. Gay Hill had the consolation of beating North Worcestershire in the Droitwich Shield.

Reynard was also on form in the match play championship, though confessed that he was "absolutely shattered" after beating Graham Hawkings in the final. In his first round match he beat sixteen year old Dean Powell from Kings Norton, after being two holes down on the fifth tee. The *Post's* reporter noted the blend of youth and experience in the field, Reynard's quarter-final victim being Alan Pugh, while Alan Price beat Roy Hobbis before losing to Reynard in the semi-finals.

The first three places in the county Open were all filled by professionals, Kevin Hayward beating David Dunk by one stroke. Peter Swinburne was the leading amateur, in fourth place.

The county team had a most disastrous season, finishing in tenth place in "The Six" and bottom of the Midland league, having halved one game against Staffordshire. Philip Guest of The Worcestershire won the President's Shield while the first recipient of the Chandler Shield was Matthew Farmer, who at that time was a member of North Worcestershire. He assisted the second team to a slightly better season than the senior team, two matches being won, against Warwickshire and Nottinghamshire, although the remaining three were defeats.

Nationally, David Eddiford reached the last sixteen in the English Amateur Championship and Clive Marsh of Rose Hill was elected captain of the National Association of Public Golf Courses.

Comments had been made at previous meetings on the clothing worn by our county teams, which was not as smart as that of other counties. The council meeting was informed in March 1985 of a reduced surplus in the annual accounts because a "considerable amount of money" had been spent on players' clothing. Our teams would now be equipped with trousers, shirts, sweaters and badges. When asked if these would be as good as the kit worn by the other counties, the president replied that the other Midland counties did not supply trousers and that Worcestershire would be turned out as well as all the other counties.

The 1985 annual meeting was held at North Worcestershire and produced the first tie for thirty years, due to Simon Pimley's 72 for Blackwell's team which helped them to a score of 303, the same as Moseley, whose team had scored consistently well. This club's "B" team prevailed in the contest for the Jubilee Shield. Pimley then went on to take the gold medal with a "blistering" second round of 66, which also gave him the G.D. Carr Cup and the Philip Padmore Trophy. Chris Norman and Nick Hunter tied for the silver medal, the latter also becoming the youths champion. Nick then went on to win the match play championship, beating Philip Guest in the final.

The county team finished in fifth place in "The Six", a long way behind the winners, Warwickshire, whose team included internationals Andrew Carman and Peter McEvoy, future tour professionals Paul Broadhurst and Carl Suneson, and Tony Allen and Martin Biddle. Despite this strength they finished fourth in the national finals.

The first team had a much improved season in the Midland league, finishing joint runners-up one point behind Nottinghamshire, one of the two teams to beat them, the other being Warwickshire. Although the second team beat Nottinghamshire in a close match, they could only tie with Warwickshire and Shropshire and Herefordshire and lost to Derbyshire and Staffordshire. David Eddiford won the President's Shield and Alan Price the Chandler Shield.

David then scored a signal victory by eleven strokes in the county Open, which was played over his home course at Droitwich. The leading professional, Hamish Macdonald, also of Droitwich, was thirteen strokes behind Eddiford. Chris Norman won the Secretaries Bowl. The Droitwich club recorded another success when Eddiford and Andrew Terry won the prestigious Finney Shield at Harborne.

Terry Shingler, partnered by Paul Eales, won the Winchelsea Foursomes; Mike Reynard won the West Midland Amateur Championship, while Alan Guest of Gay Hill was the first winner of the *Birmingham Post & Mail* Blue Arrow championship. Moseley tied with three other clubs in the English champion club title, losing on a count-back.

The year ended on a very tragic note with the death by his own hand of Simon Pimley, the county champion and match secretary, who was also the club champion at Blackwell, which he had been for four consecutive years.

An equally great loss was the passing of Dr. William Tweddell whose contribution to the game at national, county and club level has already been described.

Ray Baldwin wrote to the secretary suggesting draft proposals of changes in the constitution, Roy Chandler and Dick Mirams adding their thoughts via

County First Team 1986
Back row, left to right: Graham Hawkings, Terry Martin, Charles Smith Matthew Farmer, Chris Norman, Michael Reynard, Steve Green
Front row: Andrew Thomson, Tony Jowle, Will Painter (captain), David Eddiford, Terry Shingler

letters, as none could attend the meeting held prior to the council meeting. It was agreed to hold a further meeting to discuss the proposals when all the interested parties could attend. This had not taken place by the time of the council meeting in March 1986, when Harley Roberts announced his retirement as president after fourteen years in the office.

He had played in ninety-three county matches, won five gold medals, four silver medals and three bronze medals. He won each of the G.D. Carr Cup, the Worcestershire Open and the Midland Counties Gold Medal three times. Harley played for England sixteen times, played in the finals of the English Amateur Championship and won the Seniors Open Amateur Championship at Turnberry. He also served as president of the Midland Counties Golf Association and captained Worcestershire for four years.

His successor was another long-serving member, Roy Chandler, who had not long before retired as match secretary.

1986 was made memorable by the success of the boys' team. Having qualified at Sleaford for the first English Boys County Championship, they won the final at Sandy Lodge under the guidance of Jimmie Gray.

The men's team did not achieve anything close to that in their "Six", finishing in ninth place. A win over Shropshire and Herefordshire and a tie with Derbyshire were the best results in the league, in which they finished fourth. The second team's results were similar in all but the margins of defeat. The one encouraging feature of the first team's season was that Darren Prosser, in his first full season in the team, won the President's Shield. Andrew Price of Kings Norton won the Chandler Shield.

Sixteen teams were entered for the Tomson-James Cup when the annual meeting was held at Kidderminster, Blackwell emerging victorious thanks to solid play from David Kelley and Terry Shingler. Kidderminster were three strokes in arrears, Matthew Houghton scoring 74. He had made his county debut the previous year. The Jubilee Shield was won by The Worcestershire's "B" team.

David Eddiford won his second gold medal, a shot ahead of Richard Lane. He also took the G.D. Carr Cup for the second time and the youths' championship, in what was a particularly good year for Droitwich, for John Bickerton won the boys' championship.

Having assisted Gay Hill to their third victory in the Brand Hall Gold Vase in four years, Peter Adams won the match play championship at Kings Norton, defeating Graham Hawkings by 4 and 3 in the final. Gay Hill were less fortunate in the Boulton Salver, losing to Kidderminster by one stroke, Nick Hunter and Matthew Houghton combining well to score 140.

The county captain and secretary, Will Painter, claimed what was possibly a unique achievement when he became the county's Open champion, as he was unaware of any other county having a secretary as captain and champion. He beat Matthew Houghton by four strokes but modestly pointed out that the county's two leading professionals, David Dunk and Kevin Hayward, were not playing. The leading professional was Chris Thompson in joint seventh place.

During the year the Abbey Hotel Club affiliated to the Union, bringing the number of clubs to twenty-six. It also saw the passing of Neville Seers, a vice-president, and H.L. Hill, a long-serving committee member. Seers had been the captain of Kings Norton in 1936 and had won forty-two of the club's trophies, nineteen of them while a "veteran". He won the county championship in 1952. Peter Ricketts recorded that he had "a relaxed happy-go-lucky disposition and unfailing good humour", despite his "tigerish feats" on the golf course.

The annual subscription to the Union was increased to £1.50 in 1987, which included 60p for the EGU. There had been a deficit of £1,203 the previous year. The 1987 accounts showed a surplus of £2,048. The increase had been passed by the November council meeting in November 1986, when the president read a letter from the secretary of Kings Norton, requesting, on behalf of the members, details of county matches and stroke play competitions and lists of teams at all levels. Roy Chandler considered it a good idea in principle but it would be an arduous task.

Mr. James Fairlie of Kings Norton pointed out that some members of his club were interested and would come to support the teams if they knew when and where they were playing. Chandler replied that the fixtures were notified at the council meetings and team selection was such that players had to be called in on Saturday because of cry-offs. As a result of this the executive agreed that the Union purchase a photo-copier for Brenda Smith to assist her in dispersing the requested information to the clubs.

There was evidence that the standard of golf in the county was improving, as indeed it was throughout the country, and the executive made a further reduction in the qualifying handicaps for county events. The limit for the county championship was now to be 7, the Boulton Salver 10, the Brand Hall Gold Vase 12, and 14 for the Droitwich Shield.

Will Painter was re-elected as captain for a third term, Fred Savage entered his second year as second team captain and the vacancy for match secretary was filled by Graham Hawkings.

Although Derek Lawrenson tipped Kidderminster as favourites in the *Birmingham Evening Mail*, Moseley won the Tomson-James Cup at Worcester, Charlie Smith scoring 68, Chris Norman 69, Darren Prosser 72 and Matthew Farmer 76 for the lowest aggregate, 284, in the seventy-one years the competition had been running. The next day Darren and Chris tied for the gold medal, the former winning the play-off by a single stroke, giving Chris the silver medal but also the G.D. Carr Cup. But for a number of three-putts, Chris could well have reversed the positions. Peter Adams won the bronze, J.G. Bennett of Fulford Heath won the Philip Padmore Trophy and Prosser the youths' championship. Lawrenson had fancied Kidderminster's chances as Matt Houghton had finished sixth in the English Amateur Stroke Play Championship (the Brabazon Trophy) at Ganton which had been played the previous weekend.

Kidderminster was more successful in the Boulton Salver. Playing on their own course Jonathon Rose and Alastair Westbury returned a score of 138, Will Painter and Roy Stephenson were third with 144, but Matt Houghton and Nick Hunter had a very disappointing 150 by their standards. The club also had a good result in the Brand Hall Gold Vase, tieing with Cocks Moors Woods, who included the young Richard Sadler in their team. Kidderminster's "A" team also won the Droitwich Shield.

The match play championship was an all Moseley affair; in the semi-finals Chris Norman beat John Bickerton by one hole and Charlie Smith beat Peter Adams 3 and 2. The final was a tense affair, Norman winning by one hole.

Kevin Hayward, who missed the Worcestershire Open in 1986, underlined his superiority to his colleagues by winning this year's event with a score of 139 over the Stourbridge course. An amateur, Rob Stevens of Kings Norton, was second. Charlie Smith won the Secretaries Bowl. As there was no sponsor the costs were shared by the Union and the professionals' association.

The county team improved on the previous year's position in "The Six", finishing in fifth place at Coventry. Warwickshire were the Midland qualifiers and finished second in the national final.

One win, against Shropshire and Herefordshire, a tied match with Warwickshire, two losses and an abandoned game with Derbyshire after we had won the foursomes 3-2, were the results of our efforts in the Midland league. The second team managed a tie with Shropshire and Herefordshire but lost all their other matches. Darren Prosser retained the President's Shield, while Glen Lowe of Kings Norton won the Chandler Shield, with Bill Thompson runner-up. The first team had suffered the loss of Nick Hunter and Graham Hawkings, both of whom had turned professional, starting a trend that was to continue into the next two decades.

An unusual reason for increasing annual subscriptions to the Union was raised at the November council meeting. The county professionals had written asking for support and it was proposed to increase the subscription to £2, the extra 40p to be put to "promote and enhance the standard of professional golf throughout Worcestershire". The extra money would increase cash prizes in stroke and match play events and provide a fund for training assistant professionals, which in its turn would benefit junior amateurs. Several arguments were raised against the scheme, nobody spoke in its favour and the president felt it incumbent upon him to inform the WAPG that the Union could not support the idea. The executive committee had already debated this issue and considered that any increase should benefit amateur and junior golf. Ray Baldwin pointed out that the Union existed purely for amateur golf.

Doug Humphries, president of Kings Norton, raised the matter of publicity for county matches. He felt that the match play championship at his club would have been better supported if there had been information displayed about the event. Jim Fairlie picked up on the reply he had received at the previous meeting and wanted to know if clubs were informed if players cried off for county matches, and said that if club captains were aware of team selections they could encourage their members to play. He was also keen to know why players were reluctant to turn out for the second team. Fred Savage replied that many of them thought it "second rate" to play for the second team under the impression that they were good enough for the first team.

The executive received the message and at the March council meeting in 1988 delegates were informed that fixture cards had been printed providing all the details of fixtures and events. Furthermore the captains and presidents of clubs holding a county match would receive an invitation to watch and have lunch. Hopefully they would bring other supporters with them.

John Wharrad replaced Graham Hawkings as match secretary and Fred Savage was elected first team captain, David Glover taking over the second team from him. He enjoyed a very good season, the second team winning four matches, losing only to Staffordshire. They finished second in their league, purely on points average. David Glover attributed the success to the improved team spirit arising from the provision of team shirts and sweaters. Unfortunately, the first team lost all their matches, some by very close margins. They finished fifth in "The Six" at Erewash Valley and once again Warwickshire were the Midland qualifiers. They also managed to win the final, the first Midland win since they won in 1977. In his end-of-season report Fred Savage highlighted the fact that Darren Prosser and John Bickerton had reached such a standard that they were playing in the major amateur events and therefore were not always available for county selection. Despite this, John won the President's Shield, while Michael Daw of Warley won the Chandler Shield.

Darren reached the quarter-finals of the Amateur Championship and played in the Open Championship. He played for England and Eire Youths at number one against Europe, England Youths against Scotland and represented England in the French Nations Cup which he won with James Cook of Warwickshire. He also won the Howitt Bowl and the Kings Norton Boys Championship.

John Bickerton won the inaugural Kings Norton Oak Trophy after a tie with Chris Norman and the *Birmingham Post and Mail* Midland Clubs Champion of Champions. He also played for the England Youths team.

Another county player, Rob Stevens, won the English Universities Championship and Tony Jowle was appointed captain of the Midland Golf Union for the following year.

Moseley retained the Tomson-James Cup at Stourbridge, Colin Wykes replacing Darren Prosser in the team, as Darren had moved to Kings Norton to take advantage of the practice facilities there. The Moseley "B" team won the Jubilee Shield.

In the individual championship Darren Prosser won the gold medal with a score of 139 which also made him the youths' champion. With a score of 70 in the team event he also won the G.D. Carr Cup. John Bickerton won the silver medal and there was a three-way tie for the bronze medal. Terry Shingler was not available for the play-off in which Robert Woodward of Stourbridge beat Matt Houghton.

John then teamed up with Simon Braithwaite to win the Boulton Salver for Droitwich, and with Brian Bishop, Andrew Terry and C. Asplin to win the Brand Hall Gold Vase. Gay Hill "A" won the Droitwich Shield. His final county success of the year was the match play championship, in which he beat D. Henn of Halesowen 5 and 3.

By the time of the county Open in September, Darren Prosser had played a lot of golf, to which Derek Lawrenson attributed his lack-lustre double bogey finish at Moseley to give the title to David Eddiford by two shots. At the time the eighteenth at Moseley was the short par 4 over the pond. Prosser was still recovering from losing a four hole lead with ten holes left to play in the British Youths Championship while Eddiford was a last minute replacement. The fact that amazed Lawrenson most was that only ten players broke 150 for the tournament, nine of whom were amateurs. The professional who did manage that feat was Kevin Hayward who finished third on 145. Lawrenson had noted a similar occurrence at the Warwickshire Open a few days before. His report was the only extended piece on a Worcestershire event in the local papers all year.

Lawrenson followed Darren's career closely in 1989, although some of our other players received coverage in the press. Darren won the Southport and Ainsdale Trophy and the Scrutton Jug for the player with the best aggregate in the Brabazon and Berkshire Trophies. This earned him selection for the Walker Cup team, the first representative from Worcestershire since Michael Lunt in 1963. Darren prepared for the experience by entering an amateur tournament in South Carolina, the state adjacent to Georgia where the Walker Cup was to be contested at Peachtree.

He was one of four Midlanders in the team, the others being Andrew Hare from Lincolnshire, Russell Claydon from Cambridgeshire and Peter McEvoy. All four were selected for their counties in the Midland "Six" which was held at Glen Gorse, Leicester, Warwickshire qualifying once again. Worcestershire improved considerably by finishing third.

At Peachtree, Darren was paired with Russell Claydon in the opening foursomes against David Martin and Robert Gamez, the Americans winning 3 and 2. Then the most terrible thing happened – Darren began to feel unwell, was omitted from the remaining matches and was found to have contracted chicken pox. This developed into M.E. on his return to England, by which time he had turned professional. It took some time to get to the root of his malaise and Darren's professional career did not get off to a very happy start. However, he had the honour of being a member of the first Great Britain and Ireland team to win the Walker Cup in the United States, perhaps the most memorable achievement of the decade.

A very sad event of 1989 was the death of Harley Roberts, which was reported in an affectionate piece in the *Birmingham Post* by Michael Blair.

Kings Norton entered a formidable team for the Tomson-James Cup, which was played for at The Worcestershire. Darren Prosser's 70 was supported by David Eddiford 71, Peter Swinburne 75 and Rob Stevens 77 for a winning total of 293. Moseley and The Worcestershire shared second place and the home club won the Jubilee Shield.

Thunderstorms curtailed the individual championship to a single round, during which Simon Braithwaite returned the winning score of 67, followed by John Bickerton and Andy Carter with 68, Carter winning the play-off for the silver medal. Mike Reynard won the G.D. Carr Cup, while Braithwaite and Carter shared the Philip Padmore Trophy, the former also receiving the colts' championship trophy.

The Boulton Salver was held at Droitwich and the home club's 'D' team, John Mole and Tony Cox, won on a count-back from Rose Hill's "A" team of D.B. Glover and T. Doyle. It is worth noting that foursomes is not as popular a format as it should be and certainly a frustrating one for municipal golfers. The members of those clubs who support the county are therefore worthy of especial praise. Another successful municipal player during the season was Michael Daw of Warley, who won the match play championship, beating Phil Shurmer of The Worcestershire at the 19th hole.

There was another home club win when Gay Hill won the Brand Hall Gold vase, with M.S. Duggan 68, M.J. Duggan 70, C. Clarke 70 and J. Mangan 77 for an aggregate of 285 nett. The final of the Droitwich Shield also took place at Gay Hill, when Kings Norton "A" beat Droitwich "A".

Kevin Hayward won the county Open at Kidderminster with a score of 141. John Bickerton was the leading amateur two strokes behind, Bob Cameron of Abbey Park and Andrew Terry tieing for third place.

Third place in "The Six" was repeated in the Midland league, with wins against Nottinghamshire and Derbyshire, both by considerable margins. One of the three losses was by the odd point, the other two by four points. David Eddiford won the President's Shield. The second team could not repeat the success of the previous year, winning only one match, against Warwickshire. Bill Thompson won the Chandler Shield.

John Bickerton represented England Youths against Scotland and in the French Nations Cup, which England won. He also won the Champion of Champions and the Failand Cup.

Thanks largely to the achievements of Darren and John, Worcestershire figured again in the national selectors' deliberations. Was this a good omen for the new decade?

Chapter Eight

New Decade – New Clubs

THE FIRST county event of 1990 was Worcestershire's first annual dinner. As all the other Midland counties now held such an event, it was felt that it was time we repaid the hospitality shown to our officials by our neighbouring unions. The banqueting room at Kings Norton Golf Club was booked for 9th February. Members of all clubs in the Union were eligible to attend, at a cost of £14. The principal guest was the secretary of the EGU, Mr. Keith Wright.

The reaction was favourable and the president informed the council meeting in March that the dinner would be repeated the following year, when it was hoped that the president of the EGU would be able to attend. Between 160 and 170 were accommodated at this first event. Eventually the optimum number was calculated at around 260. The first dinner produced a deficit of £114, a situation that became a perennial one, but which was resolved by a subsidy from county funds.

The new captain was David Rodway, in a non-playing capacity, and Bill Thompson took over the second team. John Wharrad was unable to continue as match secretary and the position was left vacant until Michael Herman-Smith stepped into the breach.

Although Darren Prosser was now a professional, Rodway had a talented squad of players to choose from. Unfortunately so had most of our opponents. Worcestershire came third in "The Six" at South Staffs, when Warwickshire once again progressed to the national final, which they won for the second time in three years. They did not qualify again until 2000, when they finished fourth.

The only win in the league was at the expense of Staffordshire; the other matches were all lost, some quite heavily. On the other hand, the second team won all but one of their matches, losing only to Staffordshire, and finished second to Shropshire and Herefordshire, who won one more match point, in the league. Rob Stevens won the President's Shield and David Nevett the Chandler Shield.

Thanks to a Kings Norton player missing two important putts Moseley regained the Tomson-James Cup on their home course. The Worcestershire "B" retained the Jubilee Shield. Despite incurring four penalty shots David Eddiford won the gold medal the next day with two rounds of 70, which also earned him the G.D. Carr Cup and the Philip Padmore Trophy. Matthew Houghton was second on 146 and so became youths' champion. The bronze medal went to John Bickerton who improved on a morning round of 77 with 71 in the afternoon. This was David Eddiford's last amateur medal, for later in the season he turned professional, creating selection problems for his captain.

There was a new record winning score in the Boulton Salver when Dudley's pairing of Graham Nicklin and Mark Williams scored 131, nine below the par at Droitwich. The Brand Hall Gold Vase was held at Fulford Heath and Halesowen recorded their first success for fifteen years in this competition. Kings Norton's "A" team won the Droitwich Shield, beating Stourbridge 2 and 1 in the final at Droitwich.

The match play championship was held at The Worcestershire in August and John Bickerton beat David Eddiford in the final by one hole. He may have considered himself lucky to be there, for only a few days previously he had rather an alarming experience.

The oldest amateur stroke play tournament in England is the Midland Amateur Championship, initiated in 1895. It was renamed the Midland Closed Amateur Championship in 1976, when the seventy-two hole tournament was played at Little Aston and Sutton Coldfield, qualifiers playing a round on both courses on the first day. Those making the cut played thirty-six holes at Little Aston. In the early days of the competition the winner held the Spencer Newey Memorial Trophy, but this was stolen in 1982. Among the early winners from Worcestershire were Edward Blackwell and Frank Woolley, R.P. Humphries, Eric and Douglas Fiddian, Stanley and Michael Lunt, Harley Roberts and Tony Jowle. In 1990 the most recent winner from a Worcestershire club was David Russell in 1973. Many of today's successful tour players have featured prominently in the event over the years, recent winners being David Howell and Luke Donald.

The defending champion in 1990 was James Cook from Leamington. He set a new course record of 66 in the third round, but he was a stroke behind John Bickerton when a thunderstorm disrupted play. John was about to attempt a birdie putt when he was struck by lightning, the shock running up through his putter into his arm. Instead of walking in, John regained his calmness and holed the putt. He finished nine under par and won the championship by eight strokes, Cook having fallen back to finish fourth. John later told Derek Lawrenson that it was the second time he had been struck. This performance assisted John's selection for the England Youths team.

The only other significant performances by Worcestershire players were Peter Swinburne's joint first in the Dunhill Masters national final, in which he was placed second on a count-back, and Simon Timmins of Gay Hill who won the *Birmingham Evening Mail* Champion of Champions tournament.

In his captain's report at the November meeting David Rodway spoke of his selection problems. David Eddiford chose to play for pay during the year and John Bickerton was only available for one match because of fixture clashes. The Union had written to the EGU recommending that county matches throughout the country should be played on the same dates, as they were in the Midlands. This would ensure the best players were available for their counties and that the international players and potential national team members could compete against each other, thus gaining practice and experience for events such as the Walker Cup. It would also remove the clashes with important stroke play events.

David also felt that more coaching was required for the county players and requested extra funds for this purpose. It was proposed to raise the annual subscription to £2.50, an increase of 80p, which included an extra 40p to the EGU and 40p to cover the cost of the coaching, the national union having requested £1 per member from each county.

Another Worcestershire and England stalwart, Stanley Lunt, died during the year. He had made a tremendous effort on the county's behalf during his competitive years and made his mark on innumerable honours boards.

The handicap limits for county competitions were reviewed for the 1991 season. Players wishing to play in the county championship would now require a handicap of 5 or better but the existing limits remained for the other competitions. Despite the congestion of fixtures which had so frustrated our captain, Ray Baldwin announced that the MGU, at the suggestion of Tony Jowle, was introducing a new competition, the Midland Counties Closed Championship, as some county players were unable to meet the handicap requirement of the Midland Amateur, with which the Closed Championship had run conjointly. The new event was first played in 1992.

The Vale Golf and Country Club became affiliated to the county Union during the year and was soon holding events on its championship course, including the revived Midland Open in 1992. It was not until 1993 that the county used the facility.

Despite the air of optimism about the coming season 1991 started on a low note: because of the Gulf War the executive decided it would be inappropriate to hold a celebration and the second county dinner was cancelled. The president assured delegates at the March council meeting that it would take place in 1992.

However, the coaching scheme began on schedule and Kevin Hayward showed great enthusiasm for his task. Unfortunately the final results were little better than those of a year before, two matches being tied, the friendly with Gloucestershire and the league match with Warwickshire which David Rodway was particularly pleased with. He was less impressed with the result against Nottinghamshire as Worcestershire gained a solitary point. Nevertheless, he felt that although they finished bottom of the league once again, the players had given of their best. They played well in "The Six" to finish in sixth place at Coxmoor. The team comprised John Bickerton, Will Painter, Rob Stevens, Neil Swaffield, Alan Robinson and Terry Martin. Simon Timmins of Gay Hill won the President's Shield and the Chandler Shield was claimed by Peter Adams. The second team was less successful this season, winning three matches and losing three.

Earlier John Bickerton had won the Berkshire Trophy, despite another mishap when the head flew off his driver, and was tipped for England selection, Derek Lawrenson comparing his progress with that of Darren Prosser. John had made no secret of his ultimate intention to turn professional and this is probably the reason the selectors ignored him, despite Terry Shingler's advocacy of his cause.

He led Droitwich to victory in the Tomson-James Cup at Blackwell, scoring 68, three under par. He went on to win his first individual championship and the G.D. Carr Cup using a driver and 2-wood he had borrowed from Terry Shingler, who was unable to play in the event. Matt Houghton won the silver medal for the second year in succession and Will Painter the bronze medal and the Philip Padmore Trophy. The youths' championship was won by Neil Swaffield, with Mark Butler runner-up.

Bickerton's last chance to win a county title came at the match play championship, played at Hagley in August. Unfortunately for him Alan Robinson was in top form and beat him 2 and 1.

John Mole of Droitwich had his name engraved on the Boulton Salver in 1989. He achieved this distinction again in 1991 in the company of Nigel Wood, beating A.J. Hale and Matthew Whitehouse of Worcester on a count-back when the event took place at Dudley. The Brand Hall Gold Vase was held at North Worcestershire, when Fulford Heath's team prevailed, Gay Hill being the runners-up. Moseley's "A" team won the Droitwich Shield, beating Evesham"A" in the final at Halesowen.

The county Open was held at Redditch and once again the amateurs outplayed the professionals. Mike Reynard won the Guy Bigwood Cup and the gold medal with a score of 146, one stroke fewer than Alan Robinson. Two professionals occupied third place, G. Mercer of Brand Hall and Kevin Hayward. Reynard also received the Secretaries Bowl.

As the years roll by and the Union approaches its centenary it is inevitable that men who have played important roles in its history pass away and in 1991 the death of J.W. Allen of Moseley was reported with regret in the annual report. He captained the second team from 1953 until 1959 and was made a vice-president in 1960. Fortunately no such losses were reported the following year, although Roy Chandler was unable to attend the council meeting in November. Dick Mirams took the chair, as he did again the following February. At the next council meeting, held in October, he was elected president and Michael Herman-Smith became the first elected chairman.

The rules had been changed so that a new president would only serve for two years. This would enable clubs to have more input into the county's affairs and possibly increase the amount of professional experience this more democratic system would bring. David Rodway explained that Roy Chandler, whose poor health had instigated the proposal, was only the fourth president in the Union's history.

Two new clubs were seeking affiliation; Perdiswell, who were accepted early in the year, and Ombersley, who sought to join the Union even though the clubhouse was still under construction. This brought the total of affiliated clubs to twenty-nine and by the end of the year two more, Bransford and Wharton Park, were ready to apply for county recognition. The executive was slightly worried that new clubs might not be run by people with sufficient knowledge of golf, but the secretary assured them that all the guidelines were being followed and the criteria met. Ray Baldwin, our development officer, paid regular visits to clubs seeking affiliation giving advice on both the course and the necessary articles of association and constitution.

The second county dinner was held at Kings Norton in February and was attended by "150 odd". This time the deficit was £220 but the executive was resolved to continue the event.

Jim Gray had announced his retirement as juniors' chairman and no replacement had been found. As Jim had arranged for the boys' championship to be played at Moseley, John Moreton, a member of that club, agreed to run the event. He enjoyed it so much that he volunteered to take Jim's place, in spite of not being a car owner.

David Rodway was re-elected captain for his third term, Mike Tweddell accepting the vice-captaincy. David thanked Bill Thompson for all his support and Bill handed over the second team to Peter Adams.

Three clubs in the county celebrated their centenary in 1992, Moseley, Kings Norton and Stourbridge. The last-named club staged the annual meeting, while the match play championship, the county Open and "The Six" were all held at Moseley, in addition to the boys' championship. Moseley also invited the county team, past, present and ladies, to a match. Kings

Norton, headquarters of the Midlands PGA, held the region's PGA match play championship, a WPGA Pro-Am and the English Golf Union's county finals. The club's scratch team played a team of present and past county players. As South Staffs was founded in the same year the four clubs combined to play an annual tournament for the Centenary Salver.

As the entry for the county Open had been very poor in 1991 it was felt that a meeting with representatives of the WAPG was necessary in an attempt to renew interest in the competition. Brenda Smith pointed out that she was now the only liaison with the professionals as she assisted in the running of the Worcestershire alliances. Neville Seers had resigned due to ill health ten years previously and had not been replaced. She urged the executive to appoint a member of the committee to put in occasional appearances at these meetings, which produced substantial revenue for the professionals.

The revenue from the subscription to the Union was another issue and it was decided that an increase of 50p was required, bringing another £5,500 income to the county. The juniors had required a minibus for two tournaments, and hotel accommodation, and had two extra home fixtures. A coaching officer, Bill Thompson, had also been appointed. Ray Baldwin assured the committee that any increase required by the EGU would be notified in plenty of time. Even after a substantial increase was proposed when the move to Woodhall Spa was announced, English golfers paid a fraction of the subscriptions levied from members of clubs on the Continent.

Stourbridge's centenary was celebrated with victory in the Tomson-James Cup on their own course. Their team consisted of Neil Swaffield 70, Tim Pickering 72, Andrew Claridge 74 and Robert Woodward 78 for a total of 295. The other two centenary clubs tied for second place, Kings Norton winning the Jubilee Shield.

Matthew Houghton and Simon Timmins shared the lead after the morning round in the individual championship, four strokes ahead of Mike Reynard, who produced a round of 65 in the afternoon, just one shot more than the amateur course record, and equalling that of Eric Fiddian, who scored 65 on 28th December 1931, in an official competition. Houghton and Timmins could not match this and Matthew was second for the third time in as many years, while Simon took the bronze medal. Mike's performance earned him the G.D. Carr Cup and there was a three-way tie for the Philip Padmore Trophy, Simon Timmins, the young Danny Clee and Peter Lupino scoring nett 137. Mark Butler was the youths' champion.

Stourbridge had another centenary celebration when Neil Swaffield and Robert Woodward won the Boulton Salver at Droitwich, with a nett score of 137. Halesowen made good use of their home advantage in the Brand Hall Gold Vase and returned a record score of 266 nett. Their team was P. Webb,

Alan Price, R. Wyld and James Semple. Once again Rose Hill put up a good performance to finish second, twelve strokes behind the winners. The Droitwich Shield was won by Kidderminster "A" when they beat Evesham "B" at Worcester, winning all three matches. Nick Peplow played for Kidderminster.

It was Worcestershire's turn to host "The Six" and the ten Midland counties met at Moseley on a miserable day. The county team of Mike Reynard, Matt Houghton, Richard Sadler, Alan Robinson, Mark Butler and Neil Swaffield played well but Staffordshire showed more consistency, Rob Maxfield setting a new course record of 66, while a young man from Nottinghamshire, Lee Westwood, assisted his team to second place.

Despite this good performance in "The Six" the team fared poorly in the league matches and finished in bottom place, the best result being a tie with Warwickshire. This was most disappointing after the team had beaten Gwent 12-6 in an early season friendly. Bill Thompson won the President's Shield.

The second team did little better, beating Gloucestershire in a friendly match 11-7, tieing with Warwickshire and losing the remaining games. Anthony Hill of Fulford Heath won the Chandler Shield.

Neil Swaffield was the only Worcestershire golfer to gain a title outside the county when he won the Midland Youths Championship at Stoke Rochford. He also won the county's match play championship at Moseley, defeating Phil Shurmer of The Worcestershire in the final 4 and 3.

Alan Robinson won the Worcestershire Open, also at Moseley, with a score of 142, two ahead of Mike Reynard and Duncan Webber of Evesham. The leading professionals were Kevin Hayward and Ian Clark who tied for second place on 143.

A twenty-man team of past and present county players took on the might of Kings Norton's scratch team in September. Each match was played to the eighteenth and the score calculated on holes up. Three matches were halved, one of which involved Ian Wheater, and the end result was a win for the county by four holes up, Paul Scarrett winning the last match nine holes up. This meant that Alan Pugh had to win his match, which he did, four holes up.

1992 was another thin year for press coverage of our activities, but Peter Ricketts contributed an enthusiastic profile of Ray Baldwin to the *Birmingham Evening Mail,* in which our development officer expressed some of his views on golf course design. Ray hinted that farmers might know a lot about cows but were entirely unfamiliar with the intricacies of golf course design and construction. Ray had even fired a shot across the bows of Messrs. Thomas and Alliss, demonstrating that a hole at the Belfry was unsafe. Ray advised a change and told Ricketts, "I wasn't popular but they did it." The scourge of golf course architects also designed a number of excellent courses himself,

Courtesy: J. Moreton

Bromsgrove Golf Centre

one of which was soon to become affiliated to the county Union. This was Cleobury Mortimer, which actually lay across the county boundary with Shropshire, but the club had applied for affiliation to Worcestershire because of the proximity of other local clubs with whom it was hoped to arrange matches. The club opened with nine holes, a driving range and a small, intimate clubhouse. Members from the Kidderminster area and elsewhere joined and soon the club was able to open a second nine holes. Additions were made to the clubhouse, improving changing and dining facilities. Ray Baldwin was made an honorary member and returned a few years later to add the third loop of nine holes, of which he was justly proud. Further improvements were made to the clubhouse and the club took its place on the county rota for matches and competitions.

Another new development was the Bromsgrove driving range, with its thirty-four bays and where nine holes were also open. This proved so popular that the owners, Ted Morris and his sons, were able to build a further nine holes and a clubhouse which incorporated all the facilities required – changing rooms, check-in for the range, professional's shop, bar and restaurant. It was not long before the MGU and the EGU were using the facilities for coaching their junior squads. A Golf Foundation Starter Centre was opened there for the benefit of young beginners.

The other courses to become affiliated were Wharton Park and Bransford. The latter belongs to the Bank House Hotel and is a Florida style course with abundant water hazards. Wharton Park, built over rolling, wooded terrain, has eighteen holes of which the order has been changed from the original plan, which had the ninth hole near the clubhouse, necessitating a long uphill climb through woods to play three holes followed by another trek downhill to finish the round. Again the clubhouse incorporates all the infrastructure and the professional has a spacious driving range to teach his pupils.

These new clubs brought the number of member clubs up to thirty-three. Sadly only seventeen of these were represented at the annual dinner in February 1993, and the president asked those present at the council meeting to persuade more of their members to attend in 1994. Dick Mirams had already seen his history of Moseley Golf Club published and offered to begin writing the history of the Union.

Mike Tweddell took over as captain from David Rodway. He led the team to a slightly improved position in the Midland league, in which they beat Shropshire and Herefordshire, but lost the remaining matches, although by the narrowest margin, 8-7, against Staffordshire and Derbyshire. They also lost the three friendly matches with Gwent, Gloucestershire and Leicestershire. Richard Sadler won the President's Shield. An innovation was a twelve-a-side match with the professionals, which was decided on holes up and won by the professionals, who were presented with a tankard.

"The Six" was held at the Gog Magog club in Cambridge and as an experiment and means of giving the boys experience six of the boys' team were taken to caddy for our men. It was not as successful as was hoped, Worcestershire finishing in seventh position.

The second team won three of their league matches, against Warwickshire, Staffordshire and Shropshire and Herefordshire. They also won the friendly match with Gwent. The three matches that were lost were all very close. Richard Dean won the Chandler Shield, with Anthony Hill runner-up.

The *Birmingham Post*'s golf correspondent, Derek Lawrenson was in attendance on both days of the annual meeting at Fulford Heath and filed two lengthy reports. On the first day he witnessed Kidderminster's fourth success in the Tomson-James Cup, in which Matt Houghton and John Dallaway both scored 71 and Danny Clee and Will Painter 77 each, for a total of 296, beating Moseley by one stroke. Moseley won the Jubilee Shield.

Mike Reynard had the best round of the day, 69, and was heading for a new course record, but he found the water twice on the twelfth. The following day he scored 74 and 70 to win the gold medal and the G.D. Carr Cup. Matt

Houghton had been tipped by Lawrenson to win the championship after his form in the team event, but had a disappointing day and relinquished the runner-up position he had held for the last three years. This year the silver medal was won by Chris Gadd of Kings Norton on the second eighteen holes after a tie with Simon Timmins, who therefore received the bronze medal. Gadd was less fortunate in the tie for the Philip Padmore Trophy, J.G. Bennett of the home club winning on another count-back. There was a third count-back for the youths' championship and Andrew Claridge was placed ahead of Mark Butler.

Andrew Terry and Ian Dix of Droitwich won the Boulton Salver at Stourbridge, Steve Noble and Tim Pickering of the home club being placed second ahead of N.Clarke and S.Lester of Warley by virtue of a better second round. Another municipal club featured more prominently in the Brand Hall Gold Vase, the club who originally presented the trophy to the county, Brand Hall. This event was held at Dudley whose members were celebrating the club's centenary. This club's "A" team reached the final of the Droitwich Shield, but were beaten by Stourbridge's "A" team in the final at Fulford Heath.

The match play championship was held at Kidderminster and Neil Swaffield retained the title after a close game with Alan Robinson which finished 2 and 1 in Neil's favour. Earlier in the competition Alan had a hole in one at the fifth hole and needed six extra holes to beat Simon Timmins in the semi-final.

Blackwell was also celebrating its centenary and was the venue for the Worcestershire Open. An anonymous sponsor had provided funds for the event, which produced exciting golf and a story-book finish. Paul Scarrett, a Blackwell member, tied with Ian Clark, the Hagley professional, on 142, and so won the gold medal as leading amateur. He then beat Clark in the play-off to be awarded the Guy Bigwood Cup. In third place was Ian's son and assistant, Cameron Clark, on 143. Cameron had been the captain of the county boys' team the previous year. He beat Mike Reynard by one stroke, Mike's consolation being the retention of the Secretaries Bowl for the second time.

Sixty years after his county debut and thirty years after his term as captain, John Fraser was elected president of the Union in March 1994.

When the tradition of inviting the presidents of other county unions to annual dinners was instituted, Worcestershire lagged behind in equipping their figurehead with apparel to match the uniforms of the other unions. When Dick Mirams became president in 1992 following the death of Roy Chandler he was not enthusiastic about "dressing up" as he put it. What threatened to become a "continued minute" was resolved when it was suggested that instead of copying our rivals with a red tailcoat, Worcestershire's president would wear green and Dick reluctantly agreed to

John R. Fraser (President 1994-95)

submit himself to the tailor's tape measure.

Jeff Adams and John Moreton put forward names of suitable tailors and were authorised to obtain quotes. Master tailor John Salisbury, a member of Moseley, quoted "the thick end of £300", and earned the privilege of becoming the Union's tailor.

When John Fraser attended the Derbyshire dinner two or three years later he was introduced to that county's patron, the Duke of Devonshire, who congratulated John on wearing the Duke's hunting colours!

Worcestershire's innovation in breaking with traditional red influenced our Warwickshire neighbours, who dress their president in a blue coat.

Charles Smith became the vice-captain and Tim Pickering the second team captain. Clive Mitchell, who had been installed as match secretary in 1993, was re-elected. David Rodway and Jim Gray were elected vice-presidents in recognition of their work on the county's behalf. In David's case this was still very much an on-going process, for he was the county's representative to the EGU, sitting on the finance sub-committee.

Examples of the advice he passed on to members include the effect of VAT, what to do if a club leases its course, and organisation of club employees and rates, including water rates. Later in the decade clubs were advised to develop their own water collection system in view of possible restrictions the water companies might impose in the event of drought.

Another long-serving member of the executive was profiled by Dennis Shaw in *Amateur Golf*, the EGU magazine. Brenda Smith completed forty years with the county during the year. At the November council meeting she was presented with a quantity of Royal Worcester china to the acclamation of the delegates.

Sadly, Roy Chandler, whose illness had occasioned the new rule restricting the president to a two year term, died during the year.

Home advantage had frequently influenced the outcome of the Tomson-James Cup and Gay Hill were the winners in 1994, for the club's first time.

The team was Nigel Taylor, Peter Adams, Simon Timmins and M.S. Duggan. Their score of 303 was six strokes better than that of Droitwich. Eighteen teams had entered and the same number contested the Jubilee Shield, Worcester being the winners, with Gay Hill's "B" team second.

The individual title was won by Richard Sadler with a score of 139, which also gave him the Philip Padmore Trophy. Alan Robinson was second and won the G.D. Carr Cup. Mike Reynard won the bronze medal and James Toman of Worcester the youths' championship. Richard started his second round birdie, par, eagle, and finished strongly, despite a double bogey at the fifth hole.

The municipal clubs maintained their support for the county's events, Rose Hill 'D' winning the Boulton Salver at Droitwich and Brand Hall retaining "their" Gold Vase at The Worcestershire. Kings Norton "A" beat Droitwich"A" in the final of the Droitwich Shield at Stourbridge.

Danny Clee, one year too old for the boys' team, beat Matt Houghton, his club-mate, one up in the final of the match play championship which was held at Wharton Park. Danny subsequently became an assistant professional there.

Paul Scarrett won the gold medal in the Worcestershire Open for the second time in succession, but was unable to retain the Guy Bigwood Cup which went to the leading professional, an assistant at Kings Norton, Spencer Edwards, who had been a member of Jim Gray's winning team in the first boys' national county finals eight years previously. Richard Sadler won the Secretaries Bowl.

The county team finished eighth in "The Six" at Belton Park, Grantham. They improved on their league position, though, coming third in the Midland league, beating Shropshire and Herefordshire, Warwickshire and Staffordshire but losing to Derbyshire and Nottinghamshire. In the friendly matches Gwent were defeated but we lost to Leicestershire and Gloucestershire. A match against the professionals was also lost early in the season, but Mike Tweddell felt that the team had benefited from the experience. Matt Houghton and Charles Smith tied for the President's Shield. Four players had earned their county blazers under a new scheme sponsored by Martyn Price, having played the requisite number of matches and won the qualifying number of points. They were Neil Swaffield, Paul Scarrett, Alan Robinson and Richard Sadler.

The second team tied for first place in their league but lost on points average. They had beaten Shropshire and Herefordshire, Staffordshire and Warwickshire, tied with Derbyshire and lost to Nottinghamshire. They also won the friendly against Gloucestershire. The Chandler Shield was won by Rob Tickell, with Oliver Darby, the boys' team captain, in second place.

Jeff Adams reported a record entry for the first of the year's two meetings, when 300 competitors played at Moseley.

There was a change of venue for the annual dinner in 1995 when it was held at Bromsgrove School. It proved an unpopular choice despite the accessibility of the location, and the original venue of Kings Norton was chosen for future functions.

Between the dinner and the council meeting the Union lost one of its best-loved and hardest working members. Bill Cunningham died after a long illness, having just managed to survive his wife's passing. He came to Birmingham in 1945 after service in the Royal Army Medical Corps and eventually entered practice in Moseley with Angus Nairn, a member of Moseley Golf Club, which Bill joined. Later he joined the practice of another Moseley member, Bob Frame. He was a county vice-president and a member of the R&A.

Another absentee was Mike Herman-Smith, who was wintering in Florida, so Denis Hayes was elected chairman in his place. Mike had brought a business-like manner to the executive meetings, which rarely overran.

Mike Tweddell was interviewed by Michael Blair in the *Birmingham Post*'s pre-season round-up of Midland golf. Mike had completed his two years as non-playing captain and handed over to Charlie Smith, who, he said, "will play if he wants to. Having had a couple of stuffed shirts as captain, the lads now have someone they know."

Charlie informed his players at the county trial that they were good enough to win the league and "The Six", saying he would dearly love to see a return to the days of the Fiddians, Dr. Tweddell, Stanley Lunt and the current president, John Fraser.

Although he did not play golf until he was twenty-four, when he played at the Lickey Hills course, Charlie Smith soon revealed a talent for the game and attained a handicap of 12. He moved to North Worcestershire, then Kings Norton and finally Moseley. He reduced his handicap to scratch one week before the new CONGU scheme came into operation and promptly went back to one.

His words at the trial obviously had a good effect on the players, for Worcestershire finished joint second in the Midland league, losing only one match. They were less successful at Peterborough Milton in "The Six". Chris Norman had to drop out at the last minute because of urgent business commitments and Danny Clee took his place, causing a slight controversy with the organiser, who eventually accepted Charlie's explanation. Danny performed well all season to win the President's Shield.

The second team, led by Tim Pickering, who won the Chandler Shield, was less successful but nevertheless enjoyed their season.

The Vale's course was now considered ready for a county event and the 1995 championship was held there, Mike Reynard taking the gold medal and G.D. Carr Cup yet again, while assisting Moseley to victory in the Tomson-

James Cup. The Worcestershire's "B" team won the Jubilee Shield and Darren Edmunds, Kings Norton, became the youths' champion. John Dallaway, Kidderminster, won the Philip Padmore Trophy and the bronze medal, Neil Swaffield having taken the silver.

Fulford Heath won the Boulton Salver to set up a run of success in this competition, while Rose Hill asserted the strength of municipal golf by winning the Brand Hall Gold Vase. Later they questioned why municipal clubs did not receive home draws in the Droitwich Shield. The reason was the difficulty of booked times and a clear field on the public courses. Rose Hill protested that this was not the case at the Lickey Hills, and the executive promised to look into the matter. Droitwich won the Droitwich Shield, beating Moseley in the final.

Another youth, James Toman, finished the season in fine form, beating Matthew Houghton in the final of the match play championship. The gold medal in the county Open was won by another young man, Cameron Clark, who shared the Union Tankard with his father Ian, for whom he worked as assistant at Hagley.

Later in the year Mike Reynard reached the final of the Amateur Championship at Hoylake, in which his opponent was Gordon Sherry. Due to a bizarre series of circumstances Mike was late on the tee for the afternoon round and was penalised one hole. Although he won the next hole, it was already too late and Mike lost rather heavily. However, his defeat of Jody Fanagan, the Irish international, in a thrilling semi-final brought him to the notice of the national selectors and Mike made his debut for England the following year against France and played in the Home Internationals.

Two more county stalwarts died during the year; Douglas Fiddian, a member of the all-conquering Worcestershire team of the 1930s, and Ronnie Morgan, who had served as match secretary and captain. Ronnie had been a prisoner of war in Stalag Luft III, where he and the distinguished golf writer Pat Ward-Thomas made their own golf balls out of the shredded rubber from plimsolls and leather cases. Using clubs dropped by the Red Cross they fashioned a course in the prison compound, utilising sand excavated by would-be escapees under the famous wooden horse for the bunkers. Play had to be suspended on one occasion when a stray shot disturbed a German officer in the latrines.

1996 proved another good year for the county team, who finished second on their own in the league, winning three matches, losing one and halving the other. The win against Staffordshire, the league winners, was particularly satisfying. Neil Swaffield won the President's Shield and decided at the end of the season that he was going to turn professional. Mike Reynard won the gold medal in the annual meeting at Kings Norton, after Steve Noble of

Stourbridge had led after the first round. Noble could only manage 77 in the afternoon and took the silver medal and the Philip Padmore Trophy, while the bronze went to a Kings Norton youth, Jonathon Hems. Simon Braithwaite won the G.D. Carr Cup after a round of 70 in the team event, which was won by Stourbridge. Kidderminster "B" won the Jubilee Shield, another young player, Nathan Bennett, making a contribution.

Danny Clee rounded off a good season by winning the match play championship, beating Simon Deakin of Kings Norton in the final, and the Worcestershire Open, taking the Guy Bigwood Cup and the gold medal. The leading professionals, who tied for second place, were Andrew Hill of Gay Hill and Graham Farr of Cleobury Mortimer.

The second team under David Nevett recorded two wins, two losses and one halved match, Paul Garey winning the Chandler Shield after making his debut in the second match.

Fulford Heath's "B" team won the Boulton Salver on their own course, having won the previous year at Blackwell. In the Brand Hall Gold Vase Simon Braithwaite set a new course record of 65 at Kidderminster; ably assisted by his team-mates, this ensured a victory for Droitwich. The Droitwich Shield was won by Stourbridge "B", who beat Wharton Park in the final at Kidderminster.

The mass defection to the professional ranks was clearly going to pose problems for the incoming captain, Peter Adams, who accepted the honour with his customary cheerfulness. This was not the only change in personnel, however. Will Painter, who had served as secretary for fifteen years, announced his retirement. He had started a family and his solicitor's practice was expanding, as was the workload of county golf secretaries arranging a plethora of new competitions and fixtures throughout the country. The time had come to follow the lead of our neighbours and appoint a paid secretary.

Chapter Nine

Under New Management

A JOB DESCRIPTION was formulated for the new appointment. The secretary would take over the duties of the assistant secretary and the match secretary, while the treasurer's role would remain separate. Brenda Smith continued to act in this capacity and Clive Mitchell relinquished the duties of match secretary. The clubs within the county were advised of the new appointment and applications were invited, Andrew Boyd being the successful candidate.

A B.Sc. in mechanical engineering from Manchester University is one of Andrew's many qualifications, which equipped him for a career with various divisions of Tube Investments before he became the senior account manager for UNYSIS in Birmingham. Early appointments with Tube Investments took him to Cyprus and Saudi Arabia, where he established a greenfield site factory in Riyadh.

Andrew did not take up golf until 1990, at the age of forty-two, having previously spent his leisure sailing. From his home in Pershore he and a friend explored the Worcestershire courses, enjoying both the game and the golf club ambience. Andrew joined The Vale and by 1995 had a handicap of 10 and became captain of the club two years later, having already served on the committee. He steeped himself in the game, its organisation and the rules, successfully completing the EGU's rules school and that of the R&A – a much sterner test.

Andrew took office in 1997 but his thunder was stolen somewhat by another county administrator. There are numerous references in this history to Ray Baldwin, to whom so many clubs are indebted for his counsel. At the beginning of 1997 Ray was presented with the Gerald Micklem Award. This was instituted in 1990 and is presented annually to a person who has made an outstanding contribution to further the interests of amateur golf in this country. In 1991 it was awarded to Sir Michael Bonallack and to Peter McEvoy in 1999.

Gerald Micklem was a highly successful amateur, an international who played in six Walker Cup matches and then became one of the finest administrators the game has known, becoming captain of the R&A, president of the EGU and president of the European Golf Association.

In view of the regard in which Micklem was held and the range of his achievements, this award can be regarded as the greatest honour that can be bestowed, not for playing golf but for enabling others to enjoy the game, on its recipient. It was only fitting that it should be given to Ray, who by this time was compiling his record of Midland golf in addition to all his other activities. It was typical of Ray that he did not sit back on his laurels but continued as enthusiastically as ever with his various projects.

Two new clubs were given provisional affiliation to the Union in 1997, Gaudet Luce and Ravenmeadow. The latter was the brainchild of David Rodway, who ensured that the practice facilities would be second to none. Gaudet Luce was the second development of the Fernyhough family who own Little Lakes. Ray Baldwin planned the original layout, which was modified by Mark Laing and extended in 2002, as was Little Lakes, three testing new holes replacing some less interesting ones. Gaudet Luce provides excellent opportunities for players in the Droitwich area to enjoy affordable golf on a course requiring thoughtful play from the better golfers.

Peter Adams, the first team captain, and David Nevett, his second team counterpart, addressed the problem arising from the defection of a number of players to the paid ranks by selecting younger and, hopefully, promising players. The youths' team had enjoyed successful seasons and a number of these players were given the opportunity to experience first and second team golf.

The first team came third in "The Six" but after a good start could only manage fifth place in the league, while David called on thirty-seven players during the season. One of these was Roy Hobbis, filling in at very short notice and contributing a valuable foursomes point. Paul Scarrett won the President's Shield and Anthony Hill the Chandler Shield.

The Worcestershire amateur champion was Simon Braithwaite, who returned an excellent score of 137, James Toman taking the silver medal and Charles Smith the bronze. Richard Sadler eliminated Simon in the match play championship and met Paul Scarrett in the final at Gay Hill. Paul had beaten Toman in the semi-final and disposed of Sadler by 5 and 4. Of the sixteen men who qualified for this event seven eventually defected to the professional game, though two were subsequently reinstated as amateurs. What may have influenced their decisions to play for pay may have been the result of the county Open – the leading professional, Daniel Clee, finished in joint seventh place and three of the would-be professionals were ahead of him. However, the winner was a true amateur, Paul Scarrett adding a second trophy to his mantelpiece.

Kidderminster "A" won the Droitwich Shield, Fulford Heath claimed the Brand Hall Gold Vase and Matthew Feavyour and Jon Hems took the Boulton Salver back to Kings Norton. This club had won the Jubilee Shield but Moseley took the Tomson-James Cup by a margin of seventeen strokes.

1998 began with a heavy defeat against Leicestershire at the Ray Baldwin designed course at Kilworth Springs. However, there was one highlight for Worcestershire when Paul Scarrett beat Gary Wolstenholme one up, thereby earning the title of "the man who beat the man who beat Tiger Woods". The second team, led by Rob Tickell, did better, winning 11-7 at Stourbridge. A match with the county professionals resulted in defeat by 4½ matches to 7½.

Peter Adams, after the previous year's experience, decided on a new "hands off" approach, seeing the team tee off in the foursomes and then leaving the course to inspect the local architecture, returning in time for lunch. This seemed to have been an inspired decision because things improved for the first team when they beat Gloucestershire 8-7 at Brickhampton Court and the second team also won at The Vale. Three weeks later Gwent were comprehensively beaten at The Rolls of Monmouth. These were promising signs for the league matches, which began in June.

Nottinghamshire travelled to Moseley, with future Walker Cup player Oliver Wilson in their team, but lost 8½-6½. Their second team did better at Rushcliffe, winning by a large margin.

The first team then entertained Staffordshire at Blackwell, inflicting a loss on the visitors 9-6. Shropshire were well beaten at Shifnal but we could only manage a halved match with Derbyshire. The final match, in October, was for the title. Warwickshire came to Gay Hill, a course they rarely enjoy, and duly lost 10-5. Worcestershire were league champions!

The second team unfortunately took the wooden spoon in their league, irregular availabilities not assisting selection.

The county amateur championship produced a surprise winner, David Glover of Droitwich. David had played for the second team a few years previously but declined the invitation to play in the six-man team in the Midland qualifier. The youths' champion was Chris Heeley of Moseley and Matthew Houghton won the G.D. Carr Cup. Moseley won the Tomson-James Cup while Worcester took the Jubilee Shield. Matthew also won the match play championship, beating Jon Hems 3 and 2 in the final at Blackwell.

"The Six" was held at Cavendish Golf Club, Buxton, and was won by Staffordshire, eight strokes ahead of Cambridgeshire and thirty-two ahead of Worcestershire in sixth place. Mike Reynard tied for the best individual score on 137, but lost on a count-back over the last nine holes.

Peter Adams with the Midlands League Trophy

As a prelude to the county Open a Pro-Am was held at The Worcestershire on 2nd September, the winning team coming from Fulford Heath. David Down, the club's professional, had the best score in this event and was assisted in the team competition by Robert Sharp, Martin Wilkinson and Colin Hales. Unfortunately he could not repeat this form the next day and slipped to twenty-fourth place, David Eddiford pipping Spencer Edwards for first place on a count-back on 140, while Jon Hems was leading amateur on 141, again winning on a count-back from club-mate Matthew Feavyour, whose consolation was the Secretaries Bowl. Matthew also shared the President's Shield with Paul Scarrett.

Fulford Heath also featured prominently in other county events, winning the Brand Hall Gold Vase and retaining the Boulton Salver, the latter through the efforts of Vic Pailing and Anthony Hill, who had also won the Chandler Shield – again.

The newly formed seniors team under Norman Bolton played Leicestershire at Park Hill in a fourball match and won handsomely. Norman had a very experienced team to call upon and they responded with enthusiasm. They also played, and beat, the boys' team but lost to Warwickshire at Nuneaton. The county had taken over representative matches from the Senior Golfers Society and fixtures were arranged with our neighbouring counties for the following year.

In 1999 the county amateur championship was held at Redditch, by now recognised as one of the most demanding of the county's courses. After a first round of 76 Paul Scarrett was lying behind seven other players but in the afternoon he was one of two players to return a score of 70 and so beat Jon Rose by two strokes. The other 70 was the result of an amazing round by a sixteen year old from Kidderminster, which placed him joint seventh and earned him the youths' championship and the G.D. Carr Cup. Richard Wassell had not done well in the boys' championship earlier in the year but his subsequent performances earned him and his club great credit. His performance in the team championship helped Kidderminster win the

Jubilee Shield, while Moseley and Kings Norton tied for the Tomson-James Cup, the former club earning the right to represent Worcestershire in the EGU Champion Club competition after a nine hole count-back.

The new captain, Craig Pates, had tied with Richard Wassell in the championship and had no hesitation in picking him for the first team match against Derbyshire. Although he lost his foursomes, Richard earned a valuable point in his singles match. He was less successful a month later against Staffordshire, despite winning his foursomes, partnered again by friend and club-mate Nathan Bennett. The season had not begun very promisingly with a loss against Gloucestershire but there were more encouraging signs a week later when Gwent were beaten at Gay Hill. The first three league matches were all victories, which put Worcestershire in a good position to win the league. However, a lacklustre performance at Coventry Hearsall presented the match to Warwickshire 10½-4½. We still had a chance to repeat the previous year's success but Nottinghamshire were not to be denied and administered a stern beating at Sherwood Forest by the same margin inflicted upon us by Warwickshire. Matthew Feavyour won the President's Shield, a quarter of a point ahead of Matthew Houghton.

The second team managed a half with Gloucestershire but were savagely routed by Gwent at Newport. A further defeat at the hands of Derbyshire was also a dispiriting experience. They recovered with a much better performance against Staffordshire, who were also giving their younger players experience, Worcestershire winning 11-7. The other win was against Warwickshire at Evesham. Richard Turner, a left-hander from Moseley, won the Chandler Shield, also by the margin of a quarter of a point, from Rob Tickell. Richard Wassell was not far behind, with three points from only two appearances.

The seniors lost to Staffordshire and to the county boys, but beat Warwickshire fairly comfortably.

Although Mark Butler was the leading professional with Ian Clark in the Open Pro-Am at Moseley, his Dudley team could only finish third to Spencer Edwards' Bromsgrove team and the Moseley team led by Gary Edge. Spencer was in better form the next day, scoring 69 in his second round to return a total of 141. This placed him in a tie with leading amateur Charles Smith, past captain of both county and the host club. He had finished nearly two hours before Edwards and his loyal supporters had been encouraging premature celebrations. As a result the three hole play-off was something of a shock. The tenth, eleventh and eighteenth holes were used. Charlie managed to halve the tenth, scrambled another half on the par 3 eleventh but then hit his drive to the wrong side of the trees on the right of the eighteenth. His escape attempt hit a tree and a par was good enough for Edwards to take the Guy

Bigwood Cup. Mike Reynard was third and Gary Edge the second professional in fourth place. Mike had opened with 68 but slipped to a 74 on his own course.

Richard Wassell was prominent in Kidderminster's performance in the Brand Hall Gold Vase, which they won by one stroke from Little Lakes. This joined the Droitwich Shield in the club's trophy cabinet. Fulford Heath's 'C' team of D. Cashmore and P. White took the Boulton Salver.

Richard Sadler ended his amateur career by winning the match play championship at Stourbridge, Matthew Houghton, Anthony Otway and Paul Scarrett falling to him before the final in which he despatched Clayton Harris by 5 and 3. Clayton had eliminated Richard Wassell, Jon Hems and Simon Deakin in his matches. He turned professional a year later.

Golfers throughout the county and beyond its boundaries were saddened towards the end of the year when John Fraser passed away. He had been associated with the county for well over sixty years. He had a formidable record at his club, The Worcestershire, to whom he presented his impressive collection of trophies. As president he attended as many matches as was humanly possible and the boys' team in particular benefited from his wise and friendly encouragement. His funeral at St Andrews church, close to the common where John first hit a golf ball, was attended by a mighty gathering who were played in and out of the church by a piper.

Whether the year 2000 is regarded as the beginning of a new millennium or the end of an old one is immaterial; for the Worcestershire Union it presented some remarkable achievements.

Roy Hobbis marked his fifty year association with the county by his election as president at the March council meeting. He also found a new lease of life when he joined the British Golf Collectors Society and played in a number of matches with his hickory shafted clubs, demonstrating that a classic swing will obtain the best results from any type of golf club. He was not the only long-serving player to be honoured.

One of the county's greatest players, the country's oldest surviving Walker Cup player and a member of the all-conquering county team of the 1930s, Eric Fiddian was given Honorary Life Membership of the Union. Despite his exemplary playing record Eric modestly never sought high office, steadfastly refusing the county presidency and would only speak of his golfing achievements when really pressed. Had it not been for an injury incurred while about his family's business who knows what further feats he might have performed? Two years later a similar honour was conferred on Brenda Smith in recognition of her long and devoted service.

Matthew Houghton became the first Worcestershire player to record one hundred first team appearances. His junior club-mate and protégé Richard

Wassell, who had sprung to attention the previous year, fulfilled his potential by taking all the trophies on offer at the county amateur championship. This was held at his home club, Kidderminster, and Richard's score of 146 was good enough for the gold medal, the youths' championship, the Philip Padmore Trophy and with the previous day's 73 in the team championship, the G.D. Carr Cup. As he later finished second amateur in the county Open he also won the Secretaries Bowl.

Other Kidderminster players to perform well in these events were Nathan Bennett, who won the silver medal in the amateur championship, and assistant professional Neil Turley, who won the Guy Bigwood Cup for the county Open title, Clayton Harris being the leading amateur.

Richard and Matthew were both selected for "The Six" at Brocton Hall, joined by Mike Reynard, Paul Scarrett, Craig Moss and Matthew Feavyour. Worcestershire finished fifth. This was also the position they occupied in the Midland league, due to "goal average" – three teams each earned four points but Worcestershire's match points were fewer than Nottinghamshire's and Derbyshire's. Staffordshire were first and Warwickshire second, one of their defeats being inflicted by Worcestershire. Paul Scarrett won the President's Shield with the excellent record of six points out of a possible seven-and-a-half, including five singles wins. Similar reckoning settled the second team league, except that we were placed sixth despite winning two matches as opposed to one by fifth-placed Staffordshire. Anthony Hill, the captain, won the Chandler Shield for the fourth time.

The Tomson-James Cup was won by Blackwell, Alan Robinson, Tim Bostock and Paul Scarrett combining well to score 225; King Norton won the Jubilee Shield, the boys' captain, Richard Davies returning their best score, 74. Bostock and Robinson were also runners-up for the Boulton Salver, losing a count-back to R. Howarth and P. Walters of Fulford Heath. Richard Davies reached the final of the match play championship but was beaten by Michael Wood of Wharton Park.

The Brand Hall Gold Vase was held at Gay Hill and the home club finished six strokes better than Kings Norton, Peter Adams playing his part in his club's victory.

Seniors golf took a further step forward with the inaugural seniors' foursomes which was held at Worcester and won by two home players, Ken Murton and John Richardson, with a score of 71. The nett winners were also from the host club, David Evans and D. Tipper. John Wharrad had presented tankards for the winners and the Worcestershire Senior Golfers Society presented salvers for the nett prizes.

Norman Bolton's seniors' team had a good season, winning four matches but only halving with Shropshire and Herefordshire. Despite this fine record they finished tenth in the MGU seniors' county championship, but only nineteen strokes behind the winners.

The year ended sadly with the death in November of Dick Mirams, a staunch supporter of the Union for over fifty years. He made his county debut for the second team in 1947, became captain of that team, and later the first team, and eventually president of the Union and the first to wear the green dinner jacket at county dinners. He wrote the centenary history of Moseley and the preliminary drafts of this history. Dick had also been a cricketer of some ability. By profession a solicitor, he was a quiet, meticulous character who set and expected the highest standards from all who worked and played with him. Right up to the end of his life he and his wife Marjorie made the effort to attend county matches, a fact much appreciated by the players.

Paul Scarrett took over the first team captaincy in 2001 from Craig Pates at the start of the new year and Brian Bishop succeeded Norman Bolton as seniors' captain. Paul also accepted a second responsibility when he agreed to set up and run the county's website, which, it was hoped, would increase awareness of the Union's activities among its affiliated members.

Paul's first season in charge brought an improvement in results, the first team winning three of its league games to finish in third place, losing second place to Warwickshire on goal average – again. He introduced new blood into the team, Matthew Pates keeping his family in the picture with two singles wins in the final games. Lee Richardson won the President's Shield despite missing one league match. This improvement was not reflected in "The Six" at Hollinwell where we finished in last place.

The second team suffered badly from availabilities, no fewer than twenty-four players representing the county, and they failed to win a single match despite Anthony Hill's sterling performance in retaining the Chandler Shield. The result was particularly sad because the season had opened with a good win against Leicestershire, although the next friendly match against Gloucestershire resulted in a narrow defeat.

The county amateur championship was played at Stourbridge and Mike Reynard, suffering from a cold, returned the excellent score of 135. As he was playing off a plus 2 handicap, he did not win the Philip Padmore nett trophy, which went to Andrew Terry of Droitwich, but Mike's 70 in the team championship assured him of the G.D. Carr Cup. Matthew Feavyour was the youths' champion, lying third in the main event. Kidderminster and Blackwell tied for the Tomson-James Cup, the count-back putting Blackwell in the national club finals. The winning score was 213, Blackwell's being accumulated by Tim Bostock 71, Alan Robinson 73 and Paul Scarrett 69, while Kidderminster were represented by Richard Wassell 69, Nathan

Bennett 73 and Matthew Houghton 71. Later in the season Wassell won the match play championship at Evesham, beating Alan Sykes of Cleobury Mortimer 3 and 2 in the final.

Moseley won the Jubilee Shield thanks to the efforts of Steven Rooney 72, John Maginnis 79 and Barry Bates 75. Barry had been professional at Moseley thirty years previously before moving to Brand Hall and then successfully applying for re-instatement as an amateur.

Evesham won the Droitwich Shield, defeating Gay Hill "A" at Stourbridge. Droitwich's 'C' team of Gavin Bourne and Ian Milroy won the Boulton Salver at Fulford Heath, the club which had made a habit of winning this trophy. Instead they took the Brand Hall Gold Vase at Halesowen, beating the home club by one stroke. Neil Turley, now playing out of Redditch, retained the Guy Bigwood Cup in the Open at Droitwich with a score of 137. Richard Wassell was the leading amateur in second place with two scores of 69 which put Mike Reynard in third place after following a first round 67 with 71. This was good enough for him to take the Secretaries Bowl, however.

The seniors' team lost narrowly to Shropshire and Herefordshire after halving the foursomes, inflicted a heavy defeat on Warwickshire and lost very heavily to the boys' team. The seniors' championship was won by Alan Guest of Gay Hill, P. Evans of North Worcestershire taking the Denis Hayes Salver for the best nett score. The team finished seventh in the seniors "Six", only seven strokes behind the winners, Northamptonshire.

At the council meeting in November Brenda Smith announced her retirement as county treasurer. In appreciation of her fifty years of loyal and super-efficient service to the Union, Brenda was made an Honorary Life Member, an honour she shares with Eric Fiddian. She agreed to continue to help with the membership scheme events so was still on the county scene in 2004. Chris Gupwell, a chartered accountant and member of Droitwich, accepted the responsibility of administering the county's funds.

Paul Scarrett was hoping for better things from his young team members for the new 2002 season, which started well with a convincing win over Leicestershire and Rutland at Luffenham Heath. Unfortunately the new president, Norman Bolton, was caught by a maliciously placed speed camera on his way to the match and blamed the author for distracting him. This was not the only bad news because Craig Moss decided he wanted to turn professional soon after the match. This was balanced, fortunately, by the decision of Joe Ferguson to switch his allegiance from Shropshire and Herefordshire to Worcestershire. By the end of the season he had won the President's Shield.

The second team's match with the same opponents also had its lighter moments. The visitors arrived a player short and Steve Brookbanks, a capable

11 handicapper from Fulford Heath and father of Matthew, who was playing for us, agreed to play for them in the foursomes. The result was a home win. The only other second team win was against Gwent who were crushed at The Vale. The remaining results were disappointing to say the least despite captain Graham Wallace's efforts to put a brave and cheerful face on things. He led by example and rightly earned the Chandler Shield. Once again availabilities were erratic but they did result in a new county record. Graham was a player short against Warwickshire but Roy Hobbis was in attendance as past president. He just happened to have his clubs in the car and so achieved the distinction of representing Worcestershire in seven decades. Another possible record was the number of players Graham had to call upon – thirty-two – eight more than Anthony Hill the previous season.

Anthony Hill's efforts with the second team over the preceding seasons earned him a place in the first team and he rose to the challenge, scoring the best points average over all the matches. He and Michael Wood scored the only foursomes point against Gloucestershire in the second friendly match, which was a heavy defeat. Somehow Paul's pairings in the foursomes were not working: in the next match against Gwent, played with eight men a side, we were 4-0 down at lunchtime. Only three points accrued from the singles in a disappointing performance.

The first league match, against Warwickshire at Moseley, showed signs of improvement; the pairings gelled and we took the foursomes 4-1. After lunch it was a different story, Warwickshire fighting back so fiercely they won seven of the singles. Only Joe Ferguson, Matt Houghton and Anthony Hill contributing points. After this match Richard Wassell decided to turn professional and was taken on by Nick Underwood at his home club.

Nottinghamshire came to Blackwell in July and led by a point at lunchtime. The singles were halved, so the foursomes settled the match in the visitors' favour. A win was finally recorded against Derbyshire at Burton-on-Trent after the foursomes had been shared. Then the foursomes hoodoo struck again against Staffordshire, who took all five matches. A rally in the afternoon enabled us to win five singles and halve two more but it was not enough. The final match against Shropshire and Herefordshire produced an improved foursomes showing and a halfway lead of two points. We managed to hold on to our lead in the afternoon to win 9-6.

The team which eventually played in "The Six" was very different from the original selection and from previous years; Richard Wassell, Lee Richardson, Joe Ferguson, Aubrey Pearson, Paul Garey and Simon Braithwaite, the new county amateur champion. It was Worcestershire's turn to hold the event and Kings Norton was the chosen venue. A disappointing sixth place was an improvement on the previous year's performance.

As well as the gold medal for the amateur championship, which was held at Blackwell, Simon Braithwaite, now re-instated as an amateur, won the G.D. Carr Cup and the Philip Padmore Trophy, scoring 70 in each of his rounds. Richard Wassell won the silver medal and the youths' championship, while Mike Reynard took the bronze medal after a countback from Lee Richardson.

Kings Norton won the Tomson-James Cup thanks to Matthew Feavyour 71, Paul Garey 73 and Bill Thompson 80. The Redditch trio of Willie Kerr 74, Chris Bromley 76 and Julian Bates 80 won the Jubilee Shield.

The fifty-fourth Worcestershire Open was played at The Vale on 12th September. A tie between two players on 146 was resolved by a three hole play-off between Richard Wassell and Anthony Hill, Richard taking the Guy Bigwood Cup and thereby demonstrating that his decision to play for pay had not been a rash one. Anthony Hill took the gold medal and Lee Richardson was the second amateur, fifth equal with three professionals. Two other professionals, Mark Butler, now at Sandwell Pines driving range, and Martin Payne of Cleobury Mortimer tied for third place. Simon Braithwaite, placed as twelfth amateur, took the Secretaries Bowl. The third amateur was Matthew Houghton on 149, tying with Mike Reynard but placed ahead of him by virtue of a better second round. Danny Clee of Wharton Park was on the same score, having benefited from Matt's encouragement as a junior at Kidderminster.

Michael Wood of Wharton Park gained entry to the match play championship because of a number of withdrawals and met Michael Daw of Warley Woods, who had only just qualified, in the final at Halesowen. Wood managed to win 3 and 2. His club was less successful in the Droitwich Shield, losing to Cleobury Mortimer in the final. The Redditch team of N.Hanks and A. Brown won the Boulton Salver at Droitwich, while the team from Gay Hill took the Brand Hall Gold Vase, which was played at Kidderminster.

There was a three-man play-off for the seniors' championship when David Evans, Worcester, Charles Harrison, Droitwich, and John Wharrad, Kings Norton, tied on 77, David winning the play-off. Ken Palfrey of Gay Hill had a nett 69 to take the Denis Hayes Salver. This was the first year of another seniors' competition, the match play championship, which was won by Ken Murton who beat Stan Hickin 2 and 1 at The Worcestershire. The seniors' foursomes championship was won by Len Gore and Alan Guest of Gay Hill, with 75 gross, 70 nett. R. Webb and J. Richardson of Worcester also had a nett 70, 77 gross.

The seniors' team came fourth in the "Seniors' Six", seven strokes behind Derbyshire. They showed Leicestershire no mercy in the match at Kings Norton in April, just managed to beat Nottinghamshire at Chilwell Manor, trounced Shropshire and Herefordshire at Sapey, lost by the odd match to

Matthew Houghton

Warwickshire at Robin Hood, beat Gloucestershire convincingly at Fulford Heath and experienced their heaviest defeat, by just two points, against Staffordshire. The boys' team let them off more lightly than the previous year with an honourable half, a number of youngsters gaining a valuable "blooding" in what was a very friendly but nonetheless hard-fought match.

The March council meeting in 2003 was held in The Worcestershire's new clubhouse. The lovely old farm building had been demolished as it was no longer considered safe; renovation would have been too costly and in any case it was felt that larger premises were required.

Matthew Houghton was elected captain and reminded the meeting of his formative years in the boys' team, which was organised by Norman Bolton at the time. As Norman was now the county president, Matthew reminded him of the incentive scheme whereby each boy put a pound in the kitty and the player who won his match by the highest margin took the spoils. Matthew was the first to benefit from the scheme and dutifully handed Norman his pound as his manager's ten per cent.

Matthew's first selections blended youth and experience but did not quite succeed, a narrow loss against Leicestershire and Rutland being followed by a heavier defeat administered by Gloucestershire. The league programme began with a disappointing result against Warwickshire but improved with a gripping match at Hollinwell against Nottinghamshire. The home team took the foursomes 4-1 then Worcestershire fought back, led by Joe Ferguson, and overturned the morning's deficit to win the singles 7-3 and the match by one point, Chris Heeley winning his match by 6 and 5. This was our last taste of success and the half point advantage Warwickshire held on goal average relegated Worcestershire to sixth place. Anthony Hill confirmed his right to represent the first team by winning the President's Shield, pipping Michael Wood by a quarter of a point.

Despite having to call on twenty-six players Graham Wallace's second team fared better and by September had a chance of winning their league, having beaten Nottinghamshire in July and Shropshire and Herefordshire in August, although we had lost to Warwickshire in the opening match. Four counties had a chance to claim the title at this stage and Derbyshire came to Stourbridge for an absorbing contest. The foursomes were halved then the visitors claimed four points from the first five singles. Chris Bromley earned a valuable point then the game swung further in Derbyshire's favour leaving Worcestershire needing four wins from the last four games. We won three of them and so the match was tied. Richard Gurney, aged fifteen, won his first match at senior level to ensure the tie, playing with considerable maturity. He had earlier won the boys' championship after a play-off with Matthew Pates, and the St Andrews boys' championship.

As Nottinghamshire had beaten Warwickshire on the same day the final round of matches in October would decide the final positions. We travelled to Enville and led by one point after the foursomes but sadly lost momentum and the match in the singles, consigning us to third place. This time the goal average worked in our favour and Derbyshire were placed fourth. The ever-reliable Chris Bromley won the Chandler Shield. He had qualified as a greenkeeper at Duchy College in Cornwall and was now assistant head greenkeeper at his home club, Redditch. Another greenkeeper, Graham Wallace, the captain, was second. He had moved to Puckrup Hall as course manager and joined Ombersley to retain his Worcestershire eligibility.

As the county ladies were celebrating their centenary during the year a match was arranged at The Worcestershire which included members of both junior teams. Male honour was preserved with a win by four matches to two.

The county amateur championship returned to Moseley and was won by a home club member, seventeen year old Adam Norman, son of Chris, with a score of 143. When it was discovered that the runner-up also belonged to a Warwickshire club and had played in that county's championship, Thomas Hollis, another young player, was promoted to second place. The Tomson-James Cup produced another tie, between Moseley and Blackwell, the former club earning the right to represent the county in the national club championship as a result of the count-back. Droitwich captured the Jubilee Shield.

The G.D. Carr Cup was won by Paul Scarrett, his 70 in the team event giving him a one stroke advantage over Norman and Hollis. Ian Milroy of Droitwich won the Philip Padmore trophy. Paul missed the county Open at Worcester, which was won by Mark Butler, with Jon Jones of Cleobury Mortimer second. Joe Ferguson was the leading amateur in third place, relegating Thomas Hollis to fourth on a count-back, but losing the Secretaries Bowl to Thomas by the odd stroke. Four professionals tied for fourth on 143, one stroke ahead of Richard Wassell.

Bromsgrove had an excellent season in the other county events; the club's "A" team, J. Barratt and S. Winters, won the Boulton Salver at Redditch and Barratt was joined by P. Williams, M. Dale, C. Fox and I. Barber in the team which won the Brand Hall Gold Vase at Worcester. Droitwich "A" beat Kidderminster "A" in the Droitwich Shield, which was played at Blackwell.

Tony Jowle crowned a memorable season by winning the seniors' championship at Kidderminster. By dint of regular practice he had won a number of competitions during the season but was especially happy to take the Neville Carroll Salver on this occasion. Willie Kerr of Redditch was runner-up and home player Alan Stanyer won the Denis Hayes Salver for the best nett score. Ken Murton retained the seniors' match play championship, beating Norman Bolton in the final. Ken also won the John Wharrad Claret Jugs with John Richardson in the foursomes championship, the Aberdovey Salvers for the best nett score going to Gordon Bailey of Worcester and Moseley's Alan Pugh.

In team events the seniors had a mixed season, coming ninth in the seniors "six", which was disappointing after the previous years' placings. Leicestershire were beaten in a close match, Nottinghamshire were annihilated, winning only one greensomes match. Our team beat Shropshire and Herefordshire, lost to Warwickshire in a close game and went down heavily to both Gloucestershire and Staffordshire. Incoming captain Len Gore arranged the match with the boys' team at Gay Hill, which the juniors won 4-1. It was agreed to move this fixture to the beginning of the season to allow both teams to prepare for the next season's competitive golf. This was duly arranged and the boys won a resounding victory.

The 2004 season began with the sad loss of Ray Baldwin, the epitome of Midland golf. His life was celebrated in a memorial gathering at Kings Norton and attended by friends and golfing colleagues from far and wide. Ray had tendered his resignation as secretary of the Midland Golf Union only days before his death. His various duties were then shared out among administrators from the Midland counties.

After a disappointing start to the season, in which the opening friendly matches were lost by narrow margins, Matt Houghton's team performed splendidly in "The Six" at Woodhall Spa, finishing joint third, a great improvement on the previous year.

In June the first county newsletter was launched with the aim of making club members more aware of county events and personalities. The president, Brian Peplow, provided an introduction and a summary of the early season's activities filled the four sides, with enough photographs to catch the eye.

There was a tie for the amateur championship between Joe Ferguson and James Toman, now re-instated as an amateur. This was not resolved until some time later because of Joe's commitments on the amateur circuit, James prevailing in a tense play-off.

The first league match against Nottinghamshire at Blackwell resulted in defeat, three points separating the teams. A slight improvement brought a loss by one point against Shropshire and Herefordshire at Worfield, a score we reversed against Derbyshire at Stourbridge. We then despatched Staffordshire comfortably at Trentham, putting Worcestershire in a much more favourable position in the Midland league. This came to a climax at Kidderminster against Warwickshire who suffered their only defeat of the season. This placed them top of the table but moved Worcestershire up into second place, a fitting result after Matt Houghton's efforts to blend experience with youth; Luke Rogers and Steven Clark from the home club recorded wins, while Matthew Pates inflicted a defeat by 8 and 6 on his opponent. The team assisted the new champions in their champagne celebrations.

Robert Coe was cruelly let down by late cry-offs and irregular availabilities and the second team finished last in their league, winning only one match, rather gloriously, when they beat Staffordshire 12½-5½ at Moseley.

Ken Murton was the seniors' champion at North Worcestershire and accepted the invitation to captain the seniors in the centenary year. Willie Kerr of Redditch was the runner-up, P.D. Kelley, now at Evesham, taking the Denis Hayes Salver for the best nett score. The seniors won all their matches to the delight of Len Gore who had a very experienced pool of players to call upon.

Mark Butler won the county Open on a day dominated by the professionals, the leading amateur in joint second place being Anthony Hill. The match play champion was Chris Bromley, who was taken to the fifth extra hole by Paul Scarrett. Droitwich used their home advantage to capture the Brand Hall Gold Vase one stroke ahead of Fulford Heath, and Kris Stanton and Richard Gurney combined well to take the Boulton Salver back to Kings Norton. Richard had made his first team debut during the season at the age of sixteen and produced some sterling performances, which pleased Matt Houghton who placed great faith in Richard's ability.

It was agreed that Matt continue for a third term as centenary captain. He had emphasised to his players the importance of competing in the major amateur events, in which he was a regular entrant. As well as the Brabazon and Lytham Trophies Matt entered the Open Qualifying events and in 1992 reached the final qualifying stage at North Berwick. On the relevant page of the starting sheet his name appears with that of John Bickerton amongst such company as Howard Clark, Philip Price, Jesper Parnevik, Phil Mickelson, Ben Crenshaw and Jeff Maggert.

Chapter Ten

Juniors Golf

FIFTY YEARS ago the county teams chiefly comprised veteran golfers drawing near to the close of distinguished careers in the game. It was realised that younger golfers needed to be encouraged and helped as much as possible. Dick Mirams formed a sub-committee which arranged coaching for promising junior players, some earning selection for the county second team.

It was further recognised that these boys needed more opportunities to play competitive golf against their peers and to that end Harley Roberts suggested a Midland Boys Championship.

With the support of Guy Bigwood, Dick Mirams and the Blackwell club, he then obtained sponsorship from the *Birmingham Post and Mail*, who presented the trophy which was first played for in 1950. The newspaper also printed the posters and entry forms and donated golf balls for prizes. Later this support came in the form of financial assistance.

Originally the tournament was organised and run by Worcestershire but with the formation of the Midland Golf Union that body took over the administration in 1986. However, as Ray Baldwin was the secretary of the MGU, he and Brenda Smith continued to deal with the entries. Gloucestershire had been placed in the south-west region, so that county's boys were no longer eligible to enter but Cambridgeshire and Lincolnshire were admitted to the Midland region.

The competition was held at Blackwell each year until 1987 when Longcliffe hosted it, the plan being to alternate between the two clubs. This enabled boys in the eastern section to enjoy shorter journeys to the venue. However, Blackwell was unable to stage the tournament in 1993 and it was held at Olton. Since then it has moved around the Midland counties.

The first winner was John Brockway of Kidderminster and other Worcestershire boys have been successful, particularly in the early years of the competition. Michael Lunt won in 1952, but at the time he was a member of Edgbaston. To further encourage the leading players each year a match was arranged between a team comprising them and the county team, the boys being given a two holes up start.

Ian Wheater was the runner-up in 1954 and third the following year, when Tony Jowle finished fifth, having entered from Sandwell Park. The *Birmingham Post* sent Dick Wheildon along to report on the day's play. He was critical of the boys driving with their spoons (3-woods) rather than their drivers but was generally full of praise for the standard of play.

The next winner from a Worcestershire club was David Lait of Gay Hill in 1958 and he won again two years later, by which time he was also a member of Moseley, having been the runner-up in the intervening year. Andrew Thomson came fourth in 1958 and third in 1960. The first back-to-back winner was John Preston of Halesowen and Stourbridge in 1962-63. Sadly, John died young and his parents presented the John Preston Memorial Cup, which was first awarded in 1973 for the best score by a player under the age of sixteen on the day of the competition.

Since then Worcestershire has had just four winners: Andrew Forrester from Brand Hall and Harborne in 1964, Stephen Carpenter (also Brand Hall) in 1967, Nigel Powell of Kings Norton in 1979 and Darren Prosser of Dudley and Moseley in 1985.

As the standard of junior golf improved the handicap limit was reduced and the quality of entries is reflected in the roll of honour, many players going on to be successful competitors on the professional circuit, in amateur internationals and in the Open Championship, golf's greatest tournament, for Sandy Lyle won the Midland Boys twice, in 1972 and 1975. Others who have enjoyed distinction in the game are Paul Downes, 1976, Andrew Sherborne, 1978, David Gilford, 1981, Jim Payne, 1986 and Steve Webster, 1993.

In 2002 Bradley Brooke of Redditch tied for first place but was placed runner-up on a count-back, there being no play-offs in MGU events.

In 1957 schoolboys under the age of eighteen were allowed to enter county competitions but were not allowed to win sweep money.

The county boys' championship was instituted in 1958, R.A. Biggs of Worcester being the first winner of the John Mansell Memorial Cup for the best gross score. Dick Mirams and his wife Marjorie presented a salver for the team returning the best three scratch scores. The Donald Rigbey Cup for the best nett score was claimed by Andrew Thomson. There are now age group prizes and the most recent innovation is a nett team event, the prize for which is entry to a competition at Woodhall Spa, headquarters of the English Golf Union. The county champion club tournament for juniors was first played in 2002 and Worcestershire was represented by Redditch Golf Club. Their boys led after the first round but finished a very creditable second after thirty-six holes on the Bracken course.

Courtesy: J. Moreton

John Fraser (president) and Richard Davies (Kings Norton), boys' match play champion, 1997

When John Fraser was president he inherited a considerable sum and graciously donated a cup and ten replicas for a boys' match play knockout competition. The first sixteen gross scores are put into an automatic draw for a two-day event. The first competition for the John Fraser Cup was held at John's club, The Worcestershire, in 1998 and was won by Craig Moss of The Vale, who received the trophy from its donor.

The boys' teams played friendly matches against neighbouring counties and in 1965 Ray Baldwin and Jack Richards of Warwickshire presented the Baldwin-Richards Shield for the Midland Boys Four Counties event, the other counties being Gloucestershire, Staffordshire and Warwickshire. Our team has had mixed success in this event, which is hosted in turn by each county.

A similar event was launched in 1972 by Bill Cunningham, then our junior organiser, and Albert Evans, the Welsh international and Walker Cup selector. The Severnside Tournament was originally contested by Worcestershire, Glamorgan, Gloucestershire and Monmouthshire, which subsequently became Gwent. Originally the counties took turns to stage the tournament but since 1979 it has been held at the splendid Ross-on-Wye Golf Club. Worcestershire did not manage to win this until 1994, by which time John Moreton was the junior organiser. He immediately informed Bill of the victory to the latter's immense delight. Sadly Bill died a few months later, so

Winning Severnside Team, 1996

it was fitting that his county won the shield in his lifetime. Further successes came in 1996 and 2002, this last time by the odd half point.

Similarly to the Four Counties event several players have embarked upon distinguished amateur and professional careers, including Bradley Dredge and Philip Price of Wales. David J. Russell and John Bickerton also played in the tournament for our team.

John was also a member of the team which recorded Worcestershire's most momentous achievement in junior golf.

In 1986 the English Golf Union instituted the Juniors Team Championship. The four regions hold qualifying tournaments for their constituent counties, the winner of each region progressing to the national final. Each team comprises six players and originally the best four scores in each of the two rounds counted. In 1999 this was changed to the best five rounds for Midland qualifying. It was felt that if the Midland counties were to compete against the likes of Yorkshire, Lancashire or Surrey who all have infinitely more clubs from which to select their teams, the very best team had to represent the Midlands.

Jim Gray and John Scott took the six lads to Sleaford in Lincolnshire for the inaugural qualifying event. They were Darren Prosser, Spencer Edwards, Glen Lowe, Jonathon Reid, Stuart Band and Craig Clarke. Darren Prosser led the way with rounds of 76 and 71 and the team score of 623

Courtesy: J. Moreton

John Fraser, John Moreton and winners of the Under 15 Championship, Tolladine, 1994

beat Lincolnshire by one stroke, Craig Clarke chipping in for a birdie at the eighteenth hole. This put Worcestershire into the final at Sandy Lodge, Hertfordshire.

As a reserve was permitted in the final the team of seven was augmented by John Bickerton and Neil Swaffield, replacing Stuart Band. Jonathon Reid was the reserve.

Jim and John wrote a short report on each match. On the first day we were drawn against Gloucestershire, to whom we had lost in the Severnside Tournament. The inclusion of John Bickerton was the factor which persuaded Jim that we could beat them. However, the result was a halved match after Worcestershire had won the foursomes 2-1.

The next day we met Sussex, the favourites with two internationals in their team. The foursomes were halved, then our boys made a supreme effort and won 6-3.

The final match was against the northern qualifiers, Durham, who had lost to Gloucester. A win was essential and it duly materialised by a resounding eight matches to one. Worcestershire were the first English Boys Champions!

Since then we have had mixed results, one or two disasters being matched by some sterling performances which put us in second or third place, one or two strokes behind the winners.

Courtesy: J. Moreton

Matthew Brookbanks (Fulford Heath), Cunningham Trophy winner 2003, with president Norman Bolton and Moseley president Hilary Rice

As an example of the improvement in boys' golf in the intervening years, when it was Lincolnshire's turn to hold the qualifier eleven years later in 1996, Worcestershire's score was seven strokes better at Sleaford than in 1986 but we could only finish fourth. This was despite staying at the same accommodation as Jim's team on the previous visit, an omen that did not fulfil itself.

The Midland Boys league was formed in 1990 with east and west divisions, the winners of each section playing off in a final. Worcestershire played against Warwickshire, with whom we already had played friendly matches, Shropshire and Herefordshire and Staffordshire. Derbyshire was moved from the east to the west division in 2002 to permit Cambridgeshire to join the eastern division.

The foundations laid by Dick Mirams and Bill Cunningham led to a full programme of matches and tournaments for the under eighteens. The older boys, known initially as colts, up to the age of twenty-four, also played friendly matches. In 1992 the age limit was reduced to twenty-one and a league was formed. However, counties were not always able to field full-strength teams for various reasons and selected the youths for their second teams instead, so this league was discontinued in 1998.

When Bill Cunningham died in 1995 his daughter kindly donated his old Gibson putting cleek to the county for use as a trophy. This was

Courtesy: J. Moreton

Luke Rogers (Kidderminster), Fraser Cup winner 2003, with Norman Bolton and Hilary Rice

mounted on a handsome oak board to which are attached shields bearing the name of the boy who gains most points in county boys' matches. It was first presented at the county championship that year to Oliver Darby. At the presentation one older player, who shall be nameless, began to laugh while John Moreton was explaining what the trophy was for and describing Bill's long connection with the county. He later apologised, his excuse being that he was remembering all the fun he and his team mates had had with Bill, probably a more fitting tribute than a serious obituary! Now the sons of Bill's team members are following their fathers into the county team.

Bill Cunningham learnt his golf at Kilmarnock Barassie before the Second World War. He completed his medical education at Glasgow University, where he represented the university at rugby and golf. He also edited the student newspaper, for which he once set a rude limerick competition. His entries were judged first, second and third – he was a medical student, after all. He also wrote more serious poetry as well as humorous verse and the late John Stobbs included one of Bill's poems in his anthology *At Random Through the Green* published in 1966.

During the war he served in the Royal Army Medical Corps, and on being demobbed entered into general practice in Birmingham, where the author became one of his patients. A quick diagnosis of the medical problem was usually followed by a deeper analysis of the patient's golfing ailments.

As the standard of boys' golf continued to improve it became important to foster the talents of the younger players. An under sixteen team was formed and fixtures were arranged. The salver presented by the nine-hole clubs was used as a trophy for an under fifteen championship, which rotates around five clubs, one of which, Little Lakes, now has eighteen holes. One fascinating fixture is a triangular match with Staffordshire and Shropshire and Herefordshire. Foursomes are played in the morning, six boys going to the first tee to the bemusement of any club members present, whose concern is alleviated when only three boys tee off. Singles follow in the afternoon. The Worcestershire boys scored an impressive victory when this event was held at Droitwich in 2002. They also won at Shifnal in 2000.

In 1999 Worcestershire and Shropshire and Herefordshire created another first in junior golf, when the first mixed junior inter-county match was played at Shrewsbury. As the Herefordshire ladies are affiliated to the Worcestershire Ladies Golf Association and the Herefordshire men to Shropshire selection was a delicate matter. The home team emerged victorious but the match was played in a good spirit, as the subsequent encounters have been.

The county boys and girls also meet in the Five Counties Mixed Foursomes Tournament and Worcestershire have been so successful in this event that the teams have often taken all the prizes: best team gross and nett and best individual gross and nett. The most outstanding performance was that of Chris Bromley of Redditch and Nicola Driscoll of Worcester when Derbyshire held the event at Horsley Lodge. As he was leaving home to pick up two of his team-mates, Chris witnessed a road accident which delayed his departure as his statement was required. He arrived five minutes before his tee-off time and the organisers kindly allowed him breathing space by moving his match back. He and Nicola then went round a course they had never seen before in 71 shots, one over the par figure.

The county amateur champion has been a junior on more than one occasion in recent years, Richard Wassell (Kidderminster) taking the gold medal and all the other trophies in 2000, and Adam Norman (Moseley) in 2003. Richard also won the Derek Greey Cup for the match play championship in 2000.

By the turn of the century it was realised that more intensive coaching of the boys was necessary if we were to compete with our neighbours and clubs were invited to send promising boys to an assessment day, where three professionals ran their eyes over the candidates. From these boys three squads were selected, which became the Elite, Premier and Academy squads, the last for the youngest boys. Cameron Clark, boys' captain in 1992, Graham Farr and Kevin Hayward were the original coaches. Graham

Midland League Championship winners, 1998
Back row, left to right: John Hearns (Kings Norton), Scott Law (Gay Hill)
Matthew Feavyour (Kings Norton), Paul Scarrett (Blackwell), Patrick Smith (Kidderminster)
Nathan Bennett (Kidderminster), Richard Flint (Stourbridge)
Front row, left to right: Richard Sadler (Moseley), Alan Robinson (Blackwell), Denis Hayes (president)
Peter Adams (captain), Matthew Houghton (Kidderminster), Alan Sykes (Cleobury Mortimer)

left the county and was replaced by Finlay Clark, brother of Cameron and son of Ian, the Hagley professional. At the end of 2003 Cameron was appointed professional at Moor Hall across the border in Warwickshire and Dan Cummings, Martin Griffin and David Down took his place, each being allocated to a squad.

Thanks to the generosity of the Kings Norton club each squad has four or five all day sessions on the practice ground, the short course and the putting green, with occasional excursions to other courses to improve course management techniques. When the boys graduate to senior golf their places are taken by promotion through the squads and a new intake from assessment days. It was decided at the end of 2003 that stricter parameters were needed in determining who should be invited for assessment as more young golfers were attaining respectable handicaps. Another decision was to continue coaching through the winter, when any necessary changes to technique could be made rather than in the summer when such changes could prevent progress and limit the amount of competitive golf the boys might wish to play.

Chapter Eleven

Chronicle of the Centenary Year

Brian Peplow, Centenary President

It was recognised at the end of 2004 that if the centenary year was to be a memorable one Worcestershire had to put out the strongest teams possible at first and second team level. A team sub-committee was set up to address the problem of selection and communication with the players, who were invited to a meeting at Bromsgrove in January of the New Year. This produced a positive response, which the sub-committee considered very seriously. Matthew Houghton urged his players to enter the major amateur tournaments to help them rise to a higher level in the game, explaining the thrills he had experienced in such events as Open Qualifying and the Brabazon Trophy.

This was a few days after the annual dinner at which 280 diners sat down at Kings Norton.

The Centenary sub-committee had also been busy and Matthew Houghton obtained a Bobby Jones Calamity Jane putter, encased in a fine cabinet, for presentation to the Amateur champion. Ball markers and pitch-mark tools were also ordered as souvenirs for participants in the competitions intended for Club members.

The players then met for a medal at Bewdley Pines on a cold, wet Saturday and enjoyed evenings of "a bucket of balls and chips" at Bromsgrove. When the first friendly matches against Leicestershire and Rutland took place both teams recorded fine wins, ten points to five at Kings Norton by the first team,

Boys versus Gwent at Worcester Golf and Country Club. The first outing of the Boys County Blazers

while the seconds travelled to Market Harborough and improved on the first team performance by half a point.

The spring also brought the reintroduction of the County Card Scheme, to which initially thirteen clubs subscribed, with another eighteen in Warwickshire and forty-three clubs in Gloucestershire participating. At a fee of £12 to the county, club members stood to benefit and club secretaries could rest in the knowledge that visiting golfers using the scheme would be members of established clubs with bona fide handicaps.

Droitwich retained the Kidderminster Cup, the senior knock-out foursomes competition suggested by the eponymous club the previous year.

The second friendly matches of the season were not as successful as the first; both teams lost nine points to six against Gloucestershire, Rob Coe pursuing his youth policy in the second team in which one or two players were found wanting.

The Boys team, however, began the season in great style, beating the assistant professionals for the very first time at Evesham, the traditional venue for this match. As one of the assistants had to leave at lunchtime to report for work, his place was taken by the recently retired Nick Underwood. His one birdie was insufficient to hold the EGU Elite Squad member Richard Prophet, who had five and beat Nick 6 and 4. Four other singles matches

Left to right: Richard Gurney (Kings Norton, England under 21 Squad, third in the Midland Order of Merit), Matt Houghton, Joe Ferguson (County Champion, England Squad, second in the Berkshire)

ended in the boys' favour at the 18th hole, after the morning foursomes had been shared. The boys then donned their new blazers, sponsored by the Allied Irish Bank and Malcolm Jeffs, to whom the county owes its thanks.

A slightly under strength team then played the Gwent Boys at Worcester and managed an honourable tie, three members of the team being under sixteen and securing vital points. The boys returned to Worcester the following day to administer the ritual beating of the County Seniors.

They were less fortunate in the Midland Boys Four Counties Tournament at Moor Hall, losing to Gloucestershire in the first round, Andrew Goodyer and Simon O'Dell of Moseley being the only winners, two other boys halving their matches. Sunday morning brought better things as Staffordshire were beaten five matches to three, but the boys were no match for Warwickshire, the champions, only the captain, Matt Pugh, and Steven Lane, winning their matches. One week later they suffered another defeat against Warwickshire in the Midland Boys League.

A halved match with Herefordshire men followed, Richard Milner from Stourbridge making a spectacular debut, winning both foursomes and singles at Little Lakes.

Strong, swirling winds led to high scoring in both the team and individual championships at The Worcestershire but Joe Ferguson, James Toman and

Winners of the Captain and Guest event
Left: David Nevett. Right: Alex Bishop, captain Droitwich

Left to right: Dan Parry, Brian Peplow (president) and Malcolm O'Dowd (North Worcestershire)

Left: Garmon Ingman. Right: John Fletcher, (Stourbridge)

Brand Hall Gold Vase winners, Kidderminster
Left: Kevin Woodham. Right: Alan Stanyer

The Droitwich Shield winning team from Kidderminster
Left to right: Matt Houghton, County captain
Bob Hunter, Kidderminster president, James Toman
Aubrey Pearson, Joe Ferguson, Luke Rogers
Steven Clarke, Brian Peplow

Kidderminster Cup winning team from Droitwich
Left to right: Professor Sandy McNeish, captain Blackwell Golf Club, Bryn Harrington, Charles Harrison
John Mole, Brian Bishop, David Glover, John Swann

Steven Clark combined well to win the Tomson-James Cup for Kidderminster with a score of 219, Kings Norton's challenge being thwarted by a back injury sustained by their third player. The home Club's B team produced consistent scoring to win the Jubilee Shield, Andy Dunster returning the final card to complement the efforts of Julian Bouchet and Phil Shurmer.

In the individual championship the early pace was set by Anthony Hill of Fulford Heath with a fine 72. However home player, seventeen year old Steven Lane, finished three strokes better than this and Joe Ferguson returned a score of 70. Unfortunately Hill did not score so well in the afternoon and the interest centred on the two young men in contention. Steven continued in his tenacious manner and came in with 74 for a total of 143, which proved only good enough for the silver medal as Ferguson took just 71 strokes in the second round. As well as the gold medal he won the G.D. Carr Cup and the Centenary Trophy. Lane's consolation was the Youths Championship and the Philip Padmore Trophy. After a countback Adam Norman was awarded the bronze medal for his 146.

The following day Perdiswell Park, the Worcester municipal course, welcomed the boys under 16 team for the Club's first county event. The course was well protected by punitive rough, which the boys from the Oxfordshire League negotiated better than the home team, taking the foursomes four points to one. Unfortunately thunder and heavy rain reduced the singles to nine holes, which were completed by only eight players, Worcestershire holding the advantage when play was called off. Perdiswell Park's committee and staff are to be congratulated for their efforts to produce a well set up course, excellent catering and maximum security for the players' property.

A busy week ended with the final of the Droitwich Shield, which was held at Moseley, Kidderminster beating Kings Norton two matches to one in an exciting final, Matt Houghton and Joe Ferguson prevailing in a tense match when the Kings Norton pair found a wet bunker on the 17th and failed to escape.

The first major centenary celebration was the meeting at Kidderminster on 25th May, when the captain of every Worcestershire club and his guest were invited to play a competition in a variety of formats, followed by an excellent dinner. The winners of the team prize were Rob Shaw, Tolladine, Garmon Ingman, Stourbridge and Paul Hannah, Cleobury Mortimer. The Droitwich pairing of David Nevett and Alex Bishop won the club team prize, Garmon Ingman and John Fletcher of Stourbridge were second and Malcom O'Dowd and Dan Parry of North Worcestershire came third after a countback. Mark Atkins of Ombersley took the nett prize while the best gross score was that of David Nevett who returned an excellent 70.

Steven Lane, Boys champion

One week later the boys team travelled to St Neots for their "Six". Despite two good rounds from Steven Lane they finished well down the field, heavy rain in the second round not helping the scoring.

Rain also fell incessantly at Aberdare the following Sunday, 5th June, where the under 16 team played Glamorgan. This was an historic occasion, for it marked the county debut of Matthew Tweddell, grandson of the famous doctor and son of Michael, another past county captain. Although Matthew and his partner lost their foursomes match Matthew secured a fine win by 4 and 3 in his singles. Unfortunately only one other Worcestershire lad managed to come to grips with the course, Jack Honnor of Kings Norton winning 8 and 6. The youngest member of the team, Tom Warbrick of Redditch, struggling with a dead trolley battery, took his opponent all the way to the 18th before succumbing after a truly heroic effort. Two other matches were decided in the opposition's favour on the last green.

On the same day the first team met Shropshire and Herefordshire at Moseley, and began the league programme with a fine win, ten points to five. As the other league matches played that day were both halved, Worcestershire headed the table from the start. The second team travelled to Wormsley and were less fortunate, losing ten points to eight, Rob Coe once again having to find players on Saturday night.

The Boys team also lost to Shropshire and Herefordshire at Wharton Park, the two point advantage the visitors held after the foursomes being their winning margin as the Worcestershire boys played much better in the singles. This meant that both the first two league matches had been lost and when John Moreton received a very disappointing number of cry-offs the prospect looked bleak for the match against Derbyshire at Ashbourne on 19th June. Members of the premier coaching squad jumped at the opportunity to represent their county, however, and thanks to a pairing from the Brand Hall Municipal Club, Dale Peters and Michael Pinnock, the foursomes were won three points to two. On a sultry day on a hilly course our boys proved to have greater stamina and took the singles as well, the decisive point coming from none other than Matthew Tweddell.

The under 16 team was less successful at Lingdale against Leicestershire on 3rd July but the day was successful for the first team who beat Derbyshire handsomely at Chevin to maintain the lead in the Midland League. Rob Coe's problems continued however when an under strength second team was heavily beaten at Halesowen.

Chris Bromley, Redditch Matchplay champion 2004 and 2005, and Silver Medal winner of the Midland Golf Union Order of Merit

Richard Gurney continued to show his great potential when he qualified for the final qualifying stages of the Open Championship, his score at Lundin Links being one stroke too many to earn a place on the first tee of the Old Course. Moseley's professional, Martin Griffin, also reached the same stage and he, too, played at Lundin.

The following weekend was devoted to the Matchplay Championship, Chris Bromley retaining his title after a tense match with Chris Heeley which finished on the 19th green at Kidderminster.

The County Senior foursomes were played at Redditch on 13th July, a home pairing of Willie Kerr and Trevor Welch taking the John Wharrad Claret Jugs, while the Aberdovey Salvers were won by Terry Price and S.B. Waters from The Worcestershire. The seniors then beat Warwickshire fifteen points to three at Redditch continuing a winning vein which had begun in April with a ten points to eight win against Leicestershire. They beat Shropshire and Herefordshire by the same margin, Nottinghamshire by fourteen and a half points to three and a half, and Gloucestershire by nine and a half points to eight and a half. The only loss was against Staffordshire, who won by fifteen points to three, Worcestershire being without three of their best players who were playing for the Midlands against the North.

The Boulton Salver was held at Kings Norton and once again the winners were a home pairing of Paul Clark and M. Burrows, Steven Lane and

Luke Kimberley Under15 champion with Mike Challinor captain Habberley Golf Club

Phil Dance of The Worcestershire coming second.

The Worcestershire was the venue for the Boys Championship on Monday 25th June. The previous day Malvern was inundated by the heaviest rainfall in the country and the greenstaff were out at first light to prepare the course in an heroic attempt to repair damage to bunkers. Early rain cleared up and Steven Lane from the home Club, returned an excellent score of 70 in the first round. He continued steadily in the afternoon but Richard Prophet of Dudley improved on his morning round by scoring a fine 68 to give a total of 143. Steven had continued in his morning form but on the treacherous closing hole drove out of bounds and recorded a 7 for a score of 73 and a tie with Prophet. After consultation a three hole play-off was arranged and this time Lane made no mistakes.

Prophet's consolation was selection for the England under 16 team against Thailand at Shifnal. Sadly the Thais were too strong for the English boys and won resoundingly.

He was not the only Worcestershire player to earn national selection, as Joe Ferguson represented his country in the European Strokeplay Championship.

There was a much bigger Worcestershire entry in the English Amateur Championship. Chris Bromley and Tom Pulling both reached the fourth round.

The first team's progress in the league continued with a win against Staffordshire at Stourbridge by eight and half points to six and a half. The second team played a week later at Stone and Rob Coe was helped out by two fourteen year olds from Fulford Heath, Chris Nugent and Lee Kimberley. Although they played well they were up against considerably more experienced players. They both gained more county experience playing in the Five Counties Junior Mixed Foursomes at Chesterfield. When the result was announced it appeared that Worcestershire had once again achieved the "grand slam" of prizes. However on rechecking the cards the organiser noticed that one Worcestershire pair had signed for a wrong score and disqualified them, demoting the county to second place.

While this was taking place thirteen Worcestershire boys competed for the St Andrews Boys Championship. Seven qualified for the scratch and handicap matchplay rounds, four reaching the quarter finals on the Old Course, Richard Gurney eliminating Matt Pugh in round two. Steven Lane joined him in the scratch event, while Richard Wood and Rudy Hercik played in the handicap section. All four were eliminated after making excellent efforts and scoring well.

Lee Kimberley won the Boys under 15 Championship at Habberley with a score of 72, the club showing great enthusiasm and support for the event. Tom Warbrick of Redditch missed this competition as he was representing the county in the Reid Trophy, the EGU's Under 14 Championship. Twelve year old Tom scored 80 and 84 round the Bristol and Clifton course.

The boys' final league match was against Staffordshire at Little Aston on 14th August. Fuelled by an epic buffet breakfast the boys took the foursomes three points to two but faltered in the singles, only adding three and a half points and so lost by six and a half to eight and a half in some very tight matches. Later that week the under 16 team came third in the Triangular Tournament at Gay Hill against Shropshire and Herefordshire and Staffordshire in a very close contest, the last putt deciding the match in Staffordshire's favour after Shropshire and Herefordshire had played much better in the singles. The result was Staffordshire nineteen and a half, Shropshire and Herefordshire eighteen and a half, Worcestershire sixteen.

The older boys then travelled to Ross-on-Wye for the annual Severnside Tournament. In the first match they defeated Gwent five and a half to one and a half and, as Glamorgan and Gloucestershire had tied, were leaders. The next morning Glamorgan played excellent golf and our boys suffered by the same margin they had inflicted upon Gwent. They played much better in the afternoon but lost to Gloucestershire by the same score, three matches being decided on the 17th and two on the 18th, one a halved match in which Steven Shilton of Kidderminster had come back from four down to take twelve year old prodigy Oscar Sharp all the way home for a half. Oscar had won his first two matches by 6 and 5.

The under 16 team lost two close matches in August; after halving the foursomes against Warwickshire at Atherstone an under strength team subsided in the singles. They performed better in this format against Derbyshire at Ashbourne but the odd point deficit in the foursomes was the deciding factor. Late cry-offs gave three promising lads a chance and they all tried their hardest, Chris Lojko, Wharton Park and Will Major Mackay, Abbey & Kings Norton, showing great potential.

The Droitwich Winning Team in the Centenary Tournament
Left to right: Brian Peplow holding salver, David Glover, Andrew Sargeant, Alan Bayley Jon Jones (captain Kings Norton)

The Centenary Tournament for teams from all the county's clubs was a great success at Kings Norton, Droitwich taking the salver presented by the R&A, and David Glover returning the best gross score, 74, nett 71. His team also included Andrew Sargeant 87 nett 75 and Alan Bayley 97 nett 75. Little Lakes were second, and Kings Norton third.

David was enjoying a particularly happy season, having finished in the top twenty in the British Seniors Amateur Championship at Woburn, an event dominated by Americans.

James Newman, Droitwich, won the Boys Matchplay Championship for the John Fraser Cup at North Worcestershire, beating Andrew Cheese, Dudley, in a fluctuating final. Steve Shilton, Kidderminster, and Richard Wood, Dudley, were the losing semi-finalists.

The first team met a strong Warwickshire team at Maxstoke Park for the fourth Midland League match. No fewer than six home players turned out for Warwickshire, reversing a two point deficit after the foursomes into a near rout in the singles. The good news was that Nottinghamshire, our nearest challengers for the league title, had also lost against Staffordshire, setting up a thrilling climax to the season in October.

Third Placed team from Kings Norton
From left: Jon Jones (captain Kings Norton), Clive Gillard, Stephen Rossall, Dave Dudley

Joe Ferguson took fourth place in the County Champions Tournament at Woodhall Spa, while Richard Gurney was breaking the course record at Burnham and Berrow. Richard was subsequently selected for the English under 21 squad.

Cleobury Mortimer professional Jon Jones won the County Open after a play-off with Joe Ferguson, who won the gold medal. Had Joe checked his card more carefully he would been the champion. Tony Jowle made no such error at Blackwell to win the Seniors Championship eleven days later.

The boys finished their season well by defeating Dyfed at Dudley, an encouraging sign for next year as the eighteen year olds ineligible for 2006 were omitted from the team.

The first team then travelled to Radcliffe-on-Trent for the match against Nottinghamshire which would decide the league championship. A practice round was played on the Saturday and the team arrived in good heart at the course on Sunday morning. Unfortunately their luck in the foursomes ran out and the team trailed by four points to one at lunchtime, Joe Ferguson and Richard Gurney combining well to earn the win. A spirited fight back was mounted, Joe leading from the front and winning 5 and 4. The next four singles also fell to Worcestershire thanks to Richard Gurney, Paul Scarrett,

Presentation of The Royal and Ancient Golf Club Centenary Salver by Richard Cole-Hamilton, CBE captain of the R&A at the January dinner 2005

Adam Norman and Chris Bromley. Matt Pates and Tom Pulling produced gritty halves and Steven Clark took his opponent to the 18th before succumbing. The remaining matches were lost out in the country. Six singles points were half a point short to win the League. So Nottinghamshire won the match eight points to seven and the League on countback from Warwickshire. When the news came through that Warwickshire had beaten Shropshire and Herefordshire by nine points to six, it meant that after such a promising start to the season Worcestershire finished in third place.

The second team concluded their disappointing season by losing ten and a half points to seven and a half at Redditch. Rob Coe deserves every sympathy for his efforts to muster teams as strong as possible but he was sadly let down on a regular basis.

While the ruling bodies debate such issues as modern equipment and its effects on our golf courses and partnerships between the various custodians of the game and while more apparently prestigious tournaments are added to the fixture lists, one may well speculate on the future of county golf.

These matches give the best amateur golfers in the country the opportunity to compete head to head with each other. The standard of play continues to improve as coaching is provided at every level of the game. Worcestershire now have, once again, players considered good enough for international recognition. It is to be hoped that the county can build on this and enjoy renewed success in its second century.

This book will have gone to press before the final events in the centenary calendar, a match with the British Golf Collectors Society, wielding their hickory clubs, reminding us of how we played the game one hundred years ago. This will be followed by the Centenary Dinner at the Guildhall, Worcester. Both promise to be enjoyable events reminding us that we play the game for enjoyment as well as exercise and good fellowship.

Appendix One

Clubs, Courses & Societies

(Clubs in italics are defunct)

Alcester Golf Club

Founded 1892, 9 holes, 2476 yards

This club affiliated to the county in 1906 but later moved to Warwickshire. It ceased operation in the Second World War. It was situated on an old Roman Camp called "Grunthills" and was three minutes from the railway station.

Abbey Hotel Golf & Country Club, Redditch

Founded 1985, 18 holes, 6499 yards, SSS 72, driving range

The course was laid out by Donald Steel and contains a site of special scientific interest. The Blake family purchased the course in 1998 and invested heavily in drainage and other course improvements. The club's professional, Robert Davies, had a successful career in the county boys' team.

Bank House Hotel Golf & Country Club, Bransford

Affiliated to the Union as Bransford Golf Club

Founded 1992, 18 holes, 6204 yards, SSS 71, driving range

The course was designed by Robert Sandow after Brian Peplow obtained planning permission for change of use and incorporates many water features. The course is bisected by a road; golfers cross via a tunnel.

Bewdley Pines Golf Club

Founded 1997, 18 holes, 5724 yards, SSS 67

The Hobday family and the father and brother of European Tour player Peter Baker took over the West Midlands Golf Club in December 1997 after the original club had failed. Investment in the course attracted a large membership and six years later the club had 450 male members and 92 ladies. A WPGA alliance was held at the club in 2003, the professionals being very impressed by the quality of the greens. The club won the Two Counties Trophy in 2002 and were runners-up the following year.

Blackwell Golf Club

Founded 1893, 18 holes, 6260 yards, SSS 71

One of the county's senior clubs, Blackwell has a rich history, including the celebrated match involving Bobby Jones, Dr. Tweddell, Eric Fiddian and Stanley Lunt in 1930. Under Guy Bigwood the county and the club enjoyed their most successful years. The club has produced several county champions, captains and officers.

Brand Hall (now Brandhall) Golf Club

Founded 1906, 18 holes, 5813 yards, SSS 68

Brand Hall was originally a private club with a very testing course. This attracted some of the best players in the Midlands as members, including the likes of Harley Roberts, past president of the Midlands and Worcestershire, who enjoyed a victorious international partnership with Charlie Stowe, Jack Mitchley, also an international, and one of the finest golfers ever, and Ted Rigby, who was never beaten by Charlie Stowe in county matches. Len Wilkes was also well-known; many regarded him as the best captain ever of the county side. When the lease expired Oldbury council refused to renew it, the club dissolved and the course became a public course, which later suffered from the building of the M5. One of the club's main trophies, the Brand Hall Gold vase, was presented to the Union in 1949. The municipal club also produced county players, such as the Newbitts, father and son.
The course was extended from 14 to 18 holes in 1910.

Brandwood House Golf & Tennis Club, Kings Heath, Birmingham

Founded 1923, 18 holes, 5433 yards, Ceased operation 1936

Dick Wheildon, the Moseley professional, assisted in the design of the course and played in the official opening exhibition match in 1926 with G.R. Buckle (Edgbaston), Michael Bingham (Stourbridge) and J. Hunt of the home club.
J. Stretton Cox, a distinguished Midlands golfers, was a member, but also joined Bloxwich and Handsworth. As a result he played for three counties each side of the Second World War, Worcestershire, Warwickshire and Staffordshire.

Brinton's Golf Club, Kidderminster

Founded 1929, Affiliated 1930, SSS 68

The directors of Brintons Carpets built a nine hole golf course, football and cricket pitches and other leisure facilities for their employees. These all disappeared during the Second World War when the land was used for agriculture and to house workshops for Birmingham craftsmen.

Broadway Golf Club

Affiliated to the Union in 1905 but switched to Gloucestershire, probably when that county formed a union the following year

Bromsgrove Golf Club

Founded 1894

According to the Bromsgrove Messenger *the club was based at Breakback from 1894 until 1903 and at Sideslow Farm, site of the modern club, from 1904 to 1912, when it returned to Breakback, closing in 1918. Sideslow measured 2537 yards, with a bogey of 38. Breakback measured 2434 yards, bogey 42.*

Bromsgrove Golf Centre

Founded 1992, 18 holes, 5969 yards, SSS 69, driving range. Designed by Hawtree & Co.

The Morris family opened nine holes and the driving range in 1992 and gradually expanded to eighteen holes with a clubhouse incorporating all facilities. The members' club was formed early in the centre's history and in 2003 won both the Boulton Salver and the Brand Hall Gold Vase. The driving range includes state of the art computerised teaching equipment. There was an earlier course on the same site – see above.

Churchill & Blakedown Golf Club, Blakedown

Founded 1926, 9 holes, 6472 yards, SSS 71

This undulating course has ten greens but eighteen tees. The clubhouse was extended in 2003-04. Seaun Orpen, a member of the club, won the British Transplant Golf Championship in 1998 and 2003. He died in 2004, aged forty-seven, having won medals in other sports.

Cleobury Mortimer Golf Club

Founded 1993, 27 holes, 6147-6438 yards, SSS 69-71, driving range

Graham and Martin Pain, with the expert assistance of Ray Baldwin, began with a nine hole course, a driving range and a basic clubhouse. As more members joined, a second nine was added and the clubhouse was enlarged. Ray Baldwin then added a third loop, utilising the land where the original driving range had been and the clubhouse was extended again. The club affiliated to Worcestershire, although it is actually in Shropshire, because local clubs with whom matches are arranged lie across the border. Links with local schools attract younger players to the club.

Cocks Moors Woods Golf Club, Kings Heath, Birmingham

Founded 1926, 18 holes, 5769 yards, SSS 67

This municipal course was designed by J.H.Taylor and Frederick G. Hawtree. Taylor opened the course in company with Dick Wheildon and Stanley Lunt of Moseley and Carl Bretherton of Handsworth, a major supporter of public golf courses. Among several fine golfers who started to play there are Roy Hobbis, Richard Sadler, another county champion, and Kevin Hayward the Kings Norton professional.

Comberton Golf Club *– see* **Kidderminster Golf Club**

Droitwich Golf & Country Club

Founded 1897, 18 holes, 6058 yards, SSS 68

The first course lay nearer to the town. It was remodelled and extended by James Braid in 1923, then by Frederick W. Hawtree in the 1970s, with some additional input from Ray Baldwin, secretary from 1972 to 1987. Many members have represented the county, including John Bickerton jun., who is now a successful European Tour professional.

Dudley Golf Club

Founded 1893, 18 holes, 5730 yards, SSS 68

The original course was laid out by Old Tom Morris. The Earl of Dudley was the first president in 1903. In 1928 the club moved to a course designed by Herbert Fowler at Oakham Road. The remodelled course and clubhouse were opened in 1968. Several members represented the county and one, Darren Prosser, played for Great Britain and Ireland the first time they won the Walker Cup in America.

Edgbaston Golf Club

Founded in 1896

The club's first course was in Warley and affiliated to WUGC at its inception. The lease was not renewed and the club moved first to Harborne and then to its present site. It became affiliated to Warwickshire in 1921.

Evesham Golf Club, Craycombe Links, Fladbury

Founded 1894, 9 Holes, 6415 yards, SSS 71

The club's first course was at Twyford, north of Evesham, but moved to Craycombe Links by the end of 1895. There are eighteen tees and at one time the course was the longest in Worcestershire. The Gray family served the club as greenkeeper and professional for 83 of the club's first 100 years. The club's affiliation to the Union lapsed in the Second World War but the club was re-admitted in 1952.

Fulford Heath Golf Club, Wythall, Birmingham

Founded 1933, 18 holes, 6179 yards, SSS 70

The course was designed by James Braid and in 1952 measured 6448 yards. The club has enjoyed considerable success in the Boulton Salver, while Anthony Hill has achieved a distinguished playing record for the county, winning the President's Shield in 2003.

Gaudet Luce Golf Club

Founded 1996, 18 holes, 6040 yards, SSS 69

A proprietary club, belonging to the Fernyhough family, who also own Little Lakes. The original design of some 6400 yards was by Ray Baldwin but was modified later by head professional Mark Laing. The club has made considerable progress since it opened and provides great encouragement to junior golfers.

Gay Hill Golf Club, Hollywood, Birmingham

Founded 1913, 18 holes, 6532 yards, SSS 72

The club's first course was laid out on rough ground at Bay Tree Farm, Headley Heath. The greens were fenced in to protect them from cattle and were allocated to members for maintenance. The club moved to Hollywood Farm in 1921 and Dick Wheildon of Moseley Golf Club helped design the course, which was extended to eighteen holes the following year. More land was acquired in 1934 and the course was extended again. The club has been a great supporter of the Union and among the members who have been prominent in the county's affairs are Jeff Adams and Peter Adams; the former has run the individual membership scheme for many years, while Peter has captained both first and second teams. Under his leadership the first team won the Midland league in 1998.

Habberley Golf Club, Kidderminster

Founded 1924, 9 holes, 5440 yards, SSS 67

The club affiliated to the Union soon after its foundation but its membership lapsed during the war. The club's fortunes improved and it was able to rejoin in the 1950s.

Hagley Golf Club

Founded 1891, 9 holes

This course was on Monument Hill, two miles from Stourbridge, on clay soil. The hazards were natural ones and play was possible all year. When Stourbridge Golf Club was having difficulties with a tenant farmer in 1898 the members were permitted to play at Hagley. In their turn Hagley members were admitted to Stourbridge when the club closed in 1906.

Hagley Golf & Country Club

Founded 1980, 18 holes, 6379 yards, SSS 72

This proprietary club, its course designed by the Hawtrees, opened with nine holes and was extended in 1987-88. A number of boys have played for the county's junior teams, including Cameron Clark, boys' captain in 1992 and now a successful club professional. The Club won the R&A rules quiz in 2002.

Halesowen Golf Club

Founded 1906, 18 holes, 5754 yards, SSS 69

The club began with a nine hole course laid out by W.P. Lewis of Kings Norton. By 1910 it was possible to add a further nine. The editor of the *Birmingham and Midland Golfer* visited the club in 1911 and was impressed by what he called "the quaintest clubhouse in the Midlands". It had been the home of the poet Shenstone and is still the club headquarters. Several important county events have been held at the club.

Hanbury Golf Club

A nine hole course was laid out by the publican of the "The Vernon Arms" for his customers. It was ploughed up for the war effort in 1939.

Headley Heath Golf Club

Founded in 1913

When affiliated to the Union, this nine hole course was close to the original Gay Hill course. The first professional was Tom Lewis, who came from Moseley. Many members were lost in the First World War and the club closed, the survivors being offered membership of Gay Hill. Part of the site is now the Druids Heath estate.

Ipsley Golf Club, Redditch

Founded 1891, 9 holes between 152 and 330 yards, par 35

The course was two miles from Redditch station.It closed in 1908 when the lease was terminated. The course was closed from May to September to permit grazing. Affiliated to the Union in 1906, it was the third club to be formed in Worcestershire. It was alongside a race course and was designed by David Brown, professional at The Worcestershire.

Kidderminster Golf Club

Founded 1909, 18 holes, 6405 yards, SSS 71

The first club to be formed in Kidderminster was at Aggborough in 1890, close to the G.W.R. station and the river Stour. Edward Blackwell joined the club in 1898. Another club was formed at Comberton in 1909, when the Kidderminster club at Aggborough closed; subsequently Comberton was renamed Kidderminster Golf Club. Although Blackwell first played for Worcestershire under an assumed name Kidderminster golfers have represented the county with distinction throughout its history, including Will Painter, who has been both captain and honorary secretary of the Union, Brian Peplow, the centenary president, and Matthew Houghton, centenary captain. Alan Lloyd and J.P. Nicholls represented England Boys in 1928.

Kings Norton Golf Club

Founded 1892, 3 x 9 holes, 3382, 3372 and 3290 yards, SSS 36

A founding club of the Union, the original course was in Kings Norton but became a housing estate in the 1970s, enabling the club to move to Weatheroak Hall and develop twenty-seven holes designed by the late Frederick W. Hawtree. From Frank Woolley at the beginning of the county's history, Kings Norton players have represented Worcestershire with distinction and many of the club's members have been equally prominent in the administration of the Union's affairs, among them Dr. Brown, Neville Seers, Stan Seymour and Roy Hobbis. Doug Humphries was president in 1996-97.

Lickey Hills Golf Course

Founded 1927, 18 holes, 6010 yards, SSS 69

It is believed golf was played on this municipal course earlier than the date given. Rose Hill Golf Club is based here and that club's success in the Boulton Salver and subsequent staging of it is recorded in chapter 7. The land for the course was presented to Birmingham City Council by the Cadbury family and the course was designed by Hawtree and Taylor. A long serving professional was Bernard Preston, who had moved from Kings Norton in 1959; he trained many successful assistants and played a prominent role in the affairs of the WPGA.

Little Lakes Golf & Country Club, Lye Head, Bewdley

Founded 1975, 18 holes, 6278 yards, SSS 70

Owned by the Fernyhough family and managed by professional Mark Laing, the club opened with nine holes, extended to eighteen in the 1990s, and was lengthened again in 2002. The county boys hold regular matches there. Other facilities include tennis courts and a swimming pool.

Madresfield Golf Course

This was a private course at Madresfield Court on Earl Beauchamp's estate, Malvern. The nine holes had a bogey of 39, were laid out by Open Champion J.H. Taylor and were said to be long, pretty and very difficult.

Malvern Link Golf Club

Founded 1921, closed c.1924

Malvern St Andrews Golf Club

The club was formed c.1926 and played on the nine holes remaining on the common after The Worcestershire had moved to the new course. It did not survive the Second World War.

Malvern Working Mens Club

Founded 1886

The club played on The Worcestershire's course. Over 100 members enlisted in the First World War. The club continued after that war but did not survive the second one.

Moseley Golf Club, Birmingham

Founded 1892, 18 holes, 6315 yards, SSS 71

The original nine hole course was extended in 1914 by the legendary Harry Colt, who returned in 1937 and designed the present fourth and fifth holes, using the lake to create the club's feature hole. Since the foundation of the Union the club has played a major part in the county's affairs, as well as providing captains of England and international players, the most celebrated being Stanley Lunt and his son Michael, both of whom won the Amateur Championship, and Scottish international Dr. William Robb. More recently Michael Reynard earned international recognition.

North Worcestershire Golf Club, Northfield, Birmingham

Founded 1907, 18 holes, 5907 yards, SSS 69

The course was designed by James Braid who laid out the first nine holes then returned to design a further nine. The new eighteen hole course was used for the county championship in 1914, after the club had rejected Warwickshire's invitation to join their union after the implementation of boundary changes. Braid opened the course in 1912, losing to Harry Vardon in the morning and in the afternoon playing with Frank Woolley in an exhibition match in which they beat Vardon and Frank Carr. The order of the course after a number of changes has now reverted to Braid's original plan.

Ombersley Golf Club, Droitwich

Founded 1991, 18 holes, 6139 yards, SSS 69, driving range

A busy proprietary club with a large membership, the club staged a WPGA alliance in 2003.

Perdiswell Park Golf Course, Worcester

Founded 1990, 18 holes, 5297 yards, SSS 68

This is a public golf course belonging to Worcester City Council. It affiliated to the Union in 1992 when still a nine hole course. In 2000 Ray Baldwin designed a further nine, fitting them in with the original holes, thereby modifying the course and making it safer.

Pershore Golf Club

Founded 1893, 9 holes

This course was situated on upland overlooking the river Avon about two miles from Pershore station. The club wound up and amalgamated with Evesham in 1904.

Pitcheroak Golf Course, Redditch

Founded 1973, 9 holes, 4561 yards, SSS 62

Redditch Kingfisher Golf Club play on the nine holes left after Redditch Golf Club's original course was partially taken for road building schemes. This is a public course run by Redditch council.

Powick Golf Club

The first mention of this club in the golfing annuals was in 1896. It appears to have ceased to exist after 1902.

Ravenmeadow Golf Club. Claines, Worcester

Founded 1998, 10 holes, 5440 yards, SSS 67, driving range

Owned by past captain, secretary and more recently chairman of the Union, David Rodway, and designed by Ray Baldwin with some input from the owner. The greens are USGA standard, giving good putting surfaces all year round.

Redditch Golf Club

Founded 1913, 18 holes, 6494 yards, SSS 72

The club was formed when the Redditch and Walkwood club (see below) lost their course, and played on the course at Plymouth Road, which is now the home of Redditch Kingfisher Golf Club. In its turn the Kingfisher club lost nine holes due to road building in the 1970s and the Redditch club moved to the present course at Lower Grinsty, where Frank Pennink had laid out one of the more difficult of the county's courses. New greens were laid at the turn of the century to USGA specifications.

Redditch & Walkwood Golf Club

Founded 1905, 9 holes

The course was situated close to the site of the present Redditch Golf Club in what is now Morton Stanley Park. The first professional was Dick Wheildon. The club was wound up in 1913 when the lease expired. Redditch Golf Club was then formed at the Plymouth Road site in the same year.

Robin Hood Golf Club

Founded in 1893

The club's first course was in Worcestershire and they were founder members of our Union. When boundary changes were implemented in 1911 the club was planning a move to its new course, previously that of Olton Golf Club, and transferred to the Warwickshire union in 1912. Dr. Frank Stableford was an early member of the club while in practice in Birmingham but did not develop his famous scoring system until he had moved to the Glamorganshire Club.

Rose Hill Golf Club – *see* **Lickey Hills Golf Course**

St Michael's Golf Club, Tenbury

First mentioned 1896, 9 holes

The course was on Oldwood Common, adjacent to St Michael's college, a mile and a quarter from the station. The club was started by the college staff and played a match against Kidderminster in 1898. Although the club co-existed happily with the racecourse, relations with the commoners were less happy and the course closed in the early 1900s. Moves to re-open it in the late 1930s were thwarted by the outbreak of war, when the land was ploughed up.

Stourbridge Golf Club

Founded 1892, 18 holes, 6231 yards, SSS 69

One of the Union's founding clubs, Stourbridge has been a major force in Worcestershire golf, particularly between the two world wars when the Humphries family, the Fiddian brothers and Dr. Tweddell were at the height of their powers. The club has also been highly influential in administration, at national as well as county level, Denis Hayes having held important positions on various R&A committees.

Tenbury Wells Golf Club

Founded 1911, 9 holes

The course was laid out on land owned by the Squire, Mr. Godson, on the outskirts of the town at the junction of Leominster Road and Morningside. A clubhouse was erected in 1921 but Mr. Godson withdrew the facility in 1927 as, it is thought, he was having disagreements with the town council about boundary fencing.

Tolladine Golf Club, Worcester

Founded 1898. 9 holes, 5174 yards, SSS 67

As the club plays on part of the original Worcester City course, it claims 1898 as its foundation date. Much of the original course was lost to the building of the hospital. Worcester City moved to Boughton Park in 1927.

Upton-upon-Severn Golf Club

The nine hole course on "The Ham", a field by the river about half a mile from the station, was first mentioned in 1938. As the field flooded every winter the course did not last very long.

The Vale Golf & Country Club, Bishampton, Pershore

Founded 1991, 18 holes, 6644 yards, SSS 72, 9 holes, 2628 yards, SSS 65

The courses were laid out for the Rimell family by Robert Sandow on open, undulating land between Pershore and Evesham. Financial difficulties led to the courses being sold to UK Golf, who later sold them on to Crown Sports. An enthusiastic membership has led to several players representing the county, and Andrew Boyd, our county secretary, is a past captain.

Warley Golf Club, Birmingham

Founded 1921, 9 holes, 2606 yards, SSS 64

The home of the Warley Woods club, the course was the first home of Edgbaston Golf Club, founded in 1896. When the lease expired in 1909 the club moved to Harborne and the golf correspondent of the *Birmingham Post* suggested that the city council "municipalise" the course. However they did not do so immediately, part being ploughed up in the First World War, then the course was re-instated in an altered form in 1921. The clubhouse in Warley Abbey was demolished in the 1950s and a temporary clubhouse was erected in 1954. It is still in use today. The club has enjoyed success in county competitions and some members have played for the county.

Wharton Park Golf Club, Longbank, Bewdley

Founded 1992, 18 holes, 6435 yards, SSS 72, driving range

Created in the golf boom of the late 1980s and early 1990s. Unfortunately the original owner wanted two nines finishing at the clubhouse, which caused a steep and long climb from the 12th green to the 13th tee and a similar trek back downhill from the 15th green to the 16th tee. This was altered by Howard Swan and the course now runs more naturally, although there are still some gentler climbs to be negotiated.

The Wigorns Golfing Society

The society was formed in 1950 by Guy Bigwood, Stanley Lunt, Bill Boulton, Stanley Elliott and Derek Greey, all major contributors to Worcestershire's eminent position in English Golf. The aim was to play golf in the traditions established in the past, playing against like-minded opposition. These included such societies as Oxford University, the Hittites, the Senior Golfers' Society, the Narwhals and the Erratics. A branch was formed in South Australia, to whom a trophy was presented. The Wigorns also hold their own competitions which are described in Charles Wade's history of the society.

Witley Court Golf Course

This was a Private 9 hole course belonging to the Earl of Dudley which was laid out around the turn of the 19th and 20th centuries. In February 1902 he invited ten of the country's leading professionals to play in a tournament which was spoilt by snow and won by Harry Vardon. The Earl retained Scottish professional Andra' Kirkaldy as his personal coach. It is not known when the course fell into disuse.

Worcester Golf & Country Club, Boughton Park

Founded 1898, 18 holes, 6251 yards, SSS 70

The club started as Worcester City Golf Club at the course now used by Tolladine. It moved to Boughton Park in 1927 on a course designed by Dr. Alister Mackenzie, who created some of his trademark bunkers there. In the late 1980s problems of public safety arose on the 1st and 14th holes and internal danger to players on four other holes. Ray Baldwin conducted a feasibility study, suggesting how the course might be lengthened, land was acquired across the Laugharne Brook, and the professional, Colin Colenso, designed three new holes. This resulted in the standard scratch score rising to 70. The clubhouse is an elegant 18th century mansion, which was damaged by fire in 1948 and subsequently restored.

The Worcestershire Captains Golfing Society

This was formed in 1974 by Ian Stuart of Stourbridge to bring together past captains of the county's clubs. As well as holding their own competitions they have a full list of fixtures encompassing Devon, Somerset, Wiltshire, Gloucestershire, Gwent, South Wales Coast, Oxfordshire, Leicestershire, Warwickshire and South Cheshire.

The Worcestershire Golf Club, Malvern Wells

Founded 1879, 18 holes, 6449 yards, SSS 71

The oldest course, not only in Worcestershire but the Midlands, was laid out on Malvern Common. Early club members were the staff and headmaster of Malvern College, and it is to Rev. James that we partly owe the inauguration of our Union. When it was felt that the course on the common was becoming too hazardous the club moved to its present site at Wood Farm in 1927. Nine holes did not survive the Second World War, but by 1972 Frederick W. Hawtree had designed nine new holes and remodelled the existing ones, the work being financed by a Sports Council grant – one of the first to be awarded. Perhaps the club's most celebrated player was John Fraser, whose connection with the county spanned sixty years, culminating in his becoming president in 1994. John was very unlucky not to have attained international recognition. Another member, Norman Bolton, became president in 2002. The old clubhouse was demolished in 2002 and the new one erected.

The Worcestershire Seniors Golfers Society

This was formed in 1973 with similar aims to those of the Wigorns. The founders were Jeff Allen, president, John Fraser, captain, John Vickerstaff, secretary (now a member of Robin Hood) and Guy Currall, treasurer. Alan Lloyd and Dick Mirams also served on the committee, while the membership included Harley Roberts, Bill Cunningham and Doug Humphries. Fixtures include the Midland region of the Association of Golf Club Secretaries, Worcestershire Lady Veterans, Leicestershire Seniors and Gwent Veterans. Since the formation of the County Seniors team the Union arranged fixtures with the senior golfers of other counties, creating a healthy, competitive circuit.

Wyre Forest Golf Centre, Kidderminster

Founded 1996, 18 holes, 5790 yards, SSS 68, driving range

This is a play and pay facility with a members' club which joined the Union in 1998.

Yardley Golf Club

This nine hole course opened in 1893 and was last recorded in 1909. At the time Yardley was in the northernmost extremity of Worcestershire. The course was about a quarter of a mile from Yardley church in the direction of Sheldon and a mile and a half from the nearest railway station.

Appendix Two

Championship

Worcestershire Amateur Championship

1906 J.M. Challinor 161
1907 F.A. Woolley 161
1908 F.A. Woolley 151
1909 G.M. Archdale 161
1910 F. Gordon Smith 161
1911 F.A. Woolley 146
1912 F.A. Woolley 149
1913 J.P. Humphries 161
1914 F.A. Woolley 161
1915-19 *Not played – First World War*
1920 R.P. Humphries 149
1921 S.C. Craven 160
1922 R.P. Humphries 153
1923 C.J. Reece 157
1924 E. Somers Smith 148
1925 S. Lunt 149
1926 G.N.P. Humphries 150
1927 S.T. Matthews 149
1928 E.W. Fiddian 143
1929 Dr. W. Tweddell 145
1930 E.W. Fiddian 143
1931 Dr. W. Tweddell 145
1932 J.S. Mitchley 146
1933 J.R. Fraser 145
1934 Dr. H.G. Marshall 146
1935 J.S. Mitchley
1936-9 *Decided by match play*
Winner Runner-up by
1936 S. Lunt Dr. W.M. Robb 4&2
1937 Dr. W.M. Robb E.W. Rigbey 5&3
1938 Dr. W. Tweddell E.W. Rigbey 2&1
1939 Dr.W. Anderson
R.H. Crump 37th hole
1940-5 *Second World War*
Resumed as stroke play 1946
1946 Dr. W.M. Robb 153
1947 H.J. Roberts 139
1948 S.L. Elliott 143
1949 Dr. W.M. Robb 143
1950 E.W. Fiddian 138
1951 J.S. Mitchley 147
1952 N.A .Seers 141
1953 J.R. Butterworth 143
1954 J.R. Butterworth 143
1955 J.R. Butterworth 152
1956 F.L. Wilkinson 147
1957 H.J. Roberts 138
1958 H.J. Roberts 142
1959 H.J. Roberts 138
1960 R.W. Sandilands 146
1961 R.A. Jowle 157
1962 J.R. Butterworth 154
1963 H.J. Roberts 143
1964 R. Hobbis 139
1965 P.D. Kelley 146
1966 A. Forrester 138
1967 M.W.L. Hampton 138
1968 A. Thomson 138
1969 A. Forrester 134
1970 J. Toddington 144
1971 J. Toddington 142
1972 T.R. Shingler 150

1973 T.R. Shingler 144
1974 R. Langridge 138
1975 D. Turner 141
1976 R. Hobbis 141
1977 S.J. Pimley 146
1978 M. Curry 147
1979 P.D. Kelley 150
1980 P.R. Swinburne 145
1981 M.C. Reynard 105 *(reduced to 26 holes)*
1982 D.J. Eddiford 143
1983 T.R. Shingler 147
1984 T. Martin 145
1985 S.J. Pimley 140
1986 D. Eddiford 144
1987 D.M. Prosser, *play-off with* C.K. Norman *141 p.o. 72*
1988 D.M. Prosser 139
1989 S. Braithwaite 68 *(reduced by rain to 18 holes)*
1990 D. Eddiford 140
1991 J. Bickerton 140
1992 M.C. Reynard 136
1993 M.C. Reynard 144
1994 R. Sadler 139
1995 M.C. Reynard 148
1996 M.C. Reynard 146
1997 S. Braithwaite 137
1998 D. Glover 138
1999 P. Scarrett 146
2000 R. Wassell 146
2001 M.C. Reynard 135
2002 S. Braithwaite 140
2003 A.C. Norman 143
2004 J. Toman, *play-off with* J. Ferguson *149 p.o. conceded.*
2005 J. Ferguson 141

Worcestershire Matchplay Championship - The Derek Greey Cup

	Winner	*Runner-up*
1975	T.R. Shingler	M. Wrigglesworth
1976	T.R. Shingler	R. Hobbis
1977	S.J. Pimley	A.J. Thomson
1978	W.R. Painter	T.R. Shingler
1979	T.R. Shingler	P. Daniels
1980	M.C. Reynard	A.J. Thomson
1981	R.A. Jowle	C.F. Smith
1982	D.J. Eddiford	N. Perry
1983	C.K. Norman	D.J. Eddiford
1984	M.C. Reynard	G.W. Hawkings
1985	N.R. Hunter	P.M. Guest
1986	P. Adams	G.W. Hawkings
1987	C.K. Norman	C.F. Smith
1988	J. Bickerton	D. Henn
1989	M. Daw	P. Shurmer
1990	J. Bickerton	D.J. Eddiford
1991	A.W. Robinson	J. Bickerton
1992	N. Swaffield	P. Shurmer
1993	N. Swaffield	A.W. Robinson
1994	D. Clee	M. Houghton
1995	J. Toman	M. Houghton
1996	D. Clee	S. Deakin
1997	P. Scarrett	R. Sadler
1998	M. Houghton	J. Hems
1999	R. Sadler	C. Harris
2000	M. Wood	R. Davies
2001	R. Wassell	A. Sykes
2002	M. Wood	M. Daw
2003	P. Scarrett	J. Ferguson
2004	C. Bromley	P. Scarrett
2005	C. Bromley	C. Heeley

Worcestershire Open Championship - The Guy Bigwood Cup

1949 J.S. Mitchley*
1950 W.R. Firkins
1951 D.W.M. Robb*
1952 F.E. Miller
1953 F.E. Miller
1954 F.E. Miller
1955 H.J. Roberts*
1956 H.J. Roberts*
1957 G.F. Reynolds
1958 F.E. Miller
1959 S. Seymour*
1960 W. Firkins jnr
1961 R.A. Jowle*
1962 H.J. Roberts*
1963 F.E. Miller
1964 F.E. Miller
1965 J.E. Wiggett *(18 holes)*
1966 J.E. Wiggett & J. Ward* *(tie)*
1967 F.E. Miller
1968 P.D. Kelley*
1969 H. Macdonald
1970 T.R. Shingler*
1971 P.D. Kelley*
1972 K. Bayliss
1973 H. Macdonald
1974 T.R. Shingler*
1975 I. Richardson
1976 R. Hobbis*
1977 S.J. Carpenter*
1978 R.A. Jowle*
1979 I. Richardson
1980 R.A. Jowle*
1981 W. Firkins
1982 M.C. Reynard*
1983 A.J. Hill*
1984 K. Hayward
1985 D.J. Eddiford
1986 W.R. Painter*
1987 K. Hayward
1988 D.J. Eddiford*
1989 K. Hayward
1990 J. Bickerton*
1991 M.C. Reynard*
1992 A. Robinson*
1993 P. Scarrett*
1994 S. Edwards
1995 C. Clark
1996 D. Clee
1997 P. Scarrett*
1998 D. Eddiford
1999 S. Edwards
2000 N. Turley
2001 N. Turley
2002 R. Wassell
2003 M. Butler
2004 M. Butler
2005 J. Jones

* Amateur

Appendix Three

Officials

County Captains

1905-20	*No Captain appointed*
1921-24	J.P. Humphries
1925-29	W. Pearson
1930-33	S. Lunt
1934-36	L.N. Wilkes
1937-47	W.C.I. Boulton *(through the war)*
1948-50	W.M. Robb
1951-52	E.W. Fiddian
1953-54	Dr.W. Tweddell
1955-56	Dr. J.L. Brown
1957-58	D.A. Fiddian
1959-60	R.G.M. Morgan
1961-62	S.S. Seymour
1963-64	J.R. Fraser
1965-68	M.S.R. Lunt
1969-71	H.J. Roberts
1972-74	R.V. Mirams
1975-76	T.R. Shingler
1977-79	R. Hobbis
1980-81	R.A. Jowle
1982-83	A.J. Thomson
1984-86	W. Painter
1987-89	F. Savage
1990-92	D.E. Rodway
1993-94	M.D. Tweddell
1995-96	C. Smith
1997-98	P. Adams
1999-2000	C.E. Pates
2001-02	P. Scarrett
2003-05	M. Houghton

Presidents

1906	Earl of Dudley
19??	Earl of Plymouth *(exact date uncertain)*
1920	Earl of Plymouth
1934-66	E. Guy Bigwood
1967-71	Dr. W. Tweddell
1972-86	H.J. Roberts
1987-91	J.R.F. Chandler
1992-93	R.V. Mirams
1994-95	J.R. Fraser
1996-97	D.T. Humphries
1998-99	D.L. Hayes
2000-01	R. Hobbis
2002-03	N.E. Bolton
2004-05	B. Peplow

Appendix Four

Roll of Honour

Amateur Champions

1927	W. Tweddell *(Stourbridge)*	1963	M.S.R. Lunt *(Moseley)*

Finalists in the Amateur Championship

1904	E.B.H. Blackwell	1964	M.S.R. Lunt
1932	E.W. Fiddian	1995	M. Reynard
1935	W. Tweddell		

English Amateur Champions

1932	E.W. Fiddian *(Stourbridge)*	1966	M.S.R. Lunt *(Moseley)*
1934	S. Lunt *(Moseley)*	1977	T.R. Shingler *(Blackwell)*

Finalists in the English Amateur Championship

1935	E.W. Fiddian	1962	M.S.R. Lunt
1948	H.J. Roberts	1968	P.D. Kelley #

Finalists in the Irish Amateur Championship

1930	D.W. Fiddian	1933	E.W. Fiddian

* Players who achieved national selection before joining Worcestershire
# P.D. Kelley represented several Clubs in Worcestershire
Stanley and Michael Lunt are the only father and son to win the English Amateur, which is apparently the reason that Moseley may incorporate the English rose in their badge.

Internationals

E.B.H. Blackwell *(Kidderminster)*	Scotland	1902-25
F.A. Woolley *(Kings Norton)*	England	1910-12
W. Tweddell *(Stourbridge)*	England	1928-30, 36
	Walker Cup	1928,36
E.W. Fiddian *(Stourbridge)*	England	1929-34
	Walker Cup	1932,34
S. Lunt *(Moseley)*	England	1932-39
A.S. Newey *(Moseley)*	England	1932
W.M. Robb *(Moseley)**	Scotland	1935
K. Frazier *(Moseley)**	England	1938
H.J. Roberts *(Stourbridge)*	England	1947, 48, 53
J.R. Butterworth *(Worcester Golf and Country Club)*	England	1954
I. Hughes *(Moseley)**	Wales	1954
M.S.R. Lunt *(Moseley)*	England	1956-66
	Walker Cup	1959-65
P.D. Kelley *(Kings Norton)*	England	1965, 66, 68
T.R. Shingler *(Blackwell)*	England	1977
D. Prosser *(Dudley, Moseley, Kings Norton)*	England	1989
	Walker Cup	1989
M. Reynard *(Moseley)*	England	1996, 97
J. Ferguson *(Kidderminster)*	England	

* Prior to playing for Worcestershire

Captains of the Royal and Ancient Golf Club of St Andrews

1925	E.B.H. Blackwell	1961	Dr. W. Tweddell, M.C., M.B., Ch.B

Presidents of the English Golf Union

1932	Spencer Newey	1949-59	E. Guy Bigwood, C.B.E., J.P.
1957	W.C.I. Boulton	1960	S. Lunt, A.F.C.

Bibliography

Newspapers and periodicals

Amateur Golf (EGU magazine, ceased publication 2000)
Berrows Worcester Journal
Birmingham and Midland Golfer
Birmingham Evening Mail
Birmingham Gazette
Birmingham Post
Bromsgrove Messenger
Golf Illustrated
Redditch Indicator
Worcester Evening News

Minute books

Worcestershire Union of Golf Clubs minute books and match books

Year Books

Nisbet's Golfing Year Book 1911
The Royal and Ancient Golfer's Handbooks (Annual)
Royal and Ancient Championship Records, 1860-1980; R&A, 1981
English Golf Union Year Books (Annual)

Golf Histories

Bathurst, P. & Behrend, J. *The Oxford and Cambridge Golfing Society* Grant Books, 1997
Behrend, J. *The Amateur*, Grant Books, 1995
Behrend, J., Lewis P.N., Mackie, K. *Champions and Guardians – The Royal and Ancient Golf Club 1884-1939*, R&A, 2001
Bromhead, J. *Droitwich Golf Club 1897-1997*, Grant Books, 1996

Dixon, C. *Robin Hood Golf Club, The First Hundred Years 1883-1983,** 1993
Drury, T. Blackwell Golf Club,* 1953
Heath, P. *Towards One Hundred Years, Edgbaston Golf Club 1896-1986* Grant Books, 1986
MacAlindin, B. *James Braid Champion Golfer*, Grant Books, 2003
Mirams, R.V. *Moseley Milestones 1892-1992,** 1993
Moreton, J.F. *The Golf Courses of James Braid*, Grant Books, 1996
Plim, D. *Golf in Redditch 1891-1991,** 1991
Ricketts, P. *The Road to Weatheroak – Kings Norton Golf Club 1892-1992* Grant Books, 1992
Robertson, S.N. *Worcester Golf and Country Club 1898-1998,** 1998
Scott, G. *A Centenary History of the Worcestershire Golf Club*, G. Scott, 1979
Simmonds, G.G. *The Walker Cup, 1922-1999, Golf's Finest Contest* Grant Books, 2000
Tuckett, M. *Fulford Heath Golf Club Into the Millennium 1933-2000*
Various: *Dudley Golf Club, 1893-1993**
Wade, C.L. *Blackwell Golf Club 1893-2000*, Grant Books, 2001
Wade, C.L. *The History of the Wigorns Golfing Society 1950-2000* Grant Books, 2000
Webb, C. *Stourbridge Golf Club Centenary 1892-1992*, Mark & Moody, 1992

Handbooks

Gay Hill, Brandwood House
Lickey Hills, Warley
Cocks Moors Woods
Municipal Courses yearbooks published by Birmingham Parks Department 1926-1935 can be viewed in Birmingham Central Library

** denotes book or booklet published by the Club*

Index

THE WORCESTERSHIRE UNION OF GOLF CLUBS

WILL HOLD ITS

First Annual Meeting

ON

THE GREEN OF THE WORCESTERSHIRE GOLF CLUB, AT MALVERN,

ON

TUESDAY AND WEDNESDAY,

MAY 15TH AND 16TH, 1906.

Executive Committee of the Council:

Mr. J. J. Tomson, Chairman; Mr. G. D. Carr, Secretary; Mr. J. G. Baker (Evesham), Mr. F. R. Burrow (Worcestershire), Capt. Eccles (Worcester City), Mr. W. R. Nash (Stourbridge), and Mr. T. W. Piggott (King's Norton).

Weather

TUESDAY, 15TH MAY.

Fine

THE COUNTY CLUB CHALLENGE PRIZE, FOR THE TOMSON-JAMES CUP. Teams of four. Clubs may not enter more than two teams. Eighteen Holes. Medal Play. Entrance Fee 10/- per team. The winning team will receive Memento Medals, and the Tomson-James Cup will be held until the next County Golf Meeting by the Club whose team is successful.

There will be an optional Sweepstake (2/6) under handicap, for players taking part in the above event.

Mr. F. R. Burrow will give a prize for the best individual scratch score in the above competition.

WEDNESDAY, 16TH MAY.

Heavy Showers & Cold

1. **A SCRATCH COMPETITION.** Thirty-six Holes. Medal Play. Entrance Fee, 5/-. The winner will receive a Gold Medal, the second a Silver Medal, and the third a Bronze Medal.
2. **A HANDICAP PRIZE** (handicap limited to 9), for the first Eighteen Holes of the day. Entrance Fee, 2/6.
3. **A HANDICAP PRIZE** (handicap limited to 9), for the second Eighteen Holes of the day. Entrance Fee, 2/6.

There will be an optional Sweepstake of 2/6 for each event.

The draw for all Competitions will be sent by post to every Competitor.

N.B.—No player may take more than one prize in the second day's play.